LITERARY MASTERPIECES

ISSN 1526-1522

LITERARY MASTERPIECES

Volume **5**

One Hundred Years of Solitude

Joan Mellen

A MANLY, INC. BOOK

GALE GROUP

Detroit
New York
San Francisco
London
Boston
Woodbridge, CT

ONE HUNDRED YEARS OF SOLITUDE

Matthew J. Bruccoli and Richard Layman, *Editorial Directors*

Copyright ©2000

The Gale Group

27500 Drake Road

Farmington Hills, MI 48331

ISBN 0-7876-3971-0

ISSN 1526-1522

Printed in the United States of America

10 9 8 7 6 5 4 3 2 1

TABLE OF CONTENTS

A NOTE TO THE READER

Think of it this way: you are about to embark on a journey. This book is, among other things, designed to be at once a reservation and a round-trip ticket. The purpose of the journey, the goal and destination, is for you to experience, as fully and as deeply as you can, a masterpiece of literature. Reading a great work is not a passive experience. It will be demanding and, as you will see, well rewarded.

by George Garrett, Henry Hoyns Professor of Creative Writing, the University of Virginia

What is a masterpiece? The answer is easy if you are dealing with the great works of antiquity—for example the *Iliad* and *Odyssey* of Homer, the tragedies of Aeschylus, Sophocles, and Euripides—works that have endured for millenia and even outlasted their original language. Closer in time there are the accepted monuments of our languages and culture, such as the plays of Shakespeare, the *Divine Comedy* of Dante, and the comedies of Molière. But here and now we are dealing with work that is nearer to us in time, that speaks to and about persons, places, and things that we either know at first hand or at least know about. These works are accepted by critical consensus (and tested in the marketplace and in the classroom) as among the most original and influential works of their times. It remains for you to experience their power and originality.

There is much to be gained from close and careful study of a great book. You will always find much more than you expected to, than you are looking for. Whether we know it and admit it or not, we are one and all constantly being changed and shaped by what we read. One definition of a literary masterpiece is that it is a great work that can touch us most deeply. It can be, is, if you are wide awake and fully engaged, a profound experience. Lighthearted or deadly serious, it is about things that matter to us. The Gale Study Guides are intended to help you to enjoy and to enlarge your understanding of literature. By an intense focus, these Guides enhance the values you discover in reading enduring works. Discovery is always an important part of the process. With guidance you will see how personal discoveries can be made and, equally important, can be shared with others studying the same book. Our literary culture is, ideally, a community. This book is meant to serve as your introduction to that community.

From the earliest days of our history (until the here and now), readers have looked for pleasure and meaning in whatever they read. The two are inextricable in literature. Without pleasure and enjoyment, there can be no permanent meaning. Without value and significance, there is no real pleasure. Ideally, the close study of literary masterpieces—comedy or tragedy, past and present—will increase our pleasure and our sense of understanding not only of the individual work in and of itself but also of ourselves and the world we inhabit.

There is hard work involved. What you have labored to master you will value more highly. And reading is never exclusively a passive experience. You have to bring the whole of yourself to the experience. It becomes not a monologue, but a dialogue between you and the author. What you gain from the experience depends, in large part, on what you bring and can give back. But, as great voices have told us since the dawn of literature, it is well worth all the effort, indeed worth any effort.

We learn how powerful words can be. The language of great voices speaking to us across time and space, yet close as a whisper, matters enormously. Sooner or later, our buildings will crumble; our most intricate and elegant machines will cough and die and become rusty junk; and our grand monuments and memorials will lose all their magic and meaning. But we know that our words, our language, will last longer than we do, speaking of and for us, over centuries and millenia. Listening to great voices, reading their words and stories in the enduring works of literature, we are given a reward of inestimable value. We earn a share in their immortality.

You will meet some memorable characters, good and bad, and you are going to participate in unforgettable events. You will go to many places, among them the Africa of Chinua Achebe, the England of Virginia Woolf, the China of Maxine Hong Kingston. You can visit 1920s Paris with Ernest Hemingway, the magical Latin America of Gabriel García Márquez, the Mississippi of William Faulkner, the dark side of San Francisco with Dashiell Hammett. Gale Study Guides are good maps to the literary territory. Envision the journey as a kind of quest or pilgrimage, not without difficulty, that can change your understanding of life.

ACKNOWLEDGMENTS

This book was produced by Bruccoli Clark Layman, Inc. R. Bland Lawson is the series editor and Jan Peter F. van Rosevelt was the in-house editor.

Production manager is Philip B. Dematteis.

Copyediting supervisor is Phyllis A. Avant. Senior copyeditor is Thom Harman. The copyediting staff includes Brenda Carol Blanton, James Denton, Worthy B. Evans, Melissa D. Hinton, William Tobias Mathes, and Jennifer Reid.

Indexing was done by Alex Snead and Cory McNair.

Layout and graphics supervisor is Janet E. Hill. Graphics staff includes Karla Corley Brown and Zoe R. Cook.

Photography editors are Charles Mims, Scott Nemzek, Alison Smith, and Paul Talbot. Digital photographic copy work was performed by Joseph M. Bruccoli.

Systems manager is Marie L. Parker.

Typesetting supervisor is Kathleen M. Flanagan. The typesetting staff includes Mark J. McEwan, Kimberly Kelly, and Patricia Flanagan Salisbury.

Following is a list of the copyright holders who have granted us permission to reproduce material in this volume of Gale Study Guides to Great Literature. Every effort has been made to trace copyright, but if omissions have been made, please let us know.

COPYRIGHTED MATERIAL IN *Literary Masterpieces, Vol. 5:* **One Hundred Years of Solitude WAS REPRODUCED FROM THE FOLLOWING SOURCES:**

Johnston, Ian. Lecture on *One Hundred Years of Solitude* in *www.mala.bc.ca/~mcneil/m4lec15a.htm.* Copyright, Malaspina University-College, 1995. Reproduced by permission.

Llosa, Mario Vargas. From "Gabriel Márquez: From Aracataca to Macondo" in *Gabriel García Márquez*. Edited by Harold Bloom. Chelsea House, 1989. Reproduced by permission.

Williamson, Edwin. From "Magic Realism and the Theme of Incest in *One Hundred Years of Solitude*" in *Gabriel García Márquez: New Readings*. Edited by Bernard McGuirk and Richard Cardwell. Cambridge University Press, 1987. Reproduced with the permission of Cambridge University Press and the author.

Wood, Michael. From *Gabriel García Márquez: One Hundred Years of Solitude*. Cambridge University Press, 1990. Reproduced with the permission of Cambridge University Press and the author.

PHOTOGRAPHS AND ILLUSTRATIONS APPEARING IN *Literary Masterpieces, Vol. 5:* One Hundred Years of Solitude WERE RECEIVED FROM THE FOLLOWING SOURCES:

Cartagena, photograph by Robert Gerstmann. From *Colombia: 200 Gragados En Cobre*. Braun & Cia, 1951.

Cover of *One Hundred Years of Solitude*. By Gabriel García Márquez. Avon Books, 1971. Reproduced by permission of Avon Books, Inc.

Dust jacket from *One Hundred Years of Solitude*, Bucharest edition, in *Para que mis amigos me quieran mas: homenaje a Gabriel García Márquez*. Siglo del Hombre Editores, 1972.

Dust jacket from *One Hundred Years of Solitude*, Budapest edition, in *Para que mis amigos me quieran mas: homenaje a Gabriel García Márquez*. Siglo del Hombre Editores, 1992.

Dust jacket from *One Hundred Years of Solitude*, Chinese edition, in *Para que mis amigos me quieran mas: homenaje a Gabriel García Márquez*. Siglo del Hombre Editores, 1992.

Dust jacket from *One Hundred Years of Solitude*, Greek edition, in *Para que mis amigos me quieran mas: homenaje a Gabriel García Márquez*. Siglo del Hombre Editores, 1992.

Dust jacket from *One Hundred Years of Solitude*, Hebrew edition, in *Para que mis amigos me quieran mas: homenaje a Gabriel García Márquez*. Siglo del Hombre Editores, 1972.

Dust jacket from *One Hundred Years of Solitude*, Rio de Janeiro edition, in *Para que mis amigos me quieran mas: homenaje a Gabriel García Márquez*. Siglo del Hombre Editores, 1972.

Dust jacket from *One Hundred Years of Solitude,* Rio de Janeiro edition, in *Para que mis amigos me quieran mas: homenaje a Gabriel García Márquez.* Siglo del Hombre Editores, 1972.

Dust jacket from *One Hundred Years of Solitude.* By Gabriel García Márquez. Harper & Row, 1970.

Covers for *One Hundred Years of Solitude,* Colombian editions, in *Para que mis amigos me quieran mas: homenaje a Gabriel García Márquez.* Siglo del Hombre Editores, 1992.

Dust jackets for *One Hundred Years of Solitude,* Italian editions, in *Para que mis amigos me quieran mas: homenaje a Gabriel García Márquez.* Siglo del Hombre Editores, 1992.

Cover for *One Hundred Years of Solitude,* Venezuelan edition, by Gabriel García Márquez. Siglo del Hombre Editores, 1992.

Family tree of the Buendías. From *One Hundred Years of Solitude.* By Gabriel García Márquez. Harper & Row, 1970.

House in Aracataca where Gabriel García Márquez was born, photograph. *El Espectador.*

Gabriel García Márquez, as a young journalist, photograph. El Espectador.

Gabriel García Márquez, photograph. AP/Wide World Photos. Reproduced by permission.

Gabriel García Márquez, swamped by media in Mexico City, photograph. UPI/Corbis-Bettmann. Reproduced by permission.

Rio Magdalena, photograph by Robert Gerstmann. From *Colombia: 200 Gragados En Cobre.* Braun & Cia, 1951.

Santa Marta, photograph by Robert Gerstmann. From *Colombia: 200 Gragados En Cobre.* Braun & Cia, 1951.

ABOUT *ONE HUNDRED YEARS OF SOLITUDE*

CITATION

One Hundred Years of Solitude was first published in June of 1967 in Buenos Aires, Argentina, as *Cien años de soledad,* by Editorial Sudamericana. It was first published in the United States by Harper and Row in 1970, translated by Gregory Rabassa.

PLOT SUMMARY

Gabriel García Márquez has called *One Hundred Years of Solitude* his "least mysterious" book, his easiest to read. Intentionally he sought to make the action comprehensible: "I tried to lead the reader by the hand so as not to get him lost at any moment."[1]

The novel, generally episodic in structure, is the story of the rise and fall of a family. José Arcadio Buendía and Úrsula Iguarán travel to a village just beyond the mountains and within reach of an "ashen, foamy, dirty sea"[2] to found the village of Macondo. They pass an old Spanish galleon, indicating the incursions upon the land by Spain through its "explorers," who were really pirates and adventurers. Yet, the world is still "recent" (1). In its early days Macondo has only three hundred inhabitants. It is "a truly happy village where no one was over thirty years of age and where no one had died" (10).

A group of gypsies arrives, bringing with them magic that both fascinates José Arcadio Buendía and condemns him to solitude. He sets up "the laboratory of an alchemist" (5) in a small room in the rear of the house. He is inspired by Melquíades, one of the gypsies, who seems to have supernatural powers. Meanwhile, in order to support the family, Úrsula goes into the business of baking candies.

José Arcadio Buendía and Úrsula Iguarán have three children: Colonel Aureliano Buendía, the hero of this novel (if it could be said to have a hero), and the first human being born in Macondo; his

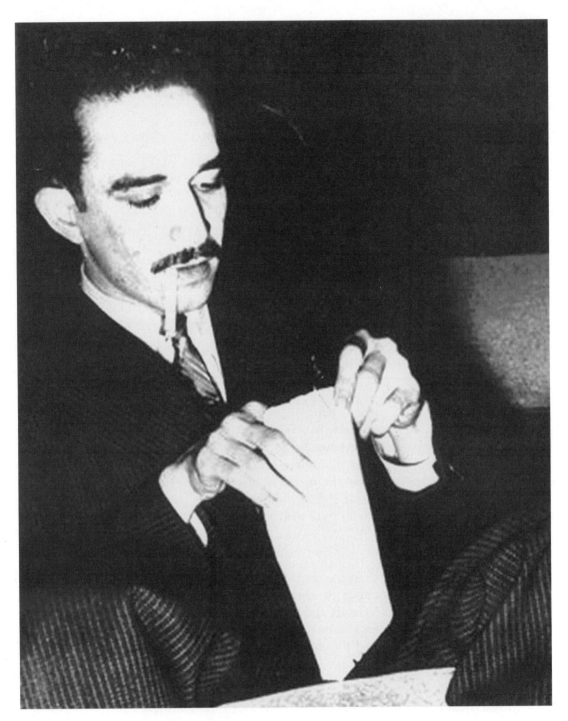

Gabriel García Márquez when he was a reporter for the Bogotá newspaper *El Espectador* in the early 1950s

older brother, José Arcadio; and a daughter, Amaranta. Each brother conceives his first child with a prostitute named Pilar Ternera. Her child with Aureliano is named Aureliano José. José Arcadio, having left Pilar pregnant with his son, Arcadio, runs away with the gypsies.

Colonel Aureliano Buendía becomes a famous warrior fighting valiantly in thirty-two civil wars, and becomes the father of seventeen more sons, all named Aureliano, all by different mothers. These are women who in wartime steal into his tent at night to partake of his genetic bounty, his strength. By the end of the novel all of the illegitimate Aurelianos will be murdered.

One day a child named Rebeca arrives at the Buendía house. She is eleven years old and is carrying a bag containing her parents' bones, and a letter that says she is a distant relation. Rebeca becomes the child most affectionate toward Úrsula. When José Arcadio returns, having been around the world as a sailor, tattooed and selling his sexual favors, he marries Rebeca. Because they are related, Úrsula banishes them for "an inconceivable lack of respect" (102). Amaranta refuses the proposal of the man with whom she is in love, Pietro Crespi, out of a masochistic need to refuse what she desires most, and he commits suicide as a result.

Arcadio, the son and only child of José Arcadio, marries a quiet woman named Santa Sofía de la Piedad and they have three children: a daughter, Remedios the Beauty, and twin sons, Aureliano Segundo and José Arcadio Segundo. Aureliano Segundo continues the family line by marrying a cold, beautiful, repressed, and repressive woman named Fernanda del Carpio. José Arcadio Segundo resembles his great uncle Aureliano more than he does the Arcadios of the family.

Fernanda and Aureliano Segundo have three children: Renata Remedios, known as "Meme," José Arcadio, and Amaranta Úrsula, who goes to Europe and becomes a modern woman, although she partakes of the abiding strength of her great-great-grandmother, Úrsula Iguarán. That original Úrsula feared for her family only one thing: the sin of incest. She and her husband are in fact cousins.

A Buendía ancestor had been born with a pig's tail. Should incest be committed by family members, and another child be born with a pig's tail, that would be the end of the Buendía family. At the age of one hundred, Úrsula wants to raise a child who would "restore the prestige of the family" (205). She decides that "this one will be a priest," and be "Pope someday" (205). When she finally dies, she is

CREATING UTOPIA

"We, the inventors of tales, who will believe anything, feel entitled to believe that it is not yet too late to engage in the creation of the opposite utopia. A new and sweeping utopia of life, where no one will be able to decide for others how they die, where love will prove true and happiness be possible, and where the races condemned to one hundred years of solitude will have, at last and forever, a second opportunity on earth."

Gabriel García Márquez

From García Márquez's Nobel Prize lecture, "The Solitude of Latin America," delivered to the Swedish Academy, 8 December 1982 (©The Nobel Foundation, 1982).

between one hundred fifteen and one hundred twenty-two years of age.

Renata Remedios (Meme) bears a child named Aureliano by a local mechanic named Mauricio Babilonia. That Aureliano, whose parents never marry, falls in love with his aunt, Amaranta Úrsula, Meme's sister. They lock themselves inside the Buendía mansion becoming "more and more integrated in the solitude of a house that needed only one last breath to be knocked down" (440).

The last Aureliano is born. He is lusty like the Arcadios yet has the "open and clairvoyant eyes of the Aurelianos" (442). When he is turned over, he does indeed have "something more than other men." They lean over and discover—"It was the tail of a pig" (443). The curse holds true: the child born of their incestuous union, also named Aureliano, is eaten by red ants and the Buendía line comes to an end.

The plot of *One Hundred Years of Solitude* contains more than just the personal histories of the members of the Buendía family; it encompasses as well the fate of the community of Macondo, which suffers a decline and fall parallel to that of the Buendías. One day early in the life of Macondo a magistrate named Don Apolinar Moscote arrives in this cooperative society where no law is needed and no one has even died a natural death. José Arcadio chases him away, but Don Moscote returns with soldiers to reinforce his order that the fronts of every house be painted blue, the color that stands for the Conservative Party. His child-daughter, Remedios, is the one with whom José Arcadio's son Aurelito, or little Aureliano, falls in love. In reaction to the politics of his Conservative father-in-law, Aurelito becomes Colonel Aureliano Buendía, eventually the supreme commander of the Liberal rebels.

García Márquez does not choose between Conservatives and Liberals. Arcadio, having been left in his childhood to solitude, becomes a brute, no matter that he is a Liberal. Unlike his uncle, Colonel Aureliano Buendía, who faced a firing squad and lived, Arcadio deservedly faces a firing squad and dies thinking of his uncle's dead wife, Remedios. Only at the moment of his death does he begin "to understand how much he really loved the people he hated most" (129). Arcadio dies shouting, "Long live the Liberal Party!" (131).

Even Colonel Aureliano Buendía, the most admirable of the Buendía men, becomes "capable of anything" (171), and executes a good man, the Conservative general José Raquel Moncada. General Moncada's name suggests the Moncada barracks attacked by Fidel Castro in 1953, sounding the first shot of the Cuban Revolution. Deconstructing revolutionary cant, García Márquez has the colonel, now corrupted, address General Moncada "'Remember, old friend,' he told him. 'I'm not shooting you. It's the revolution that's shooting you'" (173). General Moncada has developed complete contempt for Colonel Aureliano Buendía. He does not bother to get out of his bed when the colonel enters the room. "'Go to hell, friend'" (173), is his reply.

The earlier depictions of violence clearly refer to the civil wars of the nineteenth century and the heartbreaking years of La violencia (literally, "The Violence"), the period of Liberal-Conservative fighting in which thousands died and that lasted from ca. 1948 to 1965. With these allusions, however, García Márquez seems to move the frame of reference to the guerrilla movements that had begun fighting in Colombia a few years before the book was published in 1967. He achieves this end by invoking, however, not the leftist guerrilla groups within Colombia, but the Cuban Revolution.

The Liberal Party ultimately demands that Colonel Aureliano Buendía negotiate away everything it has stood for, rendering Liberals no different from the Conservatives against whom they have fought so many bloody wars:

> They asked first that he renounce the revision of property titles in order to get back the support of the Liberal landowners. They asked, secondly, that he renounce the fight against clerical influence in order to obtain the support of the Catholic masses. They asked, finally, that he renounce the aim of equal rights for natural and illegitimate children in order to preserve the integrity of the home. (182)

"'That means,' Colonel Aureliano Buendía said, smiling when the reading was over, 'that all we're fighting for is power'" (182). He prepares to sign the papers and renounce all of the political principles for which they have been fighting for twenty years, saying "The important thing is that from now on we'll be fighting only for power" (183). When his friend Colonel Gerineldo Márquez softly objects, saying "this is a betrayal" (183), Colonel Aureliano Buendía becomes enraged. He sentences his best friend to death for "high treason" (183). Only Úrsula's threat to kill Colonel Aureliano Buendía herself convinces her son to stay the execution; her final remark as she leaves the room is: "It's the same as if you'd been born with the tail of a pig" (184).

Colonel Aureliano Buendía spends the next two years trying to end the war. After the armistice, the president refuses to award any military pensions to former combatants, whether Liberal or Conservative, until each case is examined by a special commission and the award is approved by Congress. Colonel Aureliano Buendía knows what this means. "They'll die of old age waiting for the mail to come" (184), he thunders. Having grown old, Colonel Aureliano Buendía secretes himself in his father's old laboratory, making gold fishes,and leaving "the workshop only to urinate under the chestnut" (277). All he can conclude is that "the secret of a good old age is simply an honorable pact with solitude" (216).

The persistent civil wars have weakened Macondo and left the community vulnerable. Its disintegration is accomplished by the arrival and departure of the banana company, modeled on the United Fruit Company, which takes land to make its plantations, exploits the local workers, and then calls in the national army to break their strike. Even in his solitude Colonel Aureliano Buendía begins to realize, as García Márquez swiftly moves his story into the twentieth century, that his real fight may well have been against the "gringos" of North America, who bring so much destruction with their banana company. "One of these days," he shouts, "I'm going to arm my boys so we can get rid of these shitty gringos" (257).

The saga of José Arcadio Segundo—who learns the truth about the massacre, how three thousand bodies were loaded onto two hundred freight cars, like bananas, and dumped into the sea—reflects the years of La violencia. The departure of the banana company is followed by four years, eleven months, and two days of rain. By the time the rains stop, the community has died.

The final revelation in the novel is that the gypsy Melquíades's manuscript, over which many Buendías have poured during the course of the story in an effort to penetrate its meaning, turns out to be the story of the Buendías, the novel *One Hundred Years of Solitude* itself. The parchments, "as if they had been written in Spanish" (446), which of course they had, tell "the history of the family, written by Melquíades, down to the most trivial details, one hundred years ahead of time" (446). As García Márquez did in writing the novel, Melquíades "had not put events in the order of man's conventional time, but had concentrated a century of daily episodes in such a way that they coexisted in one instant" (446). So in the plot of his novel García Márquez reveals his own methodology at the end.

In his solitude, the last solitude of the Buendías, Aureliano, out of narcissism, becomes fascinated by the story of his own origins: "the instant of his own conception among the scorpions and the yellow butterflies in a sunset bathroom where a mechanic satisfied his lust on a woman who was giving herself out of rebellion" (447). He becomes so consumed by his discovery that Amaranta Úrsula "was not his sister but his aunt" (447), though that does not change the fact of incest, that he "forgot about his dead ones" (446), leaving Amaranta unburied and the baby to be eaten by the ants, nailing up the doors and windows and ignoring the rising wind of the hurricane that will wipe out Macondo.

ABOUT GARCÍA MÁRQUEZ

Gabriel José García Márquez was born in Aracataca, Colombia, on 6 March, either in 1927 or 1928. "No one knows for sure," the author has said with a smile.[3] In 1928, the year of the Santa Marta banana strike described in *One Hundred Years of Solitude,* Aracataca was a sleepy village near the Caribbean between Barranquilla and Santa Marta; it was founded by people who had fled Colombia's civil wars. As Mario Vargas Llosa has written, "When he was born, Aracataca lived off memories; his stories will take life from his memories of Aracataca."[4] One of the old plantations near where he grew up was named "Macondo," which is the Bantu noun meaning "banana."

The town had been expanded by the United Fruit Company with wooden shacks and roofs made of zinc and tin for its workers. As García Márquez describes it in *One Hundred Years of Solitude,* United Fruit created an entirely separate community for the gringos who came to manage the plantations, complete with separate schools and swimming pools. The Spanish had imported slaves to the colony of New Granada, and Caribbean Colombia, where García Márquez was born, had a large black population. The Caribbean coast was an environment mixing Guajiro Indians (the few that survived), the descendants of black slaves, immigrants from the Middle East, and of course the mestizos, who comprise sixty percent of the population of

Colombia itself. In the 1970s, traveling in Angola on a journalistic assignment, García Márquez pronounced himself a mestizo. Later he would add that he was "a mulatto," a fact he realized only late in his life.[5]

García Márquez was born into this diverse culture, tinged by magic brought from Africa and from Spain. A sense of mystery prevailed—the belief that there is much in life that is unknowable. He came to consider himself a *costeño,* or "man of the coast," a Caribbean man from a region where supernatural elements are a part of ordinary everyday life. Out of this environment García Márquez came to conclude that "you can't separate reality from fiction."[6]

The Caribbean coast of Barranquilla and Santa Marta and Cartagena de Indias was a world of many gods, a theme reflected in *One Hundred Years of Solitude* where José Arcadio Buendía becomes fascinated by daguerreotypes in his effort to find "a single image of God." Now old, José Arcadio uses the laboratory to "obtain scientific proof of the existence of God," and remains confident that "sooner or later he would get a daguerreotype of God" (58). Enraged when he becomes "convinced of His nonexistence," José Arcadio Buendía takes apart the pianola; of what point are modern inventions, is technology, in a universe abandoned by God? Reaching for proof that time exists, he goes mad (67).

As a child García Márquez heard reports of the banana strike from neighbors. Some claimed that no one had died in the massacre that followed the strike, while others were still mourning the death of an uncle or a brother who had perished.[7] In *One Hundred Years of Solitude,* the massacre is of men, women, and children, while in actuality only men had gathered that day to be shot down by General Cortés Vargas. In the novel, three thousand people die, while in reality the deaths may have numbered a few hundred; three thousand might have amounted to the entire population of the town.

Yet even this exaggeration derives from his childhood memories. One of these "was watching a very, very long train leave the plantation, full of bananas," he has said. "There could have been three thousand dead on it, eventually to be dumped in the sea."[8]

His father, Gabriel Eligio García, was a telegraph operator. His mother, Luisa Santiago Márquez Iguarán, belonged to the most prominent family in Aracataca. Her father, Colonel Nicolás Márquez, had fought in the civil wars and fathered more than a dozen illegitimate children, reflecting an appetite he would share with his fictional namesake, Colonel Aureliano Buendía.

Colonel Márquez was the leading citizen in the town of Aracataca, belonging to the most eminent family. He had fought under the great Liberal general Rafael Uribe Uribe and, as a result of his efforts, Aracataca had become a city of the Liberal persuasion. Colonel Nicolás Márquez opposed his daughter's marriage because Gabriel Eligio García was a Conservative, was illegitimate, and was known to have gone with many women. "Come have the baby in our house," the grandparents pleaded with Luisa Santiago Márquez Iguarán. After he was born, they added, "Leave Gabriel with us to raise."[9]

For the first eight years of his life, "Gabito"— as Gabriel García Márquez was called as a child—lived with his grandparents in their rambling house in Aracataca, the large and commodious house upon which the house of the Buendía family of Macondo was modeled. The original title of *One Hundred Years of Solitude* was, in fact, "La Casa" (The House). García Márquez remembered it as a haunted house:

> En cada rincon habia muertos y memorias, y despues de las seis de la tarde, la casa era intransitable. Era un mundo prodigioso de terror. Habia conversacions en clave. En esa casa habia un cuarto desocupado en donde habia muerto la tia Petra. Habia un cuarto desocupado donde habia muerto el tio Lazaro. Entonces, de noche, no se podia caminar en esa casa porque habia mas muertos que vivos. A mi me sentaban, a las seis de la tarde, en un rincon y me decian: "No te muevas de aqui porque si te mueves va a venir la tia Petra que esta en su cuarto, o el tio Lazaro, que esta in otro." Yo me quedaba siempre sentado . . . "

> (In every room there were dead people and memories, and after six o'clock in the evening, the house was impenetrable. It was a world filled with terror. There were secret conversations. In that house there was an empty room where Aunt Petra had died. There was an empty room where Uncle Lazaro had died. Then, at night, you weren't able to walk in that house because there were more dead people than living. I sat myself down in a corner at six o'clock and I told myself: "Don't move from here because if you move, Aunt Petra, who is in her room, or Uncle Lazaro, who is in the other, is going to come." I always remained seated. . . .).[10]

This passage is reflected directly in *One Hundred Years of Solitude* in the house of Rebeca, now widowed: "she had found peace in that house where memories materialized through the strength of implacable evocation and walked like human beings through the cloistered rooms" (172).

"I feel that all my writing has been about the experiences of the time I spent with my grandparents," García Márquez has said.[11] Colonel Nicolás Márquez would die waiting for the government to approve his pension and his widow would attempt to gain it for him, an event reflected in that line of *One Hundred Years of Solitude* when Colonel Aureliano Buendía cries out, "They'll die of old age waiting for the mail to come": a theme García Márquez had developed earlier in his novella *El coronel no tiene quien le escriba* (1961; translated in *No One Writes to the Colonel and Other Stories*, 1968).

Colonel Aureliano Buendía attains the same rank as had García Márquez's grandfather in the War of the Thousand Days, although his character also includes aspects of the life of Colonel Márquez's superior, General Uribe Uribe, leader of the Liberal forces. General Uribe Uribe signed the Peace of Neerlandia, as Colonel Aureliano Buendía does in the novel.

Because Colonel Aureliano Buendía was based so much on his grandfather, García Márquez identified with the character. After he finished writing the chapter in which the colonel dies, he later recalled, "I went up to Mercedes on the second floor of our house, trembling. She knew what had happened the moment she saw my face. 'The Colonel's dead,' she said. I lay down on my bed and cried for two hours."[12]

So suffused with autobiography is *One Hundred Years of Solitude* that there is even a sly joke as García Márquez compares his oldest son, Rodrigo, to the baby born with a pig's tail. "He's a real cannibal," Amaranta Úrsula says when she sees her baby for the first time, "We'll name him Rodrigo." Her husband overrules her and he decides, "we'll name him Aureliano and he'll win thirty-two wars" (442).

During García Márquez's early childhood, his grandfather was his best friend, and his presence dominates *One Hundred Years of Solitude*. He was, García Márquez has said, "the person I've gotten along with best and had the best communication with ever." His grandfather took him to the circus and introduced him to the cinema, and, he has said, "was my umbilical cord with history and reality."[13]

Yet, he knew his grandfather had once killed a man. Taking Gabito to the circus, Colonel Márquez had stopped to exclaim, "Oh! You don't know how much a dead man weighs."[14] The moment is transformed in *One Hundred Years of Solitude* when José Arcadio Buendía, the founder of Macondo, is haunted by the ghost of the man he killed, Prudencio Aguilar, who wanders the earth with "immense desolation" (23) yearning for "living people" (25). José Arcadio has an explanation for this phenomenon that reflects the words of the colonel. When Úrsula tells him she has seen the ghost of Prudencio Aguilar, he replies, "This just means that we can't stand the weight of our conscience" (25).

In the first line of *One Hundred Years of Solitude,* as he is facing a firing squad, Colonel Aureliano Buendía remembers the afternoon "when his father took him to discover ice" (1), recapitulating a childhood memory of García Márquez. His grandfather took him to the United Fruit Company store where he opened the frozen fish boxes for the child to observe for the first time in his life the miracle of ice. "But this is boiling," he said. "No, on the contrary," his grandfather told him, "it is very cold."[15]

Gabriel's aunt Francisca also lived in that spacious house in Aracataca; like Amaranta in the novel, she wove her own shroud. Exactly like the character in the novel, when the job was done, she simply laid down and died, as she had promised to do. In the town of Aracataca there was a priest who was so saintly that people said he rose off the ground whenever he raised the chalice during mass, and he became the priest who levitates when he drinks hot chocolate in *One Hundred Years of Solitude*.

The great influence on García Márquez's development of his techniques as a novelist was his grandmother, who, like Úrsula in *One Hundred Years of Solitude,* was a baker. His grandfather told him stories about "tangible things . . . items from the newspapers, war stories from the time he was a colonel on the liberal side in the Colombian civil wars."[16]

His grandmother, Tranquilina Iguarán, however, was forever telling stories in which she interwove magic and reality, making no distinction between the living and the dead. She organized life according to messages she received in her dreams and was, García Márquez would say, "a superstitious woman with a vivid imagination who terrorized me, night after night, with her stories from beyond the grave."[17] Growing up among adults, as he did, he drew comic strips and cartoons before he learned to write. These illustrated the stories his grandmother told him.

Sometimes he would convert a remark his grandmother made into fiction. One day after the departure of an electrician who was working in the house, Tranquilina Iguarán said, hitting one with a dish towel, "every time that man comes into this house, we get butterflies."[18] In *One Hundred Years of Solitude,* García Márquez has Mauricio Babilonia, the lover of Meme Buendía, trailed not just by butterflies, but, to ensure credibility, by *yellow* butterflies. Similarily, García Márquez has Colonel Aureliano Buendía organize not "many," but "thirty-two armed uprisings" (113), the better to express the theme of the meaningless repetition of the civil wars of Colombia, a century of warfare failing to accomplish anything.

From his childhood as well came the most striking example of magic realism in *One Hundred Years of Solitude.* When a local girl ran away from home with a traveling salesman, her grandmother insisted that she had in fact "gone up to heaven."[19] García Márquez transformed this story into the ascension into heaven of Remedios the Beauty. Then, fearing that this would not be believable, he added a detail. Noticing a maid next door to the house in Mexico City hanging out the wash, he found his image.[20] Remedios would rise to heaven still folding the newly laundered bedsheets.

He also drew on information he garnered as a journalist. Having learned that in 1925 the El Niño weather pattern caused the deaths of millions of birds, which were washed up onto the shores of Ecuador and Colombia, in the novel he has thousands of birds fall dead from the heavens as homage to Úrsula Iguarán when she finally dies at an age somewhere above one hundred.

The voice he employs in his writing derives as well from the stories told by his grandmother. Her voice was so solemn, so enhanced by conviction, and the expression on her face so deadpan, that he could not but believe in the reality of whatever she told him. In *One Hundred Years of Solitude,* García Márquez describes the outlandish and fantastic in the same tone of voice that he uses to describe realistic phenomena. He flashes back to the sixteenth century when the English pirate Sir Francis Drake so frightened Úrsula Iguarán's great-great-grandmother that she sat down on a lighted stove (21); he writes as if the incident were entirely true. His evidence is, after all, that her descendant is now extremely cautious.

As an impoverished young journalist in Barranquilla in the early 1950s, García Márquez lived above a brothel, where he developed friendships with several of the prostitutes; he became aware of their humanity and sympathized with their plight. One of the prostitutes from that brothel, a woman named Eufemia, was the basis for the character Nigormanta of *One Hundred Years of Solitude.*

In Barranquilla he met a group of writers at the Café Colombia, among them Ramón Vinyes, a Catalonian bookseller, and three friends. García Márquez pays homage to these three old friends, Álvaro (Cepeda), Germán (Vargas), and Alfonso (Fuenmayor) by having Aureliano in *One Hundred Years of Solitude* call them, along with Gabriel, "the first and last friends that he ever had in his life" (417). They are given the real-life first names of his friends. "Gabriel" himself, the shadow of the author, is about to embark for Europe. He carries with him, however, not, as García Márquez did in real life, Daniel Defoe's *Journal of the Plague Year* (1722), but the works of Rabelais.

García Márquez met his future wife Mercedes Barcha in Sucre when they were young, she a primary school student of thirteen. This relationship is reflected in the love of Colonel Aureliano Buendía for little Remedios; there are six grown Moscote daughters, but Aureliano wants only the one who "still wets her bed" (76). Remedios, who dies in childbirth, "a pair of twins crossed in her stomach" (94), is "the last person Arcadio" (96) thinks about when he faces the firing squad.

LOVE AND ROMANCE

"When I arrived in Bogotá, Colombia, in the 1940s from the Caribbean coast, I was 13 years old and had already lost my virginity, as was common in the region I came from. My mother, like all mothers, warned me against the two most serious threats that awaited us at Bogotá's high altitude: pneumonia and shotgun weddings.

"The threat of forced marriage was not the worst thing that could happen, for we were living in the heyday of venereal disease. In streetcars, in public toilets, everywhere, were signs reminding us: 'If you do not fear God, fear syphilis.' So the only recourse against solitude was the Saturday night dance, which provided the only sanctioned expressions of love: boleros, danced cheek-to-cheek, dates made for after mass the next day, perfumed letters, dark movie houses, pillows soaked with tears, and poetry. All of this disappeared in the 1970s, swept away by the whirlwind of unadulterated sex. I do not regret it. To the contrary, I have always believed that we were born with our pleasures numbered, and what we do not use, we lose. But the best thing is sex with all that goes with it, meaning total love."

Gabriel García Márquez

From "Love and Romance Make a Comeback," *World Press Review,* 38 (May 1991), p. 34.

Mercedes and Gabriel were separated when, as a reporter for the *El Espectador* newspaper, he was sent to Europe in 1955, where he was to remain for three years. Toward the end of *One Hundred Years of Solitude,* García Márquez grows increasingly autobiographical, as if knowing that he had accomplished his purpose in writing the novel, he could add a playful note to the work. Mercedes suddenly appears in the

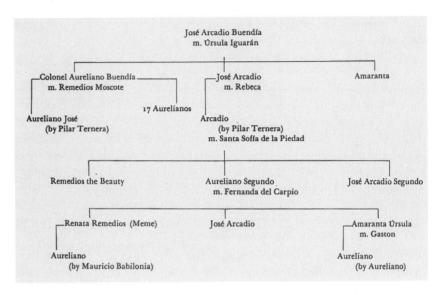

Family tree of the Buendías, the family at the center of *One Hundred Years of Solitude*

novel as a pharmacist and the "stealthy girl friend" (434) of Gabriel, who is a member of a group of intellectuals. A woman with a "thin neck and sleepy eyes" (444), she is, as in life, left behind when he goes to Europe.

Later García Márquez has Amaranta Úrsula, whose sexual relations with her nephew, Aureliano, bring the Buendía line to its end, hope to name her sons, "Rodrigo and Gonzalo, never Aureliano and José Arcadio" (410). These are the names of García Márquez's sons. Had he a daughter, she would have been named "Virginia and never Remedios" (410). The one thing in his life that he regrets, García Márquez has said, is never having had a daughter.[21]

García Márquez had called Amaranta his second favorite character because she "most resembles the original Úrsula," who was based on his grandmother, "but without the older woman's complexes and prejudices. Amaranta Úrsula is Úrsula again—but emancipated now, with the experiences of the world, with modern ideas."[22]

PEOPLE OF *ONE HUNDRED YEARS OF SOLITUDE*

Michael Wood has observed of García Márquez's writing that "there are almost no villains in his work."[23] García Márquez has said that the characters are "jigsaw puzzles of many different people, and, naturally, bits of myself as well."[24]

Úrsula Iguarán. The central figure of *One Hundred Years of Solitude* is Úrsula Iguarán, the family matriarch, an earth mother who holds together the Buendías for as long as she can, and who stays alive to do so for more than one hundred years. Not only is she the image of the strong woman, practical and enduring, but she has supernatural powers; she can, through memory, "leap back over three hundred years of fate" (22). She is the historian of the Buendías and of Colombia, the country that the Buendía family represents.

When José Arcadio Buendía tells her that "the earth is round, like an orange," she loses her patience. "'If you have to go crazy, please go crazy all by yourself.' She shouted. 'But don't try to put your gypsy ideas into the heads of the children'" (5). The strength with which she holds the family together is implied in her description: "Active, small, severe, that woman of unbreakable nerves who at no moment in her life had been heard to sing seemed to be everywhere, from dawn until quite late at night, always pursued by the soft whispering of her stiff, starched petticoats" (9).

José Arcadio Buendía. The founder of the town of Macondo and of the Buendía line, husband of Úrsula Iguarán, his "unbridled imagination" goes "even beyond miracles and magic" (2). As soon as he sees demonstration of a magnet's ability to attract metal, he wants "to extract gold from the bowels of the earth" (2). A magnifying glass at once becomes seen as a potential weapon of war. He has founded Macondo wisely, on republican principles, as a democracy and a place of fairness, but "too absorbed in his fantastic speculations" (16), he is barely aware of his two sons. Led astray by science, and its promises, he eventually smashes his laboratory and goes mad.

Prudencio Aguilar. After his rooster loses in a cockfight with José Arcadio Buendía's rooster, Prudencio Aguilar insults José Arcadio Buendía, who subsequently kills him with a spear. When the ghost of Prudencio Aguilar begins haunting him, José Arcadio Buendía decides to leave the village where he was born and travels to found Macondo.

Aureliano (Colonel Aureliano Buendía). The colonel is, Wood has written, "the novel's dark conscience."[25] "Silent and withdrawn" (15), as a young man he becomes an artist, teaching himself the art of silverwork. The times, however, convert him into a warrior, like the first ancestral Aureliano Buendía who "had exterminated the jaguars in the region" (24). The remarkable character of Colonel Aureliano Buendía was evident even before he was born:

> He had wept in his mother's womb and had been born with his eyes open. As they were cutting the umbilical cord, he moved his head from side to side, taking in the things in the room and examining the faces of the people with a fearless curiosity. Then, indifferent to those who came close to look at him, he kept his attention concentrated on the palm roof, which looked as if it were about to collapse under the tremendous pressure of the rain. (15–16)

That it is little Aureliano who touches ice at the end of the first chapter, duplicating the experience of the author, is a clue to his being as close to an alter ego for García Márquez as any character in the novel. He repeats the words little Gabito used: "it's boiling" (19).

Aureliano hears about the impending civil war from his Conservative father-in-law, Don Apolinar Moscote, who explains the politics of the civil war:

> the Liberals . . . were Freemasons, bad people, wanting to hang priests, to institute civil marriage and divorce, to recognize the rights of illegitimate children as equal to those of legitimate ones, and to cut the country up into a federal system that would take power away from the supreme authority. The Conservatives, on the other hand, who had received their power directly from God, proposed the establishment of public order and family morality. They were the defenders of the faith of Christ, of the principle of authority, and were not prepared to permit the country to be broken down into autonomous entities (104).

Don Moscote's description is a fairly accurate historical depiction of the theoretical distinctions between the two sides, although couched in decidedly Conservative rhetoric. As a humanitarian, Aureliano automatically favors the Liberal side. When Don Moscote, who is supposed to supervise elections, tampers with the ballots, destroying most of the red, or Liberal, ones, Aureliano says, "If I were a Liberal . . . I'd go to war because of those ballots" (105). Prior to the election, Don Moscote had ordered all potential weapons confiscated, including kitchen knives. When Aureliano discovers that the Conservative government is going to use the so-called weapons as "proof that the Liberals were preparing for war," he makes his final decision: "If I have to be something I'll be a Liberal," he said, "because the Conservatives are tricky" (106). Before long he has gone from being "Aurelito" to Colonel Aureliano Buendía. He organizes his "thirty-two armed uprisings" (113), only to lose them all.

Despite his inherited clairvoyance, Colonel Aureliano Buendía cannot predict the failure of his politics. After too many battles in the meaningless wars between the Liberals and the Conservatives, he becomes a man capable of anything, executing the Conservative General Moncada, a decent man, and nearly having his best friend, Colonel Gerineldo Márquez, executed as well. Cursed at by his mother for this last plan, Colonel Aureliano Buendía then "scratched for many hours trying to break the hard shell of his solitude" (184), the inhumanity with which the wars had infused his soul. Instead of killing his best friend, Colonel Aureliano Buendía tries to end the civil war. The process is one of unspeakable horror: "He went to inconceivable extremes of cruelty to put down the rebellion of his own officers, who resisted and called for victory, and he finally relied on enemy forces to make them submit" (184).

So the Colonel, paradoxically, manages to "win a defeat that was much more difficult, much more bloody and costly than victory" (185). The psychological result is that Colonel Aureliano Buendía loses affection for all other human beings: "all of that had been wiped out by the war" (188). By the time the official armistice is signed, "he had reached the end of all hope, beyond glory and the nostalgia of glory" (191).

Surviving a suicide attempt in which he shoots himself in the chest with a pistol only for the bullet to come out "through his back without harming any vital organ" (114), he lives into his old age, making gold fishes in his father's old laboratory, having "learned to think coldly so that inescapable memories would not touch any feeling" (286).

Melquíades. He is "a heavy gypsy with an untamed beard and sparrow hands" (1) and brings science to Macondo, first the magnet and then the telescope and the magnifying glass. He is "a gloomy man, enveloped in a sad aura" (6). He is also a great storyteller whose image will become "a hereditary memory" (6) to all the descendants of José Arcadio Buendía.

Melquíades is presumed dead, but after a long absence, he returns to Macondo, "which had still not been discovered by death" (54), because he cannot bear the solitude. Melquíades predicts that Macondo will become "a luminous city with great glass houses where there was no trace remaining of the race of the Buendías" (58).

José Arcadio. The elder brother of Colonel Aureliano Buendía, he has "a square head, thick hair, and his father's character" (15). He also lacks imagination. He grows into a "monumental adolescent," and "so well-equipped for life that he seemed abnormal" (27). A fortune teller, Pilar Ternera, informs Úrsula that the "disproportionate size" of his penis means that "He'll be very lucky" (28). She then proceeds to seduce him. Governed by his sensuality, José Arcadio runs away with the gypsies.

José Arcadio returns, a huge man: "He was wearing a medal of Our Lady of Help around his bison neck, his arms and chest were completely covered with cryptic tattooing, and on his right wrist was the tight copper bracelet of the *niños-en cruz* amulet" (97). Every inch of his body is tattooed, and, stranded on the Sea of Japan, he once resorted to cannibalism to survive. He is besotted by superstition, and, unlike his brother Aureliano, has little acquaintance with rationality and intellect. After he returns to Macondo, José Arcadio makes his living by selling his sexual favors to women. The minute Rebeca sees him, she rejects her longtime erstwhile suitor, the Italian immigrant Pietro Crespi as a "sugary dandy" (100). After having lived happily with Rebeca for years, José Arcadio dies mysteriously from a single gunshot wound.

Arcadio. José Arcadio's son by Pilar Ternera, Arcadio, raised indifferently, and never told his true parentage, turns out to be the cruelest of the Buendías. At first, he learns the art of silverwork from his uncle, Aureliano, then becomes a teacher. Raised with his aunt, Amaranta, he reflects the first incestuous feelings to surface among the Buendías of Macondo. Arcadio never learns who his biological parents are, and unknowingly lusts after his mother, Pilar Ternera, who tricks him into sleeping instead with Santa Sofía de la Piedad, with whom he later has three children.

Entirely without principles, Arcadio falls in love with soldiering, with the accoutrements of the military. Left in charge of the town when Colonel Aureliano Buendía goes off to war, he puts uniforms on his former pupils. He organizes a firing squad, and then employs it so capriciously that his grandmother, Úrsula, calls him a murderer. He is "the cruelest ruler that Macondo had ever known" (115). When he attempts to drag Don Apolinar Moscote out and have him shot, Úrsula intervenes and whips Arcadio mercilessly. Arcadio disobeys Colonel Aureliano Buendía's instructions to surrender the town to the Conservatives. After Macondo is devastated, he is captured and shot. As he faces the firing squad, he thinks of Remedios.

Amaranta. Úrsula's daughter, and the sister of José Arcadio and Aureliano. Amaranta is also her own worst enemy. She falls in love with the same man whom Rebeca loves, Pietro Crespi, but she keeps her feelings locked inside. Unsent love letters grow moldy at the bottom of her trunk. Vindictive, she promises herself that Rebeca, who has been raised as her sister, will marry Pietro Crespi "only over her dead body" (76).

Rebeca. A young orphan who comes to the door of the Buendías carrying a sack containing her parents' bones. She carries a letter that states that she is Úrsula's second cousin, and hence related to José Arcadio Buendía as well, but no one in Macondo recognizes the name of the sender or her parents' names. The mysteries of her origin are never revealed in the novel.

For a long time Rebeca refuses to speak and will eat only "the damp earth of the courtyard and the cake of whitewash that she picked off the walls with her nails" (46). It is Úrsula who transforms her into the most affectionate Buendía. Yet, Rebeca carries the plague of insomnia, with its deadly consequence, "a loss of memory" (48), which makes its sufferers forget how to cook and eat." Although she seemed expansive and cordial, she had a solitary character and an impenetrable heart (69), characteristics that will lead to a lifetime of loneliness. She cannot escape the trauma of her childhood and so continues to eat earth even when she is an adult.

Pietro Crespi. An Italian who arrives from the import house "to assemble and tune the pianola, to instruct the purchasers in its functioning, and to teach them how to dance the latest music printed on its six paper roles" (65). He is young and blond and handsome, a dandy in a brocade vest, despite the "suffocating heat" (66) of Macondo. With his "patent leather curls" he arouses "in women an irrepressible need to sigh" (80); he is one of those men with so much allure that every woman falls for him, including both Amaranta and Rebeca. Critic Clive Griffin has noted that he is given "a comically inappropriate name: it recalls Pedro Crespi, a major character in Pedro Calderon de la Barca's play *El alcalde de Zalamea,* who, far from being an effete Italian, was a forceful and cunning Spanish peasant."[26] The transposition is one more example of the wit and sly humor of García Márquez. After Rebeca leaves him for José Arcadio, he proposes to Amaranta, who rejects him although she loves him. He then cuts his throat.

Don Apolinar Moscote. The magistrate who demands, to Úrsula's chagrin, that the fronts of all houses be painted blue, the Conservative color, "in celebration of the anniversary of national independence" (61). Don Apolinar Moscote brings government to Macondo, along with political parties, creating the groundwork for the bloody civil wars to come.

Colonel Gerineldo Márquez. The best friend of Colonel Aureliano Buendía and a son of one of the founders of Macondo. Playfully, the author makes his own family founders of Macondo, the town he has invented. Gerineldo is the one who accompanies Colonel Aureliano Buendía at the moment of his final defeat.

"Fragile, timid, with natural good manners" he is able to bring "the atmosphere of rural peace" (149) to Macondo. When he asks Amaranta to marry him, once more self-destructively she blights her own life. "You love Aureliano so much that you want to marry me because you can't marry him" (151), she tells her ardent suitor.

Pilar Ternera. A fortune teller and the woman who sexually initiates both José Arcadio and his brother, Aureliano. She smells of smoke under her armpits, which excites her young lover José Arcadio. She is a gracious and understanding lover to both of the sons of José Arcadio Buendía, and the mother of his first two grandchildren, Arcadio and Aureliano José.

Santa Sofía de la Piedad. The daughter of small shop owners, she is paid by Pilar Ternera to go as her substitute and sleep with Arcadio, who lusts after Pilar, not realizing that she is his mother. Santa Sofía de la Piedad and Arcadio have a daughter, Remedios the Beauty, and twin sons, Aureliano Segundo and José Arcadio Segundo.

Remedios. The daughter of Don Apolinar Moscote and the child-bride of Colonel Aureliano Buendía. As soon as she reaches puberty, from the moment of her marriage, Remedios becomes a gracious woman: "From that day on the sense of responsibility, the natural grace, the calm control that Remedios would have in the face of adverse circumstances was revealed" (88). She proceeds directly from playing with dolls and wetting her bed to being a wife.

Her sweetness is such that she begins to sing at dawn. Remedios is the only person who can intervene in the arguments between Amaranta and Rebeca. She takes care of the aging and mad José Arcadio Buendía under his chestnut tree, washing him and keeping "his hair and beard free of lice and nits" (95). In Remedios, whose name is

Spanish for *remedies,* the moody Aureliano discovers "the justification that he needed to live" (95).

Aureliano José. The son of Colonel Aureliano Buendía and Pilar Ternera. When he is born, since he is illegitimate, Remedios decides that "he would be considered their oldest child" (95). Then, when Remedios dies, Amaranta adopts Aureliano José and raises him "as a son who would share her solitude" (96).

He develops incestuous feelings toward his aunt, Amaranta, as they take baths together. Aureliano José feels "a strange trembling at the sight of the splendid breasts with their brown nipples . . . and he felt his skin tingle as he contemplated the way her skin tingled when it touched the water" (156). Their infatuation ceases when Amaranta realizes she is "floundering about in an autumnal passion, one that was dangerous and had no future" (157). He is later shot in the back by a Conservative soldier and dies.

Father Nicanor Reyna. The priest who comes to Macondo to officiate at the wedding of Remedios and Colonel Aureliano Buendía and then remains in the town. When he drinks hot chocolate, he levitates. He collects money from those who come to see his miraculous levitation, and proceeds to build a church that is "the largest in the world, with life-size saints and stained-glass windows on the sides, so that people would come from Rome to honor God in the center of impiety" (90).

Remedios the Beauty. The daughter of Santa Sofía de la Piedad and Arcadio, Remedios is the "most beautiful creature that had ever been seen in Macondo" (177), although she is entirely indifferent to that fact. She is so beautiful that Úrsula must keep her secluded except to go to mass, and then her face is covered with a black shawl. Men literally die for love of her, but she remains oblivious. Although she wears a shapeless sack dress and shaves her head, she remains as beautiful as ever.

Aureliano Segundo. One of the twin sons of Santa Sofía de la Piedad and Arcadio, he marries Fernanda del Carpio. He has grown to look like the José Arcadios. Obsessed by Melquíades's books, he attempts to decipher them and is visited by the dead Melquíades. Aureliano Segundo recognizes him at once "because that hereditary memory had been transmitted from generation to generation and had come to him through the memory of his grandfather" (200). He becomes "one of the most respected men in Macondo" (204).

Aureliano Segundo and his brother share the same mistress, Petra Cotes, just as the first Aureliano and his twin brother, José Arcadio, were both initiated by Pilar Ternera. Thanks to the influence of Petra Cotes, his animals proliferate, and Aureliano Segundo becomes a rich, if wild, man. He takes the route of dissipation, of gluttony, profligacy and moral carelessness, bringing the Buendía family one step closer to destruction.

Fernanda del Carpio. She is a beautiful and repressed daughter of the interior, born in a place that sounds like Bogotá, "a city six hundred miles away, a gloomy city where on ghostly nights the coaches of the viceroys still rattled through the cobbled streets" (221). Descended from Spanish nobility, she has always been told that "One day you will be a queen" (222), but she is miserable. One of the most beautiful women in the land, she is devoid of sensuality and is inhibited and nunlike. Fernanda has been raised as a woman of the Colombian oligarchy and García Márquez does not spare her:

> At the end of eight years, after having learned to write Latin poetry, play the clavichord, talk about falconry with gentlemen and apologetics with archbishops, discuss affairs of state with foreign rulers and affairs of God with the Pope, she returned to her parents' home to weave funeral wreaths. (223)

Not surprisingly Fernanda, devoid of any sense of the practical, makes a poor wife and a horrific mother.

José Arcadio Segundo. One of the twin sons of Santa Sofía de la Piedad and Arcadio, he grows up to resemble the bony Aurelianos. He asks Colonel Gerineldo Márquez to let him witness an execution and is horrified when he thinks that the executed man is being buried alive. His earliest memory is of the man being shot. He assists the priest at mass and he becomes a Conservative, scandalizing Colonel Márquez. He opens up the river, attempting to establish a boat line between Macondo and the rest of the world but succeeds in bringing only one boat up the river. Then he takes a job as a foreman with the banana company. When the workers begin protesting working conditions, however, José Arcadio Segundo becomes a union leader and leads the workers of the banana company in their strike. The gringos soon spread disinformation about him: "Quite soon he was pointed out as the agent of an international conspiracy against public order" (320).

José Arcadio Segundo witnesses the massacre perpetrated by the banana company; unconscious and believed dead, he is transported along with three thousand corpses by freight train to the sea.

By the time he returns to Macondo, the banana company and the government have succeeded in convincing the people that there have not been any dead at all through an "extraordinary proclamation to the nation" (332). José Arcadio Segundo survives concealed in the magic room of Melquíades, somehow rendered invisible to soldiers who are searching for him.

Eventually José Arcadio Segundo goes mad, believing that every day the train left Macondo "with two hundred cars loaded with dead people: 'they were all of those who were at the station,' he shouted. 'Three thousand four hundred eight'" (361–362). Eventually, however, he becomes "the most lucid inhabitant of the house" (375) as he teaches the last little Aureliano to read and write and initiates him in the study of the parchments of Melquíades. José Arcadio Segundo also teaches him the truth of what happened in the banana strike.

Petra Cotes. A "clean young mulatto woman with yellow almond-shaped eyes that gave her face the ferocity of a panther" (205), she arrives in Macondo during the war. The twins Aureliano Segundo and José Arcadio Segundo mislead her into thinking they are one person, and she sleeps with them both at first, although José Arcadio Segundo eventually drops her. After he marries Fernanda, Aureliano Segundo continues to live with Petra Cotes.

Renata Remedios (Meme). The daughter of Aureliano Segundo and Fernanda del Carpio. Her mother calls her Renata. The Buendía family calls her "Meme," short for Remedios. Seduced by the idle pleasures and moral carelessness of the Americans (gringos), Meme rebels against the manners of Amaranta and Fernanda: "She had to make a great effort not to throw at them their prissiness, their poverty of spirit, their delusions of grandeur" (291).

She has an affair with Mauricio Babilonia. Her fate is terrible as, after her lover is killed while sneaking into the bathroom where she waits for him, her mother exiles her to a convent where she will be imprisoned forever. The cruel fate of Meme also prefigures the fall of the Buendía family:

> She was still thinking about Mauricio Babilonia, his smell of grease, and his halo of butterflies, and she would keep on thinking about him for all the days of her life until the remote autumn morning when she died of old age, with her name changed and her head shaved and without ever having spoken a word, in a gloomy hospital in Cracow. (319)

Mauricio Babilonia. A young man "sallow, with dark and melancholy eyes" and a "dreamy air" (305). He is an apprentice mechanic in the banana company garage. But Mauricio Babilonia has a "genuine elegance" (305) and he becomes the lover of Meme. He is a flawed man, bearing beneath his shirt "the rash of the banana company" (305), but wherever he goes he is surrounded by yellow butterflies. The child he fathers with Meme is named Aureliano. From the day Mauricio Babilonia is shot and killed, his spinal column shattered, Meme never again speaks.

José Arcadio. The son of Aureliano Segundo and Fernanda del Carpio and the brother of Meme. He goes away to a seminary in Europe, and Úrsula hopes that he will become a priest. When he returns, he is a vivid presence:

> His hands were pale, with green veins and fingers that were like parasites, and he wore a solid gold ring with a round sunflower opal on his left index finger. (393)

He remains, however, "an autumnal child, terribly sad and solitary," (393) the son of Fernanda. He had left the seminary long before his return to Macondo, yielding to dissipation, remembering with nostalgia his lust for Amaranta, an echo of the feelings of Aureliano José before him. When this José Arcadio discovers Úrsula's buried treasure, he wastes it in pedophilic debauchery. His asthma is relieved when Aureliano, his illegitimate nephew, purchases a remedy at the pharmacy run by Mercedes, "a girl with the stealthy beauty of a serpent of the Nile" (401) who will become the wife of Gabriel, the author.

José Arcadio and Aureliano are unable to recognize Aureliano Amador, the last of the colonel's seventeen illegitimate sons, and so the police "with their Mausers" are able "neatly" to penetrate, with bullets the cross of ashes that has remained for years on his forehead (403). José Arcadio is murdered by the children he has molested, and dies thinking of Amaranta, even as his nephew Aureliano realizes only at his death "how much he had begun to love him" (404). These are two more failures of love marking the fall of the Buendía line.

Amaranta Úrsula. The daughter of Fernanda and Aureliano Segundo, and the sister of Meme and José Arcadio, she is "Active, small, and indomitable like Úrsula" while being "almost as pretty and provocative as Remedios the Beauty" (407). Amaranta Úrsula will be the last woman of the Buendía line. She attempts to "rescue the community which had been singled out by misfortune" (408), but the Buendía propensities overwhelm her. A modern woman, she marries Gaston but is too attracted to solitude and falls in love with her nephew.

Gaston. The European husband of Amaranta Úrsula, he is an aviator and a romantic who "had come close to killing himself and his sweetheart simply to make love in a field of violets" (409). His wife, however, prefers her nephew. Gaston departs, leaving it to the Germans to create the Colombian national airline, Avianca, as they did.

Aureliano Babilionia. The last male Buendía to grow to adulthood, Aureliano is born in secret in the convent where his mother, Meme, was sent after his father, Mauricio Babilonia, was killed. After a nun delivers the illegitimate Aureliano to Macondo, his maternal grandmother, Fernanda, wishes to "throw him in the bathroom cistern" (315), but instead locks him up in Colonel Aureliano Buendía's old workshop. Like those of the Arcadios, his sex organ, "that was like a turkey's wattles" (316), is impressive. As he grows up, he possesses the "prominent cheekbones," and the firm and rather pitiless line of the lips of Colonel Aureliano Buendía (383–384).

The incest that has threatened the family since the days of Amaranta's youth is now fulfilled. Having learned the arts of lovemaking from the prostitute Nigromanta, as the young men of Colombia customarily learn from prostitutes and relatives, he returns to seduce Amaranta Úrsula. Aunt and nephew Buendía consummate their passion. Amaranta Úrsula dies giving birth to the result of their incestuous union, Aureliano, and he is that child born with a pig's tail so dreaded by Úrsula. The Buendía family line now comes to an end.

MAJOR THEMES

The underlying theme of *One Hundred Years of Solitude* is the destructive power of solitude. By the end, the last Buendías, Amaranta Úrsula and Aureliano, are left alone in the world, drifting "toward the desert of disenchantment and oblivion" (441). The fall of Macondo can be traced to the obsession with solitude that infected the first José Arcadio Buendía.

All the other themes of *One Hundred Years of Solitude* flow from this one central motif. Solitude, seemingly inevitable, is connected to the passage of time, of which García Márquez reminds the reader with persistent time cues, beginning in the first sentence of the novel, where there are two: "many

Banana plantation near the town of Santa Marta, where the 1928 banana strike fictionalized in *One Hundred Years of Solitude* took place

years later " and "that distant afternoon" (1). The next line introduces another: "at that time" (1).

Incest is another theme—incest and its link to solitude. Úrsula Iguarán and José Arcadio Buendía are cousins. The precedent for disaster befalling incestuous relations between members of this family is ever with her:

> An aunt of Úrsula's, married to an uncle of José Arcadio Buendía, had a son who went through life wearing loose, baggy trousers and who bled to death after having lived forty-two years in the purest state of virginity, for he had been born and had grown up with a cartilaginous tail in the shape of a corkscrew and with a small tuft of hair on the tip. A pig's tail that was never allowed to be seen by any woman and that cost him his life when a butcher friend did him the favor of chopping it off with his cleaver (22).

Another important theme of *One Hundred Years of Solitude* is that individuals develop their uniqueness as a result of causal connections, with one event of their lives shaping another and so contributing to the evolution of their characters. It is not heredity, but environment which shapes their temperaments and their fates. Rebeca's sad childhood leads directly to her solitary adolescence, and to a sorrowful solitude that lasts to the end of her life. Arcadio's indifferent upbringing and his illegitimacy deform his character and account for his cruelty:

> Arcadio was a solitary and frightened child during the insomnia plague, in the midst of Úrsula's utilitarian fervor, during the delirium of José Arcadio Buendía, the hermetism of Aureliano, and the mortal rivalry between Amaranta and Rebeca. (121)

He grows up without anyone really noticing him: "no one imagined how much he wept in secret" (121). He becomes corrupt, confiscating public money and using it for his own ends. If some characters are born with certain powers, like Colonel Aureliano Buendía and his clairvoyance, most become what their experience has made them.

The source of love and its power in this novel are inexplicable, another persistent García Márquez theme. In a *coup de foudre*, love at first sight, Aureliano feels an instant affection for little Remedios. When she comes to the door of his workroom "his heart froze with terror as he saw the girl at the door, dressed in pink organdy and wearing white boots" (71).

Yet, even if love arises instantaneously and seemingly without reason, it is not necessarily superficial. Aureliano's love for Remedios is powerful enough to last for a lifetime: "He wanted to stay beside that lily skin forever, beside those emerald eyes, close to that voice that called him 'sir' with every question . . . " (71). From then on "everything, even music, reminded him of Remedios" (71)—as accurate a description of the experience of falling in love as any author has offered.

That life is frequently absurd is another persistent theme of *One Hundred Years of Solitude*. The author's sense of humor is aroused as Aureliano begins to write poetry, not only "on the harsh pieces of parchment that Melquíades gave him," but also "on the bathroom walls" and "on the skin of his arms" (72). Rebeca, waiting for a letter from Pietro Crespi in a "slough of delirium" (72), behaves in a similar way. The father of Remedios puts the irrationality of love bluntly and truly: "It doesn't make sense," he argues, "we have six other daughters, all unmarried, and at an age where they deserve it, who would be delighted to be the honorable wife of a gentleman as serious and hardworking as your son, and Aurelito lays his eyes precisely on the one who still wets her bed" (76).

"Love is a disease" (75), José Arcadio Buendía shouts when he learns that his son Aureliano wishes to marry a child. But it is not the youthfulness of Remedios that upsets him. "With so many pretty and decent girls around," he argues, "the only thing that occurs to you is to get married to the daughter of our enemy" (75).

The senseless cruelty of war, another major theme in *One Hundred Years of Solitude*, is expressed in the physical transformation of Colonel Aureliano Buendía, after his years of fighting in the lost Liberal cause:

> On his waist he wore a holster with the flap open and his hand, which was always on the butt of the pistol, revealed the same watchful and resolute tension as his look. His head, with

deep recessions in the hairline now, seemed to have been baked in a slow oven. His face, tanned by the salt of the Caribbean, had acquired a metallic hardness. He was preserved against imminent old age by a vitality that had something to do with the coldness of his insides. He was taller than when he had left, paler and bonier, and he showed the first symptoms of resistance to nostalgia. "Good Lord," Úrsula said to herself. "Now he looks like a man capable of anything." He was. (170–171)

García Márquez expresses how we are different people at different stages of our lives; Colonel Aureliano Buendía has become a reflection of how he has lived.

After Colonel Aureliano Buendía returns from the civil war, the sexual and political themes merge. Ruined by war and now heartless, Colonel Aureliano Buendía has permitted the execution of the decent and good General Moncada. His bodyguards have ransacked the house of Moncada's widow. Now he orders the execution of his best friend, Colonel Gerineldo Márquez, who protested against his signing away all the principles of the Liberals in the peace treaty.

Personally allowing themselves to be guided by lust and politically infected by the pursuit of power, the Buendías have transgressed against the human solidarity which alone would ensure their survival. Yet, there is hope, if not finally for the Buendías, then for humanity. Colonel Aureliano Buendía sets his friend Colonel Gerineldo Márquez free, the friend who would rather die than see him "changed into a bloody tyrant" (184).

When Aureliano does finally cease being a warrior, he finds all normal affections gone; he cannot remember his love for his wife, Remedios, or his love for his mother, now old and worn. He is left to await his death.

IMAGES

Beginning with the ice mentioned in the first line, *One Hundred Years of Solitude* is replete with images, which appeal to the five senses, not only visual images, but images of sound, of smell, of touch, and of taste. José Arcadio Buendía and his men are forced to "eat macaws, whose blue flesh had a harsh and musky taste" (11). Their lungs "were overwhelmed by a suffocating smell of blood" (12). The world of *One Hundred Years of Solitude* is a world made richly visible by scores of such vivid images. So the band of founders of Macondo come upon "an enormous Spanish galleon. Tilted slightly to the starboard, it had hanging from its intact masts, the dirty rags of its sails in the midst of its rigging, which was adorned with orchids. The hull, covered with an armour of petrified barnacles and soft moss, was firmly fastened into a surface of stones" (12). This ship is more than a mere relic, however, for in García Márquez the strongest of his images are enlisted in the service of reiterating his major themes: "The whole structure seemed to occupy its own space, one of solitude and oblivion, protected from the vices of time and the habits of the birds" (12).

The Spanish galleon reminds the founders of Macondo of their Spanish forbears, and points as well to liberation by revealing the proximity of the sea. The galleon is alluded to later in the text in the description of the settlers of Macondo as "shipwrecked people with no escape" (26).

Many other images recur during the course of the narrative. Among these are the "gigantic chestnut tree" (9) in the courtyard which appears in the first pages and will reappear, and the almond trees planted by José Arcadio Buendía which are "broken and dusty" (43) after the invasion of the banana company. García Márquez is also fond of compiling images in lists, as in the catalogue of diseases that the gypsy Melquíades has survived:

> He had survived pellagra in Persia, scurvy in the Malayan archipelago, leprosy in Alexandria, beriberi in Japan, bubonic plague in Madagascar, an earthquake in Sicily, and a disastrous shipwreck in the strait of Magellan (6).

The gypsies provide some of the most profound imagery, as in José Arcadio Buendía's walk among the gypsies "suffocated by the mingled breath of manure and sandals that the crowd exhaled" (17).

Often the imagery borders on magic: that Amaranta and Arcadio as children drink lizard broth and eat spider eggs together predicts their later sexual attraction. García Márquez, referring to Melquíades, describes the appearance of the vegetarian: "His skin become covered with a thin moss, similar to that which flourished on the antique vest that he never took off . . . " (78). Even more vivid is the image of the dead body of Melquíades: "the body was already beginning to burst with a livid fluorescence, the soft whistles of which impregnated the house with a pestilential vapor" (78).

At times García Márquez clusters his images so there are powerful descriptions of Macondo after the rains. Amaranta Úrsula and

Aureliano, her nephew, are living in a decaying house where weeds grow in the rooms, and the heat and dust are so strong that it is impossible to breathe. The "swampy streets" are filled with "animal skeletons covered with red lilies" (355–356). A glove belonging to Patricia Brown, the wife of the most sinister of the gringo invaders, is found "in an automobile smothered in wild pansies" (356). Lizards and rats fight to the death inside the church. Petra Cotes keeps a mule in her bedroom, feeding it "on the percale sheets, the Persian rugs, the plush bedspreads, the velvet drapes, and the canopy embroidered with gold thread and silk tassels on the episcopal bed" (358). These accelerating images of devastation culminate in the image of the red ants that eat the baby Aureliano, the last Buendía.

To connect the many diverse episodes of this narrative, images are reiterated. When Amaranta Úrsula returns from Europe, she scatters the red ants "who had already taken possession of the porch" (406), and at the close of the novel red ants consume her baby. She brings to Macondo by train "fish and shellfish in boxes of ice" (410), the same sort of ice that seemed such a wonder to Colonel Aureliano Buendía when he was a boy.

García Márquez includes his political perspective through imagery as well: "Sir Francis Drake had gone crocodile hunting with cannons and . . . repaired them and stuffed them with straw to bring to Queen Elizabeth" (10–11). Desecration of the environment, and cruelty to animals, always suggest evil in the works of García Márquez. Likewise, sexuality is conveyed through vivid images, as in young José Arcadio's first sexual experience: "José Arcadio felt his bones filling up with foam, a languid fear, and a terrible desire to weep" (28).

The final images are those of destruction as Aureliano is surrounded by "prehistoric plants and steaming puddles and luminous insects that had removed all trace of man's passage" (446). The progress of the red ants cannot be postponed. The world closes in around the last surviving Buendías.

METAPHORS AND SIMILES

García Márquez has said that in *One Hundred Years of Solitude* "there isn't a single conscious symbol."[27] The novel, however, is replete with metaphors. Metaphors are so natural to the narrative that they are almost undetectable, as in the description of José Arcadio's large penis as his "enormous motley nakedness" (100). The conceit continues as José Arcadio pulls Rebeca into his hammock: "She had to make a supernatural effort not to die when a startlingly regulated cyclonic power lifted her up by the waist and despoiled her of her intimacy with three slashes of its claws and quartered her like a little bird" (101).

Figures of speech, metaphors, and similes are the means by which García Márquez tells his story in *One Hundred Years of Solitude*. The smallest moment is embellished by a comparison, the better to examine its texture and its richness. When Colonel Aureliano Buendía falls in love with the magistrate's youngest daughter, Remedios, age nine, "It was a physical sensation that almost bothered him when he walked, like a pebble in his shoe" (64).

As Wood puts it, "beliefs and metaphors become forms of fact" in *One Hundred Years of Solitude* while "more ordinary facts become uncertain." Legends are "treated as truths—because they are truths to those who believe them."[28]

Thus Úrsula engages in "the secret and implacable labor of a small ant" (13–14), a metaphor for her resilience. His sons, she tells José Arcadio Buendía, are "running wild, just like donkeys" (15), as simile follows metaphor. On the day Colonel Aureliano Buendía is to be shot, there is the "aluminum glow of dawn" (141). Later, lawyers in dark suits "flapped about the colonel like crows" (230). The carriage in which Fernanda transports her errant daughter Meme away to the convent from which she will never return is "like an enormous bat" (317). When the train comes to Macondo for the first time, a woman says the noise is "like a kitchen dragging a village behind it" (239).

Some of the metaphors are outlandish, such as Garcia's Marquez's equating the politics of Colonial Aureliano Buendía with a quack's medicinal cures; during the banana uprising Úrsula believes she is once more "living through the dangerous times when her son Aureliano carried the homeopathic pills of subversion in his pocket" (320). Other metaphors are horrific, befitting thematic urgency, as in the description of the three regiments which arrive to put down the strike of the banana company workers: "Their snorting of a many-headed dragon filled the glow of noon with a pestilential vapor" (325).

Ice is not only a frequent image in the novel, but also a metaphor as the aging Amaranta thinks of her aged rival Rebeca each morning "when the ice of her heart awakened her in her solitary bed" (236). The implaca-

Cover for a Brazilian edition of *One Hundred Years of Solitude*

bility with which Amaranta has shielded herself from pain all her life, thereby destroying her own happiness, is compared to "ice" residing in her heart. The companion metaphor to Amaranta's state is that of fire, or burning:

> solitude had made a selection in her memory and had burned the dimming piles of nostalgic waste that life had accumulated in her heart, and had purified, magnified, and eternalized the others. . . . (236)

As the massacre of the workers, women, and children is about to begin, José Arcadio Segundo is "sweating ice" (327). The crowd is "systematically being cut off all around like an onion being peeled by the insatiable and methodical shears of the machine guns" (329).

IRONY

García Márquez uses irony frequently. For his new weapon, the magnifying glass, José Arcadio Buendía puts together "a manual of startling instructional clarity and an irresistible power of conviction" (3), but this manual is for a weapon of destruction that does not work. Dramatic irony is present in the fact that despite Úrsula's repeated warnings against incest, the Buendías are continually tempted by it, and when Amaranta Úrsula and Aureliano Babilonia consummate their incestuous love, the baby with a pig's tail is born.

MAGIC REALISM

Juxtaposed with the realism of *One Hundred Years of Solitude* are instances of the technique with which García Márquez has been most closely associated: magic realism, what the Cuban novelist Alejo Carpentier first called "lo real maravilloso americano" (the magical realism of the Americans). As critic Edwin Williamson has put it, "magical realism is a narrative style which consistently blurs the traditional realist distinction between fantasy and reality."[29] Wood defines magic realism as "distortion stumbles on a truth."[30]

With the aid of nostalgia, the latent magic in the ordinary emerges so that when Pietro Crespi shows Amaranta a watercolor of Venice, "nostalgia would transform the smell of mud and putrefying shellfish of the canals into the warm aroma of flowers" (118).

García Márquez has said that "everyday life in Latin America shows us that reality is full of extraordinary things."[31] He outlined the principles of magic realism when he declared that "you cannot invent or imagine just whatever you fancy because then you risk not telling the truth and lies are more serious in literature than in real life. Even the most seemingly arbitrary creation has its rules. You can throw away the fig leaf of rationalism only if you don't then lapse into total chaos and irrationality."[32] Nowhere is the magic realism of the work more richly sensual than in García Márquez's description of the gypsies who have attracted the attention of José Arcadio Buendía:

MAKING REALITY CREDIBLE

"In Latin America and the Carribean, artists have had to invent very little. In fact, their problem has been just the opposite: making their reality credible. It's been this way since our historical beginnings; indeed, there are no writers in our literature less believable and at the same time more devoted to reality than the chroniclers of the Indies. . . .

Gabriel García Márquez

From "Latin America's Impossible Reality," translated by Eleria Brunet, *Harper's*, 270 (January 1985), p. 13.

> They were new gypsies, young men and women who knew only their own language, handsome specimens with oily skins and intelligent hands, whose dances and music sowed a panic of uproarious joy through the streets, with parrots painted all colors reciting Italian arias, and a hen who laid a hundred golden eggs to the sound of a tambourine, and a trained monkey who read minds, and the multiple-use machine that could be used at the same time to sew on buttons and reduce fevers, and the apparatus to make a person forget his bad memories, and a poultice to lose time, and a thousand more inventions so ingenious and unusual that José Arcadio Buendía must have wanted to invent a memory machine so that he could remember them all. (17)

As if it were an entirely normal occurrence, the ghost of the man José Arcadio Buendía murdered, Prudencio Aguilar, appears to Úrsula. When she tells her husband what she has seen "he did not think much of it. 'This just means that we can't stand the weight of our conscience'" (24–25), he tells her. Thus, magic is utilized to express a psychological truth. Guilt stays with human beings, and for the rest of his life José Arcadio Buendía is "tormented by the immense desolation with which the dead man had looked at him through the rain, his deep nostalgia as he yearned for living people . . . " (25). He gathers a group and crosses the mountains to found Macondo, just so that the ghost of Prudencio can "Go in peace" (25).

Other instances of magic predict the rise of science, such as baby Amaranta's basket moving "by itself," making "a complete turn around the room" (39). José Arcadio Buendía attempts no explanation. A "plague of insomnia" (41) afflicts a tribe of Guajiro Indians, foreshadowing its infection of the community of Macondo.

But the first complete moment of magic realism comes during the church service when Father Nicanor Reyna pauses to tell his congregation, "Now we shall witness an undeniable proof of the infinite power of God" (90). At this, a boy brings him "a cup of thick and steaming chocolate, which he drank without pausing to breathe" (90). He closes his eyes and rises "six inches above the level of the ground" (90).

Such a miracle inspires a response in the local population, and his acolyte collects so much money that in less than a month Father Reyna begins the construction of his massive church. He tries to convert José Arcadio Buendía under the chestnut tree, but José Arcadio Buendía rejects the "transmutation of chocolate" (91) as proof of the existence of God, demanding a daguerreotype of God as final proof.

In the work of García Márquez, magic realism is intimately connected with theme. Rebeca, upon the return of José Arcadio, is so taken with him that she falls ill with vile disease; for this author, love and disease exhibit similar symptoms: "she sucked her finger with so much anxiety that she developed a callus on her thumb. She vomited up a green liquid with dead leeches in it . . . " (100). Magic reappears near the end of the novel when Aureliano's friend Alvaro abandons Macondo, buying "an eternal ticket on a train that never stopped traveling" (433), seemingly an impossibility if one employs the standard of literal realism, but in fact true as an expression of human restlessness and the need to travel.

Equally magical, if psychologically realistic, is the moment when José Arcadio is shot:

> A trickle of blood came out under the door, crossed the living room, went out into the street, continued on in a straight line across the uneven terraces, went down steps and climbed over

curbs, passed along the Street of the Turks, turned a corner to the right and another to the left, made a right angle at the Buendía house, went in under the closed door, crossed through the parlor, hugging the walls so as not to stain the rugs, went on to the other living room, made a wide curve to avoid the dining-room table, went along the porch with the begonias, and passed without being seen under Amaranta's chair as she gave an arithmetic lesson to Aureliano José, and went through the pantry and came out in the kitchen, where Úrsula was getting ready to crack thirty-six eggs to make bread (144–145).

An umbilical cord connects a child to its mother not only before birth, but throughout life and, magically, even after death, so strong is the bond between Úrsula and José Arcadio, mother and son. So momentous is this death that the smell of gunpowder never leaves this corpse, not even after he is placed "hermetically" in a "special coffin" that is "reinforced inside with iron plates and fastened together with steel bolts" (145). The cemetery smells of powder for years until finally the banana company, which is introduced into the novel for the first time with this episode, covers the grave "with a shell of concrete" (146).

The instances of magic realism in *One Hundred Years of Solitude* are many. With the death of José Arcadio Buendía a light rain of yellow flowers falls all through the night:

they fell on the town all through the night in a silent storm, and they covered the roofs and blocked the doors and smothered the animals who slept outdoors. So many flowers fell from the sky that in the morning the streets were carpeted with a compact cushion and they had to clear them away with shovels and rakes so that the funeral procession could pass by (153).

Through this infusion of magic, García Márquez pays homage to this valiant figure, founder of the community. Although José Arcadio Buendía became disoriented by the promise of science, he expresses for García Márquez the folly of the entire human race in the twentieth century.

In *One Hundred Years of Solitude* magic appears with the notion of heredity. All of the sons of Colonel Aureliano Buendía, no matter who their mothers are, are born "with a look of solitude" (165). Equally magical is the way the characteristics of the José Arcadios and the Aurelianos begin to merge, so that the son of the colonel, Aureliano José, soon expresses the "lewd and lazy leanings" of his uncle José Arcadio.

The priest, Father Antonio Isabel, puts crosses of ashes on the foreheads of all seventeen illegitimate sons of Colonel Aureliano Buendía, crosses that will not wash off. "'From now on,'" Úrsula says, "'everyone will know who you are'" (234), a situation that will prove fatal to them all when they are tracked down by the banana company's assassins. That these crosses magically never disappear symbolizes the fact that identity—the unique identity of every individual—is immutable.

The most notorious example of magic realism in *One Hundred Years of Solitude* concerns Remedios the Beauty. It is foreshadowed when the reader is told that she is "not a creature of this world" (213), that she reaches the age of twenty without knowing how to read or write, and wanders "naked through the house because her nature rejected all manner of convention" (213). Yet, a "penetrating lucidity" permits this Remedios "to see the reality of things beyond any formalism" (214). The depth of her understanding, not her simple-mindedness, is what makes her "not a creature of this world." As Colonel Aureliano Buendía puts it, "it's as if she's come back from twenty years of war" (214).

The magic of Remedios, as if beauty were itself so unusual as to be inexplicable, begins with the power of her personal scent. The man who falls to his death admiring her body dies with "the suffocating odor of Remedios the Beauty on his skin. It was so deep in his body that the cracks in his skull did not give off blood but an amber-colored oil that was impregnated with that secret perfume" (252). People soon realize that so intoxicating is this woman that her smell keeps "on torturing men beyond death, right down to the dust of their bones" (252).

A man who manages to touch her dies soon after, as if the gods were protecting her beauty as something sacred and not to be defiled. Having "boasted of his audacity . . . the kick of a horse crushed his chest and a crowd of outsiders saw him die in the middle of the street, drowned in his own bloody vomiting" (253). The paradox is that beauty cannot exist in this world because it is immune even to love; it occurs to no one that "to conjure away her dangers, all that was needed was a feeling as primitive and as simple as that of love" (253).

No wonder then that García Márquez spares Remedios the suffering of the beautiful by rescuing her and sending her to a heaven

Dust jacket for the first U.S. translation (1970) of *Cien años de solidad*

beyond the violence of male physical desire. One day her mother, Fernanda, asks her to help fold the sheets. Remedios the Beauty begins to rise to the heavens in a miracle of levitation. Úrsula watches her great-granddaughter go:

> Úrsula, almost blind at the time, was the only person who was sufficiently calm to identify the nature of that determined wind and she left the sheets to the mercy of the light as she watched Remedios the Beauty waving good-bye in the midst of the flapping sheets that rose up with her, abandoning with her the environment of beetles and dahlias and passing through the air with her as four o'clock in the afternoon came to an end, and they were lost forever with her in the upper atmosphere where not even the highest-flying birds of memory could reach her (255).

Only magic can save José Arcadio Segundo, the witness to the banana company's massacre of three thousand citizens of Macondo. Having taken one of the colonel's golden fishes, the officer pursuing José Arcadio Segundo sees Melquíades' old room where José Arcadio Segundo is hiding with the eyes of Colonel Aureliano Buendía. Blinded by the vision of the colonel, the office fails to see the union leader sitting right there on the cot. Since only magic can save José

Arcadio Segundo, García Márquez is also making the point that in fact no one could be saved from the brutality of the Colombian hierarchy as it acted on behalf of the banana company.

After the departure of the banana company, it rains for four years, eleven months, and two days, indicating the full measure of the destruction the banana company wrought on this community. As he often does, García Márquez describes the fantastic with specific time cues, the better to make a case for believability.

Úrsula has predicted that she will die when the weather clears, but though she is more than one hundred years old she has to "make a great effort to fulfill her promise" (359). When she finally does expire, thousands of birds die and fall from the heavens as if nature were mourning the demise of this strongest figure in the Buendía family. The magic that presages her death is the means by which the author bids her, his favorite character, his affectionate farewell, as her grandson's widow, Santa Sofía de la Piedad, notices a certain confusion in nature:

> the roses smelled like goosefoot, a pod of chick peas fell down and the beans lay on the ground in a perfect geometrical pattern in the shape of a starfish, and one night she saw a row of luminous orange disks pass across the sky. (369)

After Úrsula's death, a biped with a cloven hoof makes its flamboyant appearance, a monster with a "green and greasy liquid" flowing from its wounds:

> Its body was covered with rough hair, plagued with small ticks, and the skin was hardened with the scales of a remora fish, but unlike the priest's description, its human parts were more like those of a sickly angel than of a man, for its hands were tense and agile, its eyes large and gloomy, and on its shoulder blades it had the scarred-over and calloused stumps of powerful wings which must have been chopped off by a woodsman's ax. (370)

This monster is a creature of the apocalypse, the end of time, which occurs at the close of the novel when the Buendía line is extinguished, and Macondo returns to dust. The last visitation of magic comes when the nasty children brought to the house by the final José Arcadio attempt to confiscate and destroy the parchments of Melquíades. But as soon as they lay their "hands on the yellowed sheets an angelic force lifted them off the ground and held them suspended in the air until Aureliano returned and took the parchments away from them" (399). This "angelic force" is the force that makes art immortal, since once they are deciphered the parchments turn out to be the novel, *One Hundred Years of Solitude.*

At other important moments in this novel, magic does not intervene. Signing the bitter peace of Neerlandia, Colonel Aureliano Buendía escapes to his tent where he shoots himself in the chest in exactly the circle where he thinks his heart is located, a circle that had been painted for him in iodine by his doctor. The bullet passes through the colonel's body without injuring him. No magic has been involved. "'That was my masterpiece,'" the doctor reveals "with satisfaction. 'It was the only point where a bullet could pass through without harming any vital organ'" (193).

By the end, so overwhelmingly has solitude infected the Buendías that the house needs "only one last breath to be knocked down" (440). The line seems both an exaggeration and a reality. In fact, when a journalist went to Aracataca to find *la casa* (the house) where García Márquez spent the first eight years of his life, he discovered that the place was being consumed by red ants. Life was once more imitating art, a persistent García Márquez theme.

NOTES

1. Rita Guibert, *Seven Voices: Seven Latin American Writers Talk to Rita Guibert,* translated by Frances Partridge (New York: Knopf, 1973), p. 306.

2. Gabriel García Márquez, *One Hundred Years of Solitude,* translated by Gregory Rabassa, Perenniel Classics (New York: HarperCollins, 1998), p. 13. All subsequent page citations are from this edition.

3. *Gabriel García Márquez: Magic and Reality,* written, directed, and produced by Ana Cristina Navarro, 60 mins., Films For the Humanities & Sciences, 1981, video.

4. Mario Vargas Llosa, "García Márquez: From Aracataca to Macondo," in *Gabriel García Márquez,* edited by Harold Bloom (New York & Philadelphia: Chelsea House, 1989), p. 6.

5. *Gabriel García Márquez: Magic and Reality.*

6. Ibid.

7. Regina Janes, "Liberals, Conservatives, and Bananas: Colombian Politics in the Fictions of Gabriel García Márquez," in *Gabriel García Márquez,* edited by Harold Bloom (New York & Philadelphia: Chelsea House, 1989), p. 140.

8. Peter Stone, "Gabriel García Márquez," in *Writers at Work: The Paris Review Interviews—Sixth Series,* edited by George Plimpton (New York: Viking, 1984), p. 326.

9. Claudia Dreifus, "*Playboy* Interview: Gabriel García Márquez," *Playboy* 30 (February 1983): 77.

10. Mario Vargas Llosa, *García Márquez: Historia de un Deicidio* (Barcelona: Breve Biblioteca de Respuesta: Barral Editores, 1971), p. 22.

11. Dreifus, "*Playboy* Interview": 172.

12. García Márquez and Plinio Apuleyo Mendoza, *The Fragrance of Guava,* translated by Ann Wright (London: Verso, 1983), pp. 34–35.

13. Marlise Simons, "A Talk with Gabriel García Márquez," *New York Times Book Review,* 5 December 1982.

14. Vargas Llosa, "From Aracataca to Macondo," p. 7.

15. Dreifus, "*Playboy* Interview": 76.

16. Ibid.: 74–75.

17. García Márquez and Mendoza, *The Fragrance of Guava,* p. 50.

18. Dreifus, "*Playboy* Interview": 74.

19. García Márquez and Mendoza, *The Fragrance of Guava,* p. 37.

20. Stone, *Writers at Work,* p. 324.

21. Ibid., p. 339.

22. Dreifus, "*Playboy* Interview": 76.

23. Michael Wood, *Gabriel García Márquez: One Hundred Years of Solitude* (Cambridge: Cambridge University Press, 1990), p. 9.

24. Ibid., p. 90.

25. Ibid., p. 102.

26. Clyde Griffin, "The Humour of *One Hundred Years of Solitude,*" in *Gabriel García Márquez: New Readings,* edited by Bernard McGuirk and Richard Cardwell (Cambridge: Cambridge University Press, 1987), p. 94.

27. Dreifus, "*Playboy* Interview": 174.

28. Wood, *Gabriel García Márquez,* p. 57.

29. Edwin Williamson, "Magical Realism and the Theme of Incest in *One Hundred Years of Solitude,*" in *Gabriel García Márquez: New Readings,* edited by Bernard McGuirk and Richard Cardwell (Cambridge: Cambridge University Press, 1987), p. 45.

30. Wood, *Gabriel García Márquez,* p. 4.

31. García Márquez and Mendoza, *The Fragrance of Guava,* p. 35.

32. Ibid., p. 31.

THE EVOLUTION OF
ONE HUNDRED YEARS OF SOLITUDE

*O**ne Hundred Years of Solitude* was the first novel García Márquez attempted to write. The genesis of the novel came during a trip he took when he was between the ages of fifteen and twenty-two—he has given conflicting accounts to interviewers over the years as to when the trip occurred, for example, telling Mario Vargas Llosa that he was sixteen years old at the time, Plinio Apuleyo Mendoza that he was eighteen, and Peter Stone that he was twenty-two.[1]

Raised by his maternal grandparents, after the death of his grandfather the eight-year-old García Márquez had gone to live with his parents, who were then living in Sucre. Only when his grandmother died did he return to Aracataca, with his mother. The purpose of the trip was to sell the family home in which he had been raised.

"Nothing had really changed," he noticed, "but I felt that I wasn't really looking at the village, but I was *experiencing* it as if I were reading it. It was as if everything I saw had already been written, and all I had to do was to sit down and copy what was already there . . . for all practical purposes everything had evolved into literature: the houses, the people, and the memories."[2] He also noticed something else:

> I had the sensation that I had left time, that what had separated me from the town was not distance but *time*. So I walked along the streets with my mother and I realized that she was going through something similar. We walked to the pharmacy which belonged to people who'd been close friends of the family. Behind the counter sat a lady working on a sewing machine. My mother said, "How are you, my friend?" When the woman finally recognized her, she stood up, and they embraced and cried and said absolutely nothing for more than a half hour. So I had the feeling that the whole town was dead—even those who were alive. I remembered everyone as they had been before, and now they were dead. That day, I realized that all the short stories I had

García Márquez's birthplace in Aracataca, the house where he was raised by his maternal grandparents and that was the model for the Buendía home in *One Hundred Years of Solitude*

written to that point were simply intellectual elaborations, nothing to do with my reality. [3]

The house of his maternal grandparents, Nicolás Márquez and Tranquilina Iguarán, had deteriorated in his absence. That moment is recapitulated in *One Hundred Years of Solitude* when Colonel Aureliano Buendía returns to Macondo in the middle of one of his wars and discovers that in his absence time has destroyed both the village and his house. Mario Vargas Llosa contends that it was at this moment, with this recognition, that García Márquez became a novelist: he would dedicate his life to contradicting reality, to supplanting it with another reality that he created in his imagination from the illusory model of his memories:

A partir de ese momento, García Márquez se consagrará a demostrar, mediante el ejercicio de una vocación deicida, lo que Aureliano y Amaranta Úrsula descrubren en un momento de sus vidas: *que las obsesiones dominantes prevalecen contra la muerte.*[4]

(From that moment García Márquez consecrated himself to demonstrating, by means of exercising a deictic vocation, what Aureliano and Amaranta Úrsula discover in the ultimate moment of their lives: *that strong obsessions prevail over death*).

After his trip back to Aracataca, García Márquez tried to write the novel he had envisioned. Its title was originally "La Casa" (The House). García Márquez has described its early evolution:

I wanted the whole development of the novel to take place inside the house, and anything external would be just in terms of its impact on the house. I later abandoned the title of *The House,* but once the book goes into the town of Macondo it never goes any further.[5]

The work failed to develop. After writing a few chapters he felt he "was not yet ready to write a book as big as that." García Márquez would conclude later that he then had "neither the vital experience nor the literary means to complete it."[6] What he decided to do was "start something easier and progressively learn how to write. Mostly, I wrote short stories."[7]

In 1950 García Márquez quit law school and moved to Barranquilla where he wrote a column for *El Heraldo* newspaper, titling it "La Jirafa" (The Giraffe), and using the pseudonym "Septimus," after Septimus Warren Smith, a character in Virginia Woolf's novel *Mrs. Dalloway* (1925). He became a member of an important literary circle, the Barranquilla group. He tried again to write *One Hundred Years of Solitude.* His friend Germán Vargas has described García Márquez working on "La Casa" during his first years in Barranquilla, at the beginning of the 1950s:

Vestido con un pantalón de dracón y una camiseta a rayas de colorines, García Márquez encaramado sobre una mesa de la redacción de "El Heraldo" o sentado sobre su cama de madera en un cuartucho de "el Rastcacielos," un extraño burdel de cuatro pisos, sin ascensor. . . .[8]

(Dressed in an outlandish pair of pants and a striped shirt of many colors, García Márquez seated on a table in the newsroom of "El Heraldo" or on his wooden bed in a miserable little room

WRITING *ONE HUNDRED YEARS OF SOLITUDE*

" He has rediscovered his secret book, which is growing faster than ever.... 'I'm on top of the world,' he wrote us happily in November, 1965. 'After five years of absolute sterility, the book is literally gushing from me, without any problems of words.' He says it promises to run to four or five hundred pages, a veritable marathon for him. It has visited him like an old friend. 'In a sense, it's the first novel I started to write when I was seventeen, but it's much broader now. It's not only the story of Colonel Buendía, but of his whole family, from the founding of Macondo to the day the last Buendía commits suicide a hundred years later, putting an end to the line.' There are complications along the way. Names, for instance, in accordance with Macondo's laws of recurrence, tend to appear in duplicate. A chronology of events and a genealogical table might have to accompany the book, 'because the Buendías were in the habit of naming their children after their parents, and occasionally havoc reigns. In the hundred years of history there are four José Arcadio Buendías and three Aurelianos.'"

García Márquez

From Luis Harss and Barbara Dohmann, "Gabriel García Márquez, or the Lost Chord," in *Into the Mainstream: Conversations with Latin-American Writers* (New York: Harper & Row, 1967), pp. 338-339.

of "el Rastcielos," a strange bordello of four floors without an elevator. . . .)

Unable, no matter how hard he tried, to find the appropriate voice for "La Casa," he instead wrote the novella *La hojarasca* (1955; translated in *Leaf Storm and Other Stories*, 1972). The novella is set in Macondo, marking the first appearance of this town in García Márquez's fiction, but the Macondo of *Leaf Storm* is an impoverished and desolate location, not the vibrant community that it is in *One Hundred Years of Solitude*. Narrated alternately by a retired colonel, his daughter, and her son, the novel centers around the colonel's quest to honor his promise to give a decent burial to a recently deceased doctor whom the whole town despises. Stylistically, the story is related relatively realistically, without the fantastic elements and playfulness of García Márquez's later work.

García Márquez could not find a publisher for *Leaf Storm* at first; he later recalled that

> It took me five years to find a publisher. I sent it to Editorial Losada, a publishing house in Argentina, and they sent it back to me with a letter from the Spanish critic Guillermo de Torre advising me to concentrate on other things.[9]

In the 1960s, moving again to Barranquilla, after living as a journalist in Venezuela, he tried to write *One Hundred Years of Solitude* once more. Perhaps, he believed, if he returned to the life he had led when he was a reporter, he might succeed. Nothing happened.

In Mexico in 1963 he made "a second try at the novel." He had, "a clearer idea of the structure but not of the tone. I didn't yet know how to tell the story so that it would be believed. So, again, I took to writing short stories."[10]

He has said that during those years, between 1961 and 1964, he suffered from a form of writer's block. "I'll never write again,"[11] he despairingly told Colombian poet Álvaro Mutis, his friend and fellow member of the Barranquilla group. As his friend Emir Rodríguez Monegal later commented, "García Márquez era un hombre torturado, un habitante del infierno mas exquisto: el de la esterilidad literaria."[12] (He was a tortured man during this period, an inhabitant of an exquisite hell: that of literary sterility).

One day in January of 1965 García Márquez, his wife, Mercedes, and his sons, Rodrigo and Gonzalo, were driving along in their Opel automobile on the Mexico City–Acapulco highway. Suddenly, sitting there behind the wheel, García Márquez imagined every word of the first chapter of *One Hundred Years of Solitude*. "It was," he said, "as if I had read everything that was to be in it."[13]

"It was so ripe in me that I could have dictated the first chapter, word by word, to a typist,"[14] he has said. He made a quick U-turn, drove home, and began. For the next six months, Mercedes assumed the financial responsibility for the household. "Mercedes had to be like the women in the Colombian civil wars: she had to run the household and keep life going while I campaigned."[15] Having sold the car for money to live on, he descended into his study, which he called "The Cave of the Mafia," in a withdrawal similar to José Arcadio Buendía's isolating himself in his workshop in *One Hundred Years of Solitude*.

"Don't bother me, especially don't bother me about money," García Márquez told his wife. Mercedes pawned household appliances and borrowed money from friends to keep the household going and her husband supplied with what he needed. García Márquez has frequently spoken of the lengths to which Mercedes went in enabling him to write *One Hundred Years of Solitude*. Calling her "stupendous," he told William Kennedy that she made an arrangement with the butcher to pay him in monthly installments; when there was no money for the rent, she got the landlord to agree to wait six months to be paid:

> I didn't know what my wife was doing . . . and I didn't ask any questions. But there was always whiskey in the house. Good Scotch. In that respect my life hasn't changed much since those days. We always lived as if we had money. But when I was finished writing, my wife said, "Did you really finish it? We owe twelve thousand dollars." She had borrowed from friends for a year and a half."[16]

THE CHARACTERS OF *ONE HUNDRED YEARS OF SOLITUDE*

"Three of them got completely out of hand, in the sense that their personality and their lives didn't come out as I wanted. Aureliano José's awesome passion for his aunt Amaranta took me by surprise; José Arcadio Segundo was never the banana workers' Union leader I would have liked; and José Arcadio, the apprentice Pope, turned into a sort of decadent Adonis quite out of place in the novel as a whole."

García Márquez

From García Márquez and Plinio Apuleyo Mendoza, *The Fragrance of Guava,* translated by Ann Wright (London: Verso, 1983), pp. 76-77.

His children saw him only at night when he left his study, "intoxicado de cigarillos" (intoxicated by cigarettes), as Vargas Llosa puts it.[17] Álvaro Mutis and other friends came every night to visit the writer and encourage him; the group included María Luisa Elío and Jomí García Ascot, to whom he dedicated the novel.

For *One Hundred Years of Solitude,* García Márquez engaged in extensive research. He consulted books on alchemy, navigation, poisons, disease, cookery, home medicines, and, not least, the history of Colombia and its civil wars, which figure so profoundly in the novel. He had the twenty-four volumes of the *Encyclopaedia Britannica* open by his side as he wrote.

Some of the questions he pondered were: "How can you tell the sex of a shrimp? How is a man executed by a firing squad? How do you determine quality in bananas?" Later he said that he dropped a character "because I wasn't able to find anybody who could translate seven Papiamiento phrases." There was more: he "had to look up a great deal about Sanskrit; I had to figure out the weight of 7,214 doubloons so as to be certain that they could be carried by four kids. . . ."[18] "In my dreams," he has said of the period during which he wrote *One Hundred Years of Solitude,* "I was inventing literature."[19]

He solved another basic problem when he freed himself from the confines of strict linear chronology with events following each other in time. Flashbacks and flash-forwards raise the novel to a mythic level and allow for the repetition of the behavioral patterns that will be the ultimate cause of the downfall of the Buendía family and of Macondo, the community they have founded.

But, according to García Márquez, his most significant breakthrough came when he decided to use the same deadpan tone with which his grandmother had told him some of her most fabulous stories when he was a child: "my grandmother . . . used to tell me about the most atrocious things without turning a hair, as if it was something she'd just seen. I realized that it was her impassive manner and her wealth of images that made her stories so credible. I wrote *One Hundred Years of Solitude* using my grandmother's method."[20]

Alternately, García Márquez has attributed to one of his aunts this same storytelling approach. One of his aunts was always consulted to explain odd occurrences, and she could always persuade people of the validity of her absurd responses:

> . . . one day a child approached her with an oddly shaped egg and asked her why it was so peculiar. The aunt examined it carefully and answered, "Look, you want to know why this egg has this bulge? Well, because it's a basilisk egg. Light a fire in the patio." So they built the fire and burned the egg as if it were the most natural thing in the world to do. "This 'naturalness,'" García Márquez states, "gave me the key to *One Hundred Years of Solitude* in which the most frightful, the most unusual things are told with the same dead-pan expression my aunt had when they burned the basilisk egg on the patio, without ever even knowing what it was."[21]

Previously, García Márquez has revealed, he had "tried to tell the story without believing in it. I discovered that what I had to do was believe in them myself and write them with the same expression with which my grandmother told them: with a brick face."[22]

He drew his characters from his own experiences, but also from the unlikeliest of places. The minor character of General Lorenzo Gavilán came from *La muerte de Artemio Cruz* (1962; translated as *The Death of Artemio Cruz*, 1964) by Mexican novelist Carlos Fuentes. A reader had written to Fuentes wondering about the fate of the character General Lorenzo Gavilán, which had been left unresolved in Fuentes's novel. "Fuentes checked and realized it was true. I told Fuentes it could be fixed," García Márquez later recalled. "So that is why Lorenzo Gavilán, with the belt buckle from Morelia, dies in the Macondo banana workers' strike."[23]

The character of Úrsula, and the other women characters, were derived as well from his memories of stories told to him by his grandmother. She spoke of the civil wars and of a man who went to war, telling his wife, "you'll decide what to do with your children."[24] Out of this incident he drew his portrayal of the Buendía family during the civil war depicted in his novel.

He built the character of the priest who levitates when he drinks hot chocolate with care. This priest was based on a saintly priest in

Covers (left to right) of the 1983, 1979, and 1982 Colombian publications of *One Hundred Years of Solitude*

Aracataca, of whom people said that "he rose off the ground whenever he raised the chalice during Mass." García Márquez based an episode in the novel upon this remark, but it did not sound believable to him. "If I don't believe something," he says, "neither will the reader":

> So I decided to see how believable it was with other vessels and liquids. Well, he drank all sorts of things and nothing worked. Finally, I had him drink Coca-Cola and that seemed to be just the thing! However, I didn't want to give Coca-Cola free advertising, so I gave him hot chocolate, which also proved believable.[25]

As he was writing, he realized that given his time scheme, Úrsula Buendía had grown to be two hundred years old. At various moments in the composition of the novel he was aware "that she had lived too long, and I tried to have her die. However, she continued. I always needed her for something. She had to be kept until she died naturally."[26]

It was only when he reached the last chapter that he began to have fun. "I had the feeling nobody could stop it," he said, referring to the advancement of *One Hundred Years of Solitude* toward its conclusion, "that I could do anything I wanted with it, that the book was in the bag. In that state, I was so happy, especially after the early agonies, that I started to make those private jokes."[27]

It was then that he wrote Mercedes and his friends into the novel. He remarked later that "there are many more jokes in that section than are apparent to the casual reader. Friends see them and they die laughing, because they know what each one refers to. That was a book that *had* to be finished with great joy—because, in another sense, it is a very sad book. Like life, no?"[28]

He did not have a title until he came almost to the last page of the novel. Having abandoned the title "La Casa," along with the idea of having all the action occur inside one house, he was at a loss. Then the new title came to him: "I made some calculations and discovered that more than 100 years of solitude had passed but it wouldn't have sounded right to call the book *One Hundred and Forty-Three Years of Solitude*. I rounded off the number."[29]

García Márquez had "brooded over. . . . *One Hundred Years of Solitude* for fifteen or seventeen" years.[30] Eighteen months after he had begun writing the final draft, he had produced 1,300 pages of typescript, along with diagrams and sketches. These he promptly burned, lest critics misuse them by overanalyzing the work, limiting it, and hence depriving readers of its richness.

"I threw it out," García Márquez has explained, "not only so that the way the book was constructed shouldn't be known—that's something absolutely private—but in case that material should ever be sold. To sell it would be selling my soul, and I'm not going to let anyone do it, not even my children."[31]

He has put it another way. By burning his notes, "the critics would have to take the book on its own merits and not go looking in the original papers." For anyone to have seen his background material would have been "like being seen in your underwear,"[32] so intimate does he believe the writing process to be. Often he has used the conceit of the writer as magician. Keeping his secrets of fictional composition is like "the way magicians never tell others how they make a dove come out of a hat."[33]

The Argentine publishing house Editorial Sudamericana had asked García Márquez to send it his novel in progress. The publishers did not know that they would receive the new version of "La Casa." As García Márquez was about to send his manuscript, a series of mishaps occurred. The typist, who had the only copies of the chapters of *One Hundred Years of Solitude,* was hit by a bus; the pages went flying. Unhurt, she picked herself up and reassembled the typescript. Then on the day they were to mail the typescript, García Márquez and his wife arrived at the post office only to discover that they lacked the 160 pesos necessary for postage. Mailing only half the manuscript, García Márquez had to return later in the day to send the remainder. "Well, now all we need is for this novel to be bad!"[34] Mercedes said.

García Márquez had been so poised, so ready to write this book, that when he received the galley proofs, he changed only one word, although Paco Porrua, his editor at Editorial Sudamericana, had encouraged him to make any revisions he wished. Later García Márquez would say: "I had to live for twenty years and write four books of apprenticeship to discover that . . . the story had to be told, simply, the way my grandparents told it."[35]

NOTES

1. Mario Vargas Llosa, *García Márquez: Historia de un Deicidio* (Barcelona: Breve Biblioteca de Respuesta: Barral Editores, 1971), p. 88; Gabriel García Márquez and Plinio Apuleyo Mendoza, *The Fragrance of Guava*, translated by Ann Wright (London: Verso, 1983), p. 73; Peter Stone, "Gabriel García Márquez," in *Writers At Work: The Paris Review Interviews—Sixth Series*, edited by George Plimpton (New York: Viking, 1984), p. 321.

2. Stone, *Writers at Work*, p. 321.

3. Claudia Dreifus, "*Playboy* Interview: Gabriel García Márquez," *Playboy*, 30 (February 1983): 172.

4. Vargas Llosa, *Historia de un Deicidio*, p. 93.

5. Stone, *Writers at Work*, p. 337.

6. Rita Guibert, *Seven Voices: Seven Latin American Writers Talk to Rita Guibert*, translated by Frances Partridge (New York: Knopf), p. 306.

7. Dreifus, "*Playboy* Interview": 172.

8. Quoted in Vargas Llosa, *Historia de un Deicidio*, p. 37.

9. *The Fragrance of Guava*, p. 55.

10. Dreifus, "*Playboy* Interview": 172.

11. Gene H. Bell-Villada, *Gabriel García Márquez: The Man and His Work* (Chapel Hill & London: University of North Carolina Press, 1990), p. 56.

12. Quoted in Vargas Llosa, *Historia de un Deicidio*, p. 76.

13. Dreifus, "*Playboy* Interview": 172.

14. Guibert, *Seven Voices*, p. 306.

15. Dreifus, "*Playboy* Interview": 172.

16. William Kennedy, "The Yellow Trolley Car in Barcelona: An Interview," in his *Riding the Yellow Trolley Car* (New York: Viking, 1993), pp. 258–259.

17. Vargas Llosa, *Historia de un Deicidio*, p. 77.

18. *Gabriel García Márquez: Magic and Reality,* written, directed, and produced by Ana Cristina Navarro, 60 mins., Films For the Humanities & Sciences, 1981, video.

19. Bell-Villada, *The Man and His Work,* p. 70.

20. Michael Wood, *Gabriel García Márquez: One Hundred Years of Solitude* (Cambridge: Cambridge University Press, 1990), p. 61.

21. George R. McMurray, *Gabriel García Márquez* (New York: Ungar, 1983), pp. 87–88.

22. Stone, *Writers at Work,* p. 324.

23. Marlise Simons, "A Talk with Gabriel García Márquez," *New York Times Book Review,* 5 December 1982.

24. Rita Guibert, *Seven Voices: Seven Latin American Writers Talk to Rita Guibert,* translated by Frances Partridge (New York: Knopf, 1973), p. 316.

25. Dreifus, "*Playboy* Interview": 176.

26. Ibid.: 174.

27. Ibid.

28. Ibid.

29. Ibid.: 172–174.

30. Guibert, *Seven Voices,* p. 323.

31. Ibid., p. 326.

32. Dreifus, "*Playboy* Interview": 174.

33. Ibid.

34. Ibid.: 172.

35. Wood, "Chronology," *Gabriel García Márquez,* p. x.

THEMES IN *ONE HUNDRED YEARS OF SOLITUDE*

SUMMARY OF THE THEMES IN *ONE HUNDRED YEARS OF SOLITUDE*

Gabriel García Márquez has said that a novelist writes but one book: "En mi caso, sí es el libro de Macondo, que es lo que mas se dice. Pero si lo piensas con cuidado, verás que el libro que yo estoy escribiendo no es el libro de Macondo, sino el libro de la soledad"[1] (In my case, yes, that one book is the book of Macondo, which is what is said. But if you consider it carefully, you will see that the book I am writing is not the book of Macondo, but rather the book of solitude). For García Márquez, solitude does not mean only isolation, or hermetic separation from the world. He is making a political statement as well as a personal one in using this term. "Solitude" for this author is defined as the opposite of solidarity: "The story of Colonel Aureliano Buendía—the wars he fought and his progress to power—is really a progress toward solitude," he has said. He defines "absolute power" as "total solitude."[2]

According to García Márquez, "the whole disaster of Macondo . . . comes from a lack of solidarity—the solitude which results when everyone is acting for himself alone. That's then a political concept." His main goal in *One Hundred Years of Solitude* was "to give solitude the political connotation I believe it should have."[3]

Solitude destroys the most significant and appealing personage in the story, Colonel Aureliano Buendía. In the middle of *One Hundred Years of Solitude,* the colonel falters: "Lost in the solitude of his immense power, he began to lose direction" (181). Without solidarity—or love—for other human beings, he finds life is worthless. The colonel tries to find his way out of this morass, only to fail. He senses that solitude has rendered him immune to the humanity of other people.

THE MAGNIFICENT FAMILY CHRONICLE—ONE OF
THE MOST ACCLAIMED NOVELS OF OUR TIME!
"FORCES UPON US AT EVERY PAGE THE WONDER AND
EXTRAVAGANCE OF LIFE!" *The New York Review of Books*

Cover for the first U.S. paperback edition (1971) of García Márquez's complex novel
about the Buendía family and the town of Macondo

The end of the war has returned him not to peace, but to the emptiness of solitude: "the war has done away with everything" (188). Solitude has put Colonel Aureliano Buendía beyond "the nostalgia of glory" (191). Solitude destroys the character with whom the author has the most sympathy and destroys the Buendía family and the town, Macondo. It is "the pox of solitude" (424), García Márquez implies, that has destroyed his native land, Colombia, as well.

This theme of the destructiveness of individualism, which García Márquez calls "solitude," runs through the entire novel. He seizes every opportunity to point to the dangers of narcissism, self-absorption, and sympathizing with only oneself and one's family rather than with the larger world they share with others. In one example, as a result of Úrsula's banning them from her household, Rebeca and José Arcadio have isolated themselves; after his premature death, she remains alone, enduring a physical deterioration that García Márquez attributes to solitude: "the skin of her face was wrinkled by the aridity of solitude" (235). Solitude is so awful a fate that, having died while traveling, the gypsy Melquíades returns to Macondo because he "could not bear the solitude" (54).

Yet, solitude is a constant temptation. It can be a comfort and a refuge from the travails of a long life. The colonel wraps himself in his solitude, and solitude enables Rebeca to make the wise choice of refusing to return to the house of the Buendías if it means relinquishing her happiness with José Arcadio. An ease with solitude becomes a means of enduring the trauma of old age. García Márquez writes that Rebeca "had needed many years of suffering and misery in order to attain the privileges of solitude and . . . was not disposed to renounce them in exchange for an old age disturbed by the false attractions of charity" (236–237). Solitude is associated with independence and in that context provides dignity.

Near the end of her life Amaranta experiences "the measureless understanding of solitude" (300), which at last frees her of bitterness. If solitude can harden, as it does in the case of Colonel Aureliano Buendía, it can also restore. Aureliano Segundo and Petra Cotes in their old age find their love renewed and lament "that it had cost them so much of their lives to find the paradise of shared solitude" (365). The inevitability of solitude is not wholly unwelcome.

An equally prevalent theme in *One Hundred Years of Solitude* is the similarly ambiguous attraction of nostalgia. "Macondo is a town built with nostalgia," García Márquez has explained. "The virtue of nostalgia is that it eliminates all the disagreeable aspects from one's memories and leaves only the pleasant ones."[4] However, after solitude, the greatest danger to human solidarity is nostalgia, which divorces an individual from the present, with all its urgencies. In that sense it is good that Colonel Aureliano Buendía reaches a point beyond "the nostalgia of glory," even as he settles into his final and complete solitude.

Like solitude, however, nostalgia can offer comfort. Fernanda's heart "of compressed ash" breaks open at last "with the first waves of nostalgia" (392). Only then is she offered the generous liberation the author bestows upon her: "she became human in her solitude" (392).

Solitude and nostalgia: in *One Hundred Years of Solitude,* it is almost as if these characteristics are inherited. Through "the memory of his grandfather" (200), José Arcadio, Aureliano Segundo makes contact with the old gypsy Melquíades, who appears to him as "under forty years of age" and wearing "the same old-fashioned vest and the hat that looked like a raven's wings" (200). Just as the last Aureliano is born with the "open and clairvoyant eyes of the Aurelianos" (442), so the family, and Colombia, seems doomed by a propensity toward insularity, one that reappears with each new generation.

In *One Hundred Years of Solitude,* the other major theme is the author's outrage at imperialism. In the second half of the novel he bitterly exposes the exploitation of the natural wealth of his country by the "gringos," who arrive ruthlessly "to plant banana trees in the enchanted region that José Arcadio Buendía and his men had crossed in search of the route to the great inventions" (248). So overwhelming is the destruction that the unnamed banana company—clearly based on the United Fruit Company—visits upon Macondo that Colonel Aureliano Buendía is "tormented by the definite certainty that it had been a mistake not to have continued the war to its final conclusion" (256–257).

THE MEANING OF SOLITUDE

"Solitude, the novel's central theme, knits personal destinies closely. Whatever their essence, all the characters are born condemned to suffer it. It is a universal law and no one, not even Úrsula, the Mother who lives for others, is spared it; her final blindness plunges her into the impenetrable loneliness of decrepitude. The most obvious example, emphasized by the symbolism of the act, is Colonel Aureliano's order to have traced around him a chalk circle which no one may cross. His is the solitude of power, and in that solitude, as the narrator says, Colonel Aureliano is completely isolated. Later we read that he locked himself in, as it were, and his family ended up thinking of him as if he had died. This line sums up the meaning of solitude by equating it with death."

Ricardo Gullon

From "Gabriel García Márquez & the Lost Art of Storytelling," translated by José G. Sanchez, *Diacritics,* 1 (Fall, 1971), pp. 27-32.

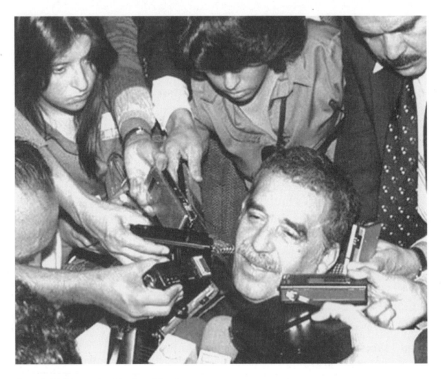

García Márquez in Mexico City in 1981

If the civil wars had led to a settlement of the issues that divided the country internally, then the country might have been strong enough to repel the foreign invasion. García Márquez does not leave his countrymen blameless for losing their native wealth. The colonel realizes that the country is being raped, but too late. "'One of these days,'" he shouts, "'I'm going to arm my boys so we can get rid of these shitty gringos'" (257). Allied with the Colombian military, the banana company takes no chances; every one of the sons of Colonel Aureliano Buendía is hunted down and murdered by secret agents.

The famous strike of 1928 follows. The army brings in troops and machine guns and fires on the helpless crowd of men, women, and children. All of this is witnessed by José Arcadio Segundo, who is told "There weren't any dead" (331), as García Márquez dramatizes the dissemination of what would later be called *disinformation*: false information deliberately spread, generally by a governmental or quasi-governmental source, to hide the truth or sway public opinion.

A plethora of other themes are developed in this encyclopedic novel. One is the simultaneity of all events in time, an idea that came to García Márquez when he read Virginia Woolf's novel, *Mrs. Dalloway* (1925), at the age of twenty; as he later told Plinio Apuleyo Mendoza, "it completely transformed my sense of time. I saw in a flash the whole process of decomposition of Macondo and its final destiny."[5]

A sentence at the close of *One Hundred Years of Solitude* encapsulates this theory of time: "Melquíades had not arranged events in the order of man's conventional time, but had concentrated a century of daily episodes in such a way that they coexisted in a one instant" (446).

To enhance this theme, García Márquez relinquishes suspense, a staple of traditional fiction, by using the flash-forward. Even as José Arcadio Buendía is planting his almond trees in an Edenic Macondo, the author shifts to a vision "Many years later" after the invasion of the banana planters, who have converted Macondo into a "field of wooden houses with zinc roofs" (43) when the trees are broken and dusty.

Only José Arcadio Segundo, who witnessed the horrible banana company massacre, is given "enough lucidity to sense the truth of the fact that time also stumbled and had accidents and could therefore splinter and leave an eternalized fragment in a room" (375). Time for García Márquez is a living entity, coexisting with human life, an enigma and a constant presence.

His aim was to create the sensation that even as events are occurring, time is standing still. It is standing still because the characters are caught in a web of narcissism, paralyzed by self-absorption, and so fail to notice the ruin of their world. García Márquez has charged his Colombian compatriots with similarly being caught in the past.

At times, García Márquez marries his theory of time to his humor. A sense of the absurdity of all human endeavor runs through *One Hundred Years of Solitude*. García Márquez manipulates the chronology of the narrative so as to surprise the reader, as if, thematically, he were suggesting that life cannot be contained by explanation, rationality, or predictability. When he writes of the orphaned Rebeca that the name Rebeca Buendía "was the only one she ever had and that she bore with dignity until her death" (47), the implication is that she will never marry. In fact, she marries a Buendía and so does not need to change her name.

This thematic perspective occurs when the reader learns, in the first line of the novel, that Colonel Aureliano Buendía will face a firing squad, implying that the author is revealing the means of death of this character. In fact, the Colonel will escape that death by firing squad and will live to so ripe an old age that he will wish for death.

The irrationality of love, and of the self-absorbed personal life, is another major theme flowing from the larger perspective on solitude in the novel. Despite the intensity of her longing for Rebeca's suitor, the Italian piano teacher, Pietro Crespi, when Amaranta gets her chance and Crespi proposes to her, she rejects him. Crespi then commits suicide, making Amaranta's proud and foolhardy behavior irreversible. Love, here as in García Márquez's later novel *El amor en los tiempos del cólera* (1985; translated as *Love in the Time of Cholera*, 1988), is compared to a disease; for all that, in both novels it is no less welcome and inevitable.

Still another theme emerges late in *One Hundred Years of Solitude* with the reflexive mentioning of literature and the function of the novel. "It never occurred to him until then," García Márquez writes, referring to the scholarly last Aureliano, "to think that literature was the best plaything that had ever been invented to make fun of people" (417). Literature can, for García Márquez, with epic force describe the rise and fall of a community; it can also zero in on the foibles of anyone. Always it can be suffused with humor.

The character Gabriel, bearing the same name as the writer of this book, in the scenes in the bookshop near the end, is the only one who "did not doubt the reality of Colonel Aureliano Buendía" (419), his own invention. Then, suddenly becoming literal, the author gives a personal reason why Gabriel does not believe that Colonel Aureliano Buendía was an invention: "because he had been a companion in arms and inseparable friend of his great-great-grandfather Colonel Gerineldo Márquez" (419).

THEMES RELATED TO GARCÍA MÁRQUEZ'S ERA

The political themes of *One Hundred Years of Solitude* offer not only a history of Colombia during the twentieth century, but a glimpse into García Márquez's own perspective. Although he comes from a Liberal background, his grandfather having been a great Liberal leader, by the end of the novel García Márquez has established that the difference between Liberals and Conservatives is in name only—a difference of whether the houses of Macondo are painted blue or red. Neither side has contributed to alleviating the suffering of the majority of the Colombian people. Both sides represent the small oligarchy that has ruled the country from the moment of its independence.

Solitude as a concept runs through the consciousness not only of García Márquez, but of many Latin American writers. Economically and culturally, each country has been isolated from the others. As José Donoso points out in his *The Boom in Spanish American Literature,* until the 1960s Latin American books were available only in the country in which they were produced, despite the fact that Spanish is the common language of the continent, with the exception of Brazil.[6] Other Latin American authors have spoken of their own isolation.

Asked about his position among Latin American writers, Guillermo Cabrera Infante has spoken of his "absolute independence and therefore great isolation." For Cabrera Infante, his solitude has been that of being "the only one of them all to have the misfortune to have experienced life in a communist country like Cuba, which from an island in a state of revolution became an increasingly bureaucratic, irrational, and totalitarian state."[7] Cabrera Infante has added that "my solitude, like my being so far away, is a luxury. Other Cuban writers can't say the same."[8]

History, and in particular Colombian history, is a dominant theme of *One Hundred Years of Solitude.* In fact, Lucila Ines Mena has argued that history and its proper understanding is "the central theme"[9] of this novel. This theme takes hold as one of the sons of Aureliano, Aureliano Triste, decides to build a railroad, linking "the town with the rest of the world" (238). For Úrsula, it is a confirmation that "time was going in a circle," for she is remembering José Arcadio Buendía's "project for solar warfare" (238).

But she is wrong. Time is moving forward in the guise of an irreversible history, and history itself—and its reliability—moves to

LATIN AMERICAN HISTORY AND *ONE HUNDRED YEARS OF SOLITUDE*

"One way of seeing Latin American history, then, is as a pilgrimage from a founding utopia to a cruel epic that degrades utopia if the mythic imagination does not intervene so as to interrupt the onslaught of fatality and seek to recover the possibilities of freedom. One of the more extraordinary aspects of García Márquez's novel is that its structure corresponds to the profounder historicity of Latin America: the tension between utopia, epic, and myth. The founding of Macondo is the founding of utopia. José Arcadio Buendía and his family have wandered in the jungle, in circles, until they encounter precisely the place where they can found the New Arcadia, the promised land of origin...."

Carlos Fuentes

From *Gabriel García Márquez and the Invention of America,* E. Allison Peers Lectures, no. 2 (Liverpool : Liverpool University Press, 1987).

Dust jacket for the Hungarian edition (1971) of
One Hundred Years of Solitude

the foreground in the last half of the novel to become a dominant theme. Chester S. Halka persuasively argues the issue of the centrality of history for *One Hundred Years of Solitude*:

> The novel makes a sharp distinction between true history and false history: true history is associated with Melquíades's writings and with a nonconventional perspective; false history is linked to the official history disseminated by state propaganda and by historians approved by the government. This distinction emerges most clearly in the aftermath of the banana-company massacre.[10]

Gerald Martin underlines this point by arguing that *One Hundred Years of Solitude* is a "demystification of Latin America's interpretation of its own history."[11] García Márquez is not only recounting the history of Colombia, but also judging it. Simultaneously, he is doing the same thing for the continent as a whole. The second half of the novel, which culminates in the disintegration of Macondo, begins with the sudden arrival of the banana company, which is represented as cause of the final defeat of the community:

> The gringos, who later on brought their languid wives in muslin dresses and large veiled hats, built a separate town across the railroad tracks with streets lined with palm trees, houses with screened windows, small white tables on the terraces, and fans mounted on the ceilings, and extensive blue lawns with peacocks and quails (245).

They have come to obliterate the local inhabitants, both culturally and economically, and, finally, when the people protest, murderously. The author's irony from the moment of the first appearance of the gringos is devastating: "No one knew yet what they were after, or whether they were actually nothing but philanthropists . . ." (245).

García Márquez criticizes the North American intervention in Colombia—not least the self-righteousness and arrogance of U.S.

actions: "Endowed with means that had been reserved for Divine Providence in former times, they changed the pattern of the rains, accelerated the cycle of harvest, and moved the river from where it had always been . . ." (245). The "dark conscience" of the novel sums up the disaster to come: "'Look at the mess we've got ourselves into,'" Colonel Aureliano Buendía said at that time, "'just because we invited a gringo to eat some bananas'" (246).

Only a fool could rejoice at the coming of the North Americans, a fool like Aureliano Segundo who "could not contain his happiness over the avalanche of foreigners" (246). The metaphor—the gringos, arrival compared to a natural disaster, an avalanche—contains the author's own judgment.

The climax of *One Hundred Years of Solitude,* the moment when Macondo truly begins its irreversible decline, comes one hundred pages from the end of the novel with the strike of the banana workers led by José Arcadio Segundo. The scene is based, of course, on the actual event of the year of García Márquez's birth. Writing strictly as a realist, he describes the grievances of the workers:

> The protests of the workers this time were based on the lack of sanitary facilities in their living quarters, the nonexistence of medical services, and terrible working conditions. They stated, furthermore, that they were not being paid in real money but in scrip, which was good only to buy Virginia ham in the company commissaries. José Arcadio Segundo was put in jail because he revealed that the scrip system was a way for the company to finance its fruit ships, which without the commissary merchandise would have to return empty from New Orleans to the banana ports (233).

THE BUENDÍAS AND MACONDO

"Our formal point of reference in this bemusing world of myth and history, even more than the place Macondo, is the Buendías' existence in it. From Aureliano's introductory memory of an afternoon spent with his father onwards, parochial genealogy acts as the guide to whatever larger message there is. The very founders of Macondo are José Arcadio's men, whose descendants exist only in so far as they have dealings with the Buendías. Later, García Márquez may convey brilliantly the sense of a moment in social and cultural history, in nineteenth-century bourgeois soirees round the pianola, for example, but in every case it is through the words, deeds and relationships of the family. We know about Liberals of the period via the Colonel, and not as a party or group. Again, a mulatto like Nigromanta is introduced because the last Aureliano at one point needed a woman like her, not because the place had the remnants of a slave population. . . . Macondo exists only as long as the family tree flourishes there."

Gordon Brotherston

From "An End to Secular Solitude: Gabriel García Márquez," in his *The Emergence of the Latin American Novel* (Cambridge: Cambridge University Press, 1977), pp. 122–135.

Cover for the 1972 Venezuelan edition of
One Hundred Years of Solitude

There is no magic about the cruelty of the North American company, although its "decrepit lawyers dressed in black" get the Colombian courts to dismiss the demands of the workers "with decisions that seemed like acts of magic" (323). When the workers attempt to present the banana company representative, Mr. Brown, with a list of their demands, the company and its lawyers go to great lengths to evade them. When Mr. Brown is summoned to court, the company declares him an imposter and has him jailed; the next time he appears in court, he is disguised as a local vendor of medicinal herbs; then the company lawyers respond to a new challenge by presenting a phony death certificate "which bore witness that on June ninth last he had been run over by a fire engine in Chicago" (324). He turns out to be "alive in the electrified chicken coop" (326). He must hide from the people whose lives he has altered forever.

The dramatization of such disinformation by authorities alludes as well to action taking place in the middle of the twentieth century by governments and their intelligence agencies. The story of Macondo, which seems to start at the beginning of time, with Macondo representing a Garden of Eden where no one has yet died, has proceeded to the moment of its composition, the late 1960s.

Disinformation—the alteration of history and current events for the political purposes of the ruling class—is now dramatized; it is not magic but strict realism when the banana company is able to prove that it "did not have, never had had, and never would have any workers in its service because they were all hired on a temporary and occasional basis" (324), which was the actual finding of the Colombian court. García Márquez uses the real name of the commander who gave the order to kill at the massacre: General Cortés Vargas.

At the end of *One Hundred Years of Solitude,* the theme of reflexivity, the merging of literary text with the author's own life, takes over. Moving into memoir, and using the actual first names of his personal friends, García

Márquez pays homage to his friends Álvaro (Cepeda), Germán (Varga), and Alfonso (Fuenmayor). He is present as "Gabriel," the only one who respects the memory of Colonel Aureliano Buendía, his own character. It is Gabriel who knows that the official version was wrong and that there had been a massacre of the banana company workers.

Gabriel and the colonel, all the good people in this novel, end up "off course in the tide of a world that had ended and of which only the nostalgia remained" (419), as confessional an autobiographical moment as García Márquez will allow himself. There is also humor in the author's offering his own point of view, spoken by the Catalonian bookseller: "The world must be all fucked up when men travel first class and literature goes as freight" (431).

THEMES COMPARED TO REPRESENTATIONS IN OTHER LITERATURE

Many of these themes in García Márquez's works, particularly those that reflect his political perspective, have also found expression in the writing of others, especially in novels with an apparent social purpose. Among Latin American writers, Miguel Ángel Asturias has dealt with the incursions of the United Fruit Company in his so-called banana trilogy: *Viento fuerto* (1950; translated as *Cyclone,* 1967); *El Papa Verde* (1954; translated as *The Green Pope,* 1971); and *Los ojos de los enterrados* (1960; translated as *The Eyes of the Interred,* 1973).

Among the innovative writers of the continent, Jorge Luis Borges has dealt in his parables with the magical and subjective qualities of time, and the futility of attempting to construct any narrow concept of the individual. However, in his writing Asturias lacks the thematic energy of García Márquez's departures from realism, and Borges lacks García Márquez's passionate political outlook. The essentially American reality of *One Hundred Years of Solitude,* the author's joy in its particularity that becomes a major theme, may be found as well in Cuban novelist Alejo Carpentier's *El reino de este mundo* (1949; translated as *The Kingdom of This World,* 1957).[12]

The theme of political disillusionment appears often in Latin American literature; the most striking example, according to Michael Wood, is Mario Vargas Llosa's *Historia de Mayta* (1984; translated as *The Real Life of Alejandro Mayta,* 1986): "where a miserably failed Peruvian revolution" not only "parallels Castro's success," but also "helps us to see how deep disillusionment has gone in Latin America."[13]

Among North American writers, the proletarian authors of the 1920s and 1930s, John Dos Passos and John Steinbeck foremost among them, have written about social inequity in terms of the warfare between labor and capital, and have depicted strikes. The theme of the self-destruction of a culturally isolated community arises in the novels of William Faulkner, particularly *Absalom, Absalom!* (1936) and *The Sound and The Fury* (1929).

Among the works of British writers, Joseph Conrad's *Nostromo* (1904), set in the imaginary Latin American country of Costaguana, contains themes similar to those of *One Hundred Years of Solitude*. Wood remarks astutely that "a feeling of unreality" in these settings "is a part of local reality, best reported by versions of the baroque."[14]

The thematic perspective of *One Hundred Years of Solitude* is so rich and suggestive that its ideas can be traced to nearly all of the great works of literature, from the Bible and the epics of Homer to William Shakespeare's plays. The colonel, like Homer's Odysseus, returns from long wars irretrievably altered. Gene Bell-Villada has compared the use in García Márquez's *One Hundred Years of Solitude* of "a ritualized clash between equally valid though mutually irreconcilable opposites," to themes in the plays of Shakespeare: the clash of ambition and loyalty in *Macbeth* (1623); of love and friendship in *Othello* (1622); and that of passion and duty in *Antony and Cleopatra* (1623).[15]

In *One Hundred Years of Solitude* José Arcadio Buendía faces the conflict between political leadership and science. Amaranta is forced to deal with the conflict between her sexual desire, which finds expression in incestuous feelings, and the inhibitions visited upon a woman of her class and culture.

The theme that magic may best express transcendent moments of experience appears in a negative sense in Franz Kafka's *The Metamorphosis* (1915), a work that strongly influenced García Márquez. But where Kafka embraces the gloom of defeat, García Márquez manages to convey an optimism that suggests that life is worth living. The theme that individual intransigence (solitude) may lead to the fall of a community is also found in the writing of Faulkner.

Traces of García Márquez's approach to character may even be found in the cinema. Wood has argued that the character of Colonel Aureliano Buendía seems to derive from motion pictures featuring Gary Cooper and Humphrey Bogart, noting that both of these actors project male images "unmoved by abstractions but provoked by cruelty, by the sight of victimization."[16]

None of these examples, however, come close to resembling the particular relationship between García Márquez's inventiveness and his themes. Macondo itself, as García Márquez concludes, may "not have a second opportunity on earth" (448). Other communities, forewarned, may do better.

NOTES

1. Mario Vargas Llosa, *García Márquez: Historia de un Deicidio* (Barcelona: Breve Biblioteca de Respuesta: Barral Editores, 1971), p. 94.

2. Rita Guibert, *Seven Voices: Seven Latin American Writers Talk to Rita Guibert,* translated by Frances Partridge (New York: Knopf, 1973), p. 314.

3. Claudia Dreifus, "*Playboy* Interview: Gabriel García Márquez," *Playboy,* 30 (February 1983): 172.

4. Ibid.

5. Gabriel García Márquez and Plinio Apuleyo Mendoza, *The Fragrance of Guava,* translated by Ann Wright (London: Verso, 1983), p. 48.

6. José Donoso, *The Boom in Spanish American Literature,* translated by Gregory Kolovakos (New York: Colombia University Press / Center for Inter-American Relations, 1977), p. 25.

7. Guibert, *Seven Voices,* p. 374.

8. Ibid., p. 397.

9. Quoted in Chester S. Halka, "*One Hundred Years of Solitude* in History, Politics, and Civilization Courses," in *Approaches to Teaching García Márquez's One Hundred Years of Solitude,* edited by María Elena de Valdés and Mario J. Valdés (New York: Modern Language Association of America, 1990), p. 41.

10. Ibid., p. 40.

11. Gerald Martin, "On 'Magical' and Social Realism in García Márquez," in *Gabriel García Márquez: New Readings,* edited by Bernard McGuirk and Richard Cardwell (Cambridge: Cambridge University Press, 1987), p. 113.

12. This point is noted by Raymond L. Williams, *Gabriel García Márquez* (Boston: Twayne, 1984), p. 77.

13. Michael Wood, *Gabriel García Márquez: One Hundred Years of Solitude* (Cambridge & New York: Cambridge University Press, 1990), p. 7.

14. Ibid., p. 5.

15. Gene H. Bell-Villada, *Gabriel García Márquez: The Man and His Work* (Chapel Hill & London: University of North Carolina Press, 1990), p. 75.

16. Wood, *Gabriel García Márquez,* p. 94.

CRITICAL RESPONSE TO
ONE HUNDRED YEARS OF SOLITUDE

CRITICAL SUMMARY

One Hundred Years of Solitude has attracted much critical attention. Because of the richness and complexity of the novel, critical commentary of the novel involves complicated arguments that draw on sophisticated theories about approaches to literature. While students can learn new ways of understanding the novel from these critics, it is important to keep in mind that great novels can be appreciated from various perspectives; a mark of a brilliant novel is the many ways it is meaningful to its readers.

It has been seen as the primary novel of "The Boom," which in the 1960s brought Latin American fiction to the world stage. It has been considered the primary work of magic realism, a literary technique originally deriving from European Surrealism of the 1920s, but now transplanted to the Latin American cultural, historical, geographical, and political context, where it has been most fully realized.

One Hundred Years of Solitude has been viewed as a work of such monumental integrity and fictional genius that it has been compared to the first great novel ever written, Miguel de Cervantes's *Don Quixote* (1605). It has been seen as biblical and mythic in its structure and in the universality of its themes. Critics have explored antecedents of Gabriel García Márquez's plot in the Bible.

Commentators have also emphasized the intersecting of myth and history in this novel. *One Hundred Years of Solitude* is notable for its encyclopedic quality; in this work García Márquez has borrowed from the disciplines of chemistry, anthropology, and history, as well as from a host of literary genres, from the epic to the modernist novel.

One Hundred Years of Solitude has been viewed as a masterpiece of modernist fiction, placed alongside the great works of James Joyce, Virginia Woolf, Franz Kafka, and in particular William Faulkner, whom García Márquez has frequently said was a fellow Caribbean writer, since

García Márquez at the Nobel Prize ceremony in 1982

he lived near the Gulf of Mexico. The characters in *One Hundred Years of Solitude,* despite being specifically related to their particular social context, have been seen as so psychologically nuanced that they can be considered simultaneously as universal figures, even as archetypes reflecting all of human experience.

CRITICAL SURVEY

Although it was published in the early 1970s and never translated into English, Peruvian novelist Mario Vargas Llosa's *García Márquez: Historia de un Deicidio* (García Márquez: History of a Deicide; Barcelona: Breve Biblioteca de Respuesta: Barral Editores, 1971) remains by far the most comprehensive and the most illuminating biographical work written about García Márquez. In his book, Vargas Llosa combines interviews with García Márquez with his own interpretations and research, producing a textual richness. He places García Márquez in his cultural and geographical context, beginning with the influence of the United Fruit Company on Aracataca, the town in which García Márquez was born.

Because history of Aracataca fueled the imagination of García Márquez, Vargas Llosa at once introduces the reader to the Atlantic coast of Colombia. He describes the growth of the labor movement in the area, culminating in the banana workers' strike of 1928, the approximate year García Márquez was born. Because the fiction of García Márquez, in particular the novel *One Hundred Years of Solitude,* is so rooted in this region, Vargas Llosa describes the history of "la zona bananera"(The Banana Zone) before he even begins to discuss the life of García Márquez:

> A falta de algo mejor, Aracataca vivía de mitos, de fantasmas, de soledad y de nostalgia. Casi toda la obra literaria de García Márquez está elaborada con eso materiales que fueron el alimento de su infancia. Aracataca vivía de recuerdos cuando él nació; sus ficciones vivirán de sus recuerdos de Aracataca.[1]

> (In the absence of something better, Aracataca was living on myths, fantasies, solitude and nostalgia. Almost all the literary work of García Márquez is an elaboration of those materials that were the substance of his childhood. Aracataca was living on memories when he was born; his fiction, in turn, would live on his memories of Aracataca.)

Vargas Llosa also provides valuable biographical information about the maternal grandfather of García Márquez, Don Nicolás Márquez. His descriptive style is similar to his style as a novelist and he offers visual images of his subjects. The grandmother of García Márquez, Doña Tranquilina, the reader discovers, was "blanca" (white-skinned) with "ojos azules, todavia hermosa"(blue eyes, still beautiful) when García Márquez was born, although she would die, "ciega y loca, como Úrsula Iguarán de Buendía"[2] (blind and mad, like Úrsula Iguarán de Buendía), the character in *One Hundred Years of Solitude* based so closely upon her.

In his comprehensive study, Vargas Llosa covers the apprenticeship of García Márquez and his early career in journalism. He discusses the articles García Márquez wrote for *Elite* (Caracas) and *Cromos* (Bogotá) as he traveled through central and eastern Europe. He also chronicles the profound effect on García Márquez and the other writers of Latin America of the Cuban Revolution in January of 1959:

> El triunfo de los guerrilleros cubanos abría una nueva etapa en la historia de América Latina; la victoria de Fidel provocó de inmediato un gran movimiento de solidaridad en todo el Continente, y sobre todo, en los medios estudiantiles e intelectuales. Fue el caso de García Márquez: como a muchos escritores latinoamericanos de su generación, la revolución cubana hizo de él, por lo menos durante un tiempo, un hombre activamente comprometido en una acción política de izquierda.[3]

> (The triumph of the Cuban guerrillas opened a new epoch in the history of Latin America; Fidel's victory inspired a large movement of solidarity throughout the continent, particularly among students and intellectuals. It was so for García Márquez: like many Latin American writers of his generation, the Cuban revolution converted him into, at least for a time, a man actively engaged in political action on the Left).

Of particular interest in this compendious study by Vargas Llosa, also a writer of considerable distinction, is his analysis of the function of the novelist: "Escriber novelas es un acto de rebelión contra la realidad, contra Díos, contra la creación de Díos que es la realidad"(To write novels is an act of rebellion against reality, against God, and against the creation of God that is reality).[4]

For Vargas Llosa, "todos los novelistas son rebeldes" (all novelists are rebels). He quotes French critic Roland Barthes to the effect that the story of any one novelist "es la historia de un tema y sus variaciones"(is the history of one theme and its variations). Such is the case of García Márquez. The common denominator of all his work is the closed world of his childhood:

Esta voluntad unificadora es la de edificar una realidad cerrada, un mundo autónomo, cuyas constantes proceden esencialmente del mundo de infancia de García Márquez. Su niñez, su familia, Aracataca constituyen el núcleo de experiencias más decisivo para su vocación. . . .[5]

(This unifying will is to build a closed reality, an independent world, whose constants essentially come from the world of García Márquez's childhood. His youth, his family, and Aracataca constitute the most decisive nucleus of experiences for his vocation . . .)

For any serious critical study of García Márquez, *García Márquez: Historia de un Deicidio* is the one indispensable work.

Michael Wood's *Gabriel García Márquez: One Hundred Years of Solitude* (Cambridge: Cambridge University Press, 1990) is a brief but excellent introduction to the work. It is particularly excellent in placing García Márquez, through *One Hundred Years of Solitude,* within his literary context. Wood compares García Márquez with Latin American contemporaries such as Alejo Carpentier and Jorge Luis Borges, and with modernist writers such as Joyce, Woolf, and Kafka.

Wood also does the best job of any non–Latin American critic in placing García Márquez and his *One Hundred Years of Solitude* within a social and political context. He notes the influence of the Cuban Revolution on writers that "it showed that the apparently changeless could be changed, and determination could achieve almost anything, against astonishing odds."[6] Wood traces the influence of this radical change of consciousness to *One Hundred Years of Solitude* wherein "despair is dismantled, held up as a superstition, an illusion of destiny."[7]

Examining *One Hundred Years of Solitude* in depth, Wood notes, echoing the author himself, that with respect to *One Hundred Years of Solitude,* García Márquez is "the most accessible of writers,"[8] and is astute in examining the nature of the magic that suffuses this work, and how it is connected to its social realism: "*One Hundred Years of Solitude* presents a world neither of hard fact nor of embraced superstition, but a world where the imaginary and the figurative are seriously entertained and not visibly discriminated against."[9] According to Wood, "beliefs and metaphors become forms of fact" while "more ordinary facts become uncertain."[10] Meanwhile, legends are "treated as truths—because they are truths to those who believe them."[11]

Gene H. Bell-Villada's *García Márquez: The Man and His Work* (Chapel Hill: The University of North Carolina Press, 1990) is a good introduction to García Márquez as a writer and to *One Hundred Years of Solitude*. Bell-Villada's approach is biographical; the best section of his book, "Backgrounds," places García Márquez in both his Colombian and his Latin American context.

Bell-Villada offers a short history of the founding of Colombia by the Spanish settlers, noting that "the initial collective roamings that precede the founding of Macondo, and José Arcadio Buendía's later search for the ocean, both correspond to this early period in Colombia's past."[12] He also gives a fine description of the culture of the Atlantic coast of Colombia, while noting that "from his most youthful literary days García Márquez was a man intensely conscious of his costeño roots, often praising them at the expense of the Bogotá style of life."[13] Bell-Villada quotes García Márquez profusely, not least in a comment he made when he was twenty-two years old: "there are cities with ships and cities without ships. That is the only acceptable distinction, the only truly essential difference."[14]

In *García Márquez: The Man and His Work,* Bell-Villada provides a strong section on the literary influences upon *One Hundred Years of Solitude,* particularly of the Bible. One chapter, "The History of Macondo," is devoted exclusively to *One Hundred Years of Solitude.*

Another general introduction to the work of García Márquez is *Gabriel García Márquez* by Raymond Williams (Boston: Twayne, 1984). Williams's book is brief, but he does place García Márquez in the context of the Boom, beginning with Alejo Carpentier's *Los pasos perdidos* (1953; translated as *The Lost Steps,* 1956), and including Guillermo Cabrera Infante's *Tres tristes tigres* (1967; translated as *Three Trapped Tigers,* 1971). There is one chapter on *One Hundred Years of Solitude,* but the most interesting part of the book is the short section Williams devotes to "García Márquez and the Colombian Tradition."

Two excellent anthologies devoted to García Márquez include important essays on *One Hundred Years of Solitude. Gabriel García Márquez: New Readings,* edited by Bernard McGuirk and Richard Cardwell (Cambridge: Cambridge University Press, 1987) is the more scholarly in approach. Of the twelve essays in this collection, four are devoted to *One Hundred Years of Solitude*: "Magic Realism and the Theme of Incest in *One Hundred Years of Solitude*" by Edwin Williamson; "Translation and Genealogy: *One Hundred Years of Solitude*" by Aníbal González; "The

Humour of *One Hundred Years of Solitude*" by Clive Griffin; and "On 'Magical' and Social Realism in García Márquez" by Gerald Martin.

The best of these essays are those by Williamson and Martin. Williamson begins by defining "magical realism" and placing it, properly, in its Latin American context. He examines its effect on the reader, moving on to connect the use of magic realism with the theme of incest, arguing that "The fundamental impetus of *One Hundred Years of Solitude* springs from the wish to *avoid* incest."[15]

Gerald Martin begins with a series of provocative quotations, beginning with one from García Márquez's short story, "Blacamán el bueno, vendedor de milagros" (1968; translated as "Blacaman the Good, Vendor of Miracles,"1972), which Martin translates as: "Although you have every right not to believe me after putting up for so long with my sly tricks and falsifications, I swear to you by the bones of my mother that what I am now about to show you is no illusion but the plain and simple truth . . . ." Martin calls *One Hundred Years of Solitude,* "perhaps, the greatest of all Latin American novels," and points out that not only is the story of the Buendía family "a metaphor for the history of the continent since Independence," but it is as well "a narrative about the *myths* of Latin American history."[16]

Martin contrasts García Márquez with Borges, only to raise larger questions inspired by *One Hundred Years of Solitude:* "My view is that the essential point of departure for any comprehensive analysis of *One Hundred Years of Solitude* must be an examination of its perception of the relation between ideology and consciousness, and between lived reality, historiography and literature."[17] He goes on to challenge the assertion that *One Hundred Years of Solitude* represents "the historical demise of social realism in Latin American fiction" and the advent of the "linguistic, experimental or post-Modernist novel."[18] The doom of the Buendía line, Martin suggests, means "that neocolonialism is at an end, remembering that the novel was written during the early years of the Cuban Revolution."[19]

Gabriel García Márquez, edited by Harold Bloom, Modern Critical Views (New York & Philadelphia: Chelsea House, 1989) also offers several essays with rich perspectives on *One Hundred Years of Solitude.* The best is "Liberals, Conservatives, and Bananas: Colombian Politics in the Fictions of Gabriel García Márquez" by Regina Janes. Janes reveals how García Márquez integrates political themes into *One Hundred Years of Solitude,* and discusses how the civil wars of the nineteenth century and "la violencia" of the twentieth are played out in this novel.

In the course of Janes's discussion, she provides valuable information about the history of Colombia, beginning with the Spanish conquerors who saw Bogotá as "El Dorado," the city of gold; she describes how three Spanish explorers headed for Bogotá from three different directions in 1538. Janes also reveals how "the life of the colonial period surfaces briefly in the house that Úrsula built in *Cien años de soledad*":

> "It was constructed for the most aristocratic of purposes, to promote and arrange the marriages of marriageable daughters, and it is filled with imported objects, Viennese furniture, bohemian crystal, tablecloths from Holland. With the guest list for the inaugural party, Macondo emerges as a town with an aristocracy and leading oligarchs, for the only people invited, we are told, are the descendants of the founders . . . the social pattern incarnated in that house can be called colonial, but it could as well be post independence and early modern, for it is a pattern that was established early and has endured long in Colombian society, reputedly one of the most traditional, aristocratic, and closed in Latin America."[20]

THE SUCCESS OF *ONE HUNDRED YEARS OF SOLITUDE*

"Many thought in Latin America, when *One Hundred Year of Solitude* was first published and achieved its enormous and instantaneous success, that its popularity (comparable in the Hispanic world only to that of Cervantes and *Don Quixote*) was due to the element of immediate recognition present in the book. There is a joyous rediscovery of identity here, an instant reflex by which we are presented, in the genealogies of Macondo, to our grandmas, our sweethearts, our brothers and sisters, our nursemaids. Today, twenty years after the fact, we can see clearly that there was more than instant anagnorisis in the García Márquez phenomenon, that his novel, one of the most amusing ever written, does not exhaust its meanings in a first reading. This first reading (for amusement and for recognition) demands a second reading, which becomes, in effect, the real reading."

Carlos Fuentes

From *Gabriel García Márquez and the Invention of America*, E. Allison Peers Lectures, no. 2 (Liverpool: Liverpool University Press, 1987).

Janes offers a panoply of source materials, including an 1883 quotation from Rafael Nuñez, twice elected president of Colombia. Decrying the devastation that the recurrent civil wars had brought to the country, Nuñez compared Colombian politics—unfavorably—to the London zoo, and repeated a North American diplomat's remark: "In Colombia they've organized anarchy itself."[21] Janes also does well in placing the efforts of Colonel Aureliano Buendía in the context of the series of constitutions that succeeded each other in nineteenth-century Colombia.

She notes that the banana episode as described by García Márquez might, with his exaggerations, be seen as "a textbook illustration of 'lo real maravilloso.'" Janes concludes that "when García Márquez moves politics from the background to the foreground of his works, he abandons realism for suprarealism and becomes a satirist."[22]

In the same collection, Roberto González Echevarría, in "*Cien años de soledad:* The Novel as Myth and Archive," usefully places *One Hundred Years of Solitude* among other Latin American novels, such as Vargas Llosa's *La guerra del fin del mundo* (1981; translated as *The War of the End of the World*, 1984), which also combine history and myth. Discussing the conjunction of myth and history, Echevarría asks: "Can Latin American history be as resilient and as useful a hermeneutic tool for probing human nature as the classical myths, and can the novel be the vehicle for the transmission of these new myths? Is it at all conceivable, in the modern, post-oral period, to create myths?"[23]

Echevarría invokes the sciences and anthropology to answer these questions. "Anthropology," he explains, "is a way through which Western culture indirectly affixes its own cultural identity."[24] In an essay rich in historical anecdotes, he points out that the Guatemalan novelist Miguel Ángel Asturias went to Paris to study ethnology under Georges Raynaud; one of his classmates was the Cuban writer Alejo Carpentier, who was then writing *¡Ecue-Yamba-O!* (Praised Be the Lord, 1933), a novel about Cuban blacks that incorporates ethnographic materials— although the book is written in Spanish, the title is in Lucumí, an African language spoken in Cuba.

According to Echevarría,

The blend of mythic elements and Latin American history in *Cien años de soledad* reveals a desire to found an American myth. . . . The lack of specificity of the various incidents, which appear to represent several related or similar events, points in this direction. The Latin American myth is this story of foundation, articulated through independence, civil war, struggle against U.S. colonialism, all cast within a genealogical line that weaves in and out, repeating names and characters.[25]

Floyd Merrell, in "José Arcadio Buendía's Scientific Paradigms: Man in Search of Himself," explores José Arcadio's experiments in the context of the scientific movements of the Western World. Merrell notes that "José Arcadio's thought, implying reversibility, periodicity, and stasis is a mirror image of the ultimate extension of classical physics."[26]

Bloom's Modern Critical Views anthology also includes Vargas Llosa's "García Márquez: From Aracataca to Macondo," a translation of some of the biographical material from the first sections of *Historia de un Deicidio.*

Of special interest to teachers and advanced students is a short book edited by María Elena de Valdés and Mario J. Valdés, *Approaches to Teaching García Márquez's One Hundred Years of Solitude* (New York: Modern Language Association of America, 1990). Several essays demonstrate how this novel is studied in various academic contexts: in humanities courses; in comparative literature courses; in history, politics, and civilization courses; in women's studies courses; in interdisciplinary courses; and in Latin American literature courses.

Chester Halka's essay placing *One Hundred Years of Solitude* in its historical context is particularly helpful, and Halka also suggests further readings for students interested in pursuing this frame of reference. In particular he cites Lucila Inés Mena's study of the novel, *La función de la historia en "Cien años de soledad"* (The Function of History in *One Hundred Years of Solitude,*1979), available, however, only in Spanish. He quotes from Mena's comparisons between Colonel Uribe Uribe, Colonel Nicolás Márquez, and Colonel Aureliano Buendía.

CRITICAL EXCERPTS

Michael Wood, "The History of Paradise," from his *Gabriel García Márquez: One Hundred Years of Solitude* (Cambridge: Cambridge University Press, 1990), pp. 24–40

This is the story of how we begin to remember.

—Paul Simon

Situations

It would be absurd, and horribly dull, to try to summarize *One Hundred Years of Solitude*, except as a rambling joke. "I merely wanted," García Márquez said to Rita Guibert, "to tell the story of a family who for a hundred years did everything they could in order not to have a son with a pig's tail, and . . . ended up having one." This is a good joke because the pig's tail is both much worried about and really a diversion. It is what the family is afraid of, and what awaits it. But between the fear and its fulfilment the whole novel takes place, and most characters don't think about the pig's tail at all. It is a lure, an instance of what Roland Barthes

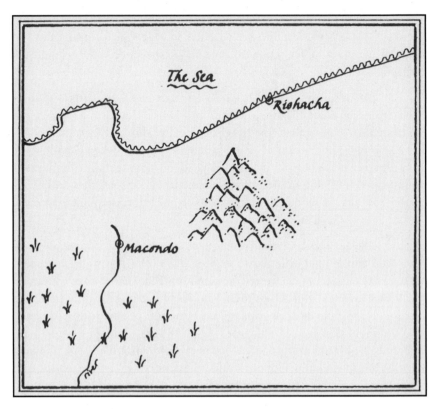

Map of the fictional setting for *One Hundred Years of Solitude* (referred to as Map I in Michael Wood's "The History of Paradise")

called "a narrative enigma." Well, it is also a sign of incest, but that is a lure too, since the incest in the book, although always hovering, is mainly metaphorical or merely flirted with.

Still, summaries apart, we do need a means of holding the book in our minds, and we see at once that it is indeed "the story of a family," the prodigious Buendías; and even more the story of a place, the human geography of the family's fortunes.

José Arcadio Buendía, with whom our story begins, is described as a young patriarch, and might be said to go even further back into the Bible, since he is the first citizen of a sort of paradise. It is an ambiguous paradise, far from perfect and not available for easy nostalgia, but its loss, nevertheless, means that much of *One Hundred Years of Solitude* reads like an elegy. From the start the tiny settlement of Macondo is offered to us as a ver-

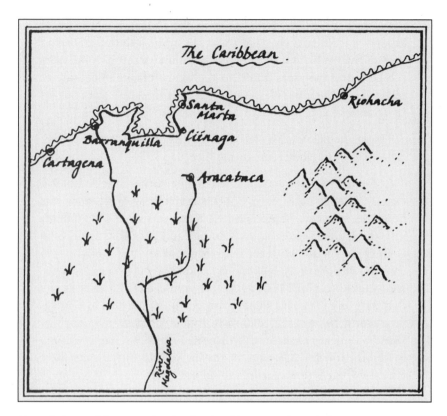

Map of the Caribbean Lowlands of Colombia (Map 2 in Wood's essay)

sion of Eden. "The world," we read, "was so recent that many things lacked names, and in order to indicate them it was necessary to point." The polished stones in the clear river are "white and enormous, like prehistoric eggs" [9:11]. There are twenty-odd mud and cane houses in the villages, homes of the twenty-odd founding families. The population soon grows to 300, but it is still a "truly happy village" where no one is over thirty and no one has died [16:18].

Where is this Eden? If we draw a map based on the information given to us in the first two chapters of the novel, we get something like Map 1.

We have no way of knowing the shape of the coastline, but we know that the sea is to the north of Macondo; that a range of mountains separates Macondo from Riohacha; that Drake is supposed to have attacked Riohacha in the sixteenth century and hunted crocodiles there; that there are swamps to the south and west of Macondo; and that roads, towns and a sort of modernity can be found two days' travel to the west, "on the other side of the swamp"[39:43]. We hear of "colonial coins" [10:12]; of "authorities," a "government," and a distant "capital" [11:13].

Northern Colombia, in which there is an "ancient city" called Riohacha, looks something like Map 2.

Macondo is the name of a banana plantation near Aracataca, García Márquez' birthplace, but this scarcely signifies, since it is now internationally famous as the name of a mythical community, the Latin America equivalent of Faulkner's Yoknapatawpha County. The point about the maps is not to say that the setting of *One Hundred Years of Solitude* is Colombia—if García Márquez had wanted to name his country he would have done so—only that its geography and history are not different; that the imagined world has a real situation in time and space. The analogy with Faulkner is exact in this respect, I think. We are not going to find the town of Jefferson on any map of Mississippi. But there isn't anywhere else on earth it could be.

The recentness of this world turns out to be a metaphor, an impression, and not a situation in time. The time indeed is relatively late, very late if we are thinking of Eden: "several centuries" later than the sixteenth, and some "three hundred years" since Drake's incursions into the Spanish Main [24:27]. An early expedition by the villagers discovers a suit of rusty armour, complete with calcified skeleton; a later expedition leads them to a great Spanish galleon, stranded some twelve kilometres from the sea, embedded among stones and draped with orchids. The armour is said to be from the fifteenth century, which it could just be, since the northeastern coastal region of South America, what is now Colombia and Venezuela, was first visited by Europeans, with and without armour, in 1499–1500. Santa Marta was founded in 1525; Cartagena in 1533.

Do we *know* we are in the Americas? Even if we don't look at the maps? We do if we are not desperate to see Macondo as a never-never land or a universal allegory. García Márquez is scrupulously quiet about large terms like nations and the year of Our Lord. But he is precise about place names, days of the week, months, seasons, political parties, peace treaties, an accordion given to a musician by Sir Walter Raleigh. We learn of the Spanish ancestry of the settlers. There are Liberals and Conservatives. There is much importation of fancy goods from Europe: furniture from Vienna, linen from Holland, glassware from Bohemia. A civil war ends with the peace of Neerlandia, which the history books (but not García Márquez) tell us was signed in 1902. There are Indians in the region, speaking their own prehispanic tongue, a people for whom this world is not at all recent. When the settlers are said to be "the first mortals" [28:31] to see the western slope of the mountains they have crossed in their pioneering journey, we need to understand the phrase, again, as a metaphor or hyperbole, a figure for feeling. They were the first mortals of European descent, the new world was not empty, just empty of their kind. Even Eden is relative in this light, a glancing joke (can one *arrive* in Eden?), and another Biblical reference confirms this sense of mischief. The founders of Macondo have travelled to a "land no one had promised them" [27:31].

García Márquez creates wide meanings by copious omissions and by the use of specific but not local details. Colombia becomes a generic, legendary Latin America, a place of innocence and isolation and charm, of high mountains and rainy tropics and ash-coloured sea, but also of internal wars, bureaucrats, booms, strikes, North American intervention, and fits of fondness for the military. It is a sub-continent carefully suspended between myth and the atlas, rather as the name Baghdad, say, used to make Westerners feel they were both in the Middle East and in the Arabian Nights. It feels recent because it keeps hiding from history. It is Eden not because it is pristine and original, but because it has forgotten the Fall. Or almost forgotten.

The settlers bring with them the very stories they hoped to leave behind. The happy village is founded on remorse, since José Arcadio Buendía killed a man who attacked his honour, and whose ghost troubled his sleep and sent him journeying. José Arcadio Buendía is above all struck by the *loneliness* of the ghost, an early sounding of the theme which dominates the book, and later, when the village is not quite so happy and someone has died, the ghost finds his way to Macondo, driven by a longing for the company of the living, and oriented by Macondo's appearance on the "motley maps of death" [75:80]. He is old now, his hair white and his gestures uncertain, and José Arcadio Buendía is startled to learn that "the dead also aged" [74:80]. Perturbed by the contradictory behaviour of time—it seems both static and changing—José Arcadio Buendía loses all sense of temporal measurement, and runs amok, frothing at the mouth, reverting to what is described as "a state of total innocence"[76:82]. It is a haunted innocence, though, since he is also barking in a strange language which turns out to be Latin: the linguistic equivalent of finding the old armour or the Spanish galleon. José Arcadio Buendía has fallen into a past he didn't know was there. Certainly only a miracle could start a man speaking a language without learning it, but even miracles have implications. There is a similar implication in another splendid gag, worthy of Cervantes, which has José Arcadio Buendía, by dint of much watching of the sun and stars, and much work with his astrolabe, sextant and compass, discover for himself that the earth is round. The discovery is authentic, all his own, so foreign to his community that no one there believes him. But this new Columbus gets his chance only because his culture has forgotten the old one, and it is of course a lovely, dizzying touch to make a group of *Americans* forget Columbus.

Macondo's innocence is also an ignorance. Paradise is a refuge, a simplification of social existence, a form of solitude. There is another Fall. Progress arrives uninvited, propelled by its incapacity for leaving things alone. The distant government, for example, stretches out an unwelcome arm in the shape of a *corregidor* (chief magistrate), complete with six ragged soldiers, ordering all the houses in the village to be painted blue, "in celebration of the anniversary of national independence" [56:61]. Independence, the nation: the very history Macondo thought it had abandoned.

But the inhabitants of Macondo also reverse their escape themselves by seeking out the once excluded world. Even Úrsula Buendía, remorselessly sceptical about her husband's inquiries, orders a pianola for her new house, which in turn attracts an Italian pianola expert, who becomes a suitor to the girls of the family. José Arcadio Segundo tries to open up river communication for the town, and brings in its first and last boat, a log-raft loaded with French prostitutes. Aureliano Triste goes off to find his fortune and returns to Macondo with the railway, "the innocent yellow train that was to bring so many ambiguities and certainties, so many pleasant and unpleasant moments, so many changes, calamities, and feelings of nostalgia to Macondo" [196:210]. The railway indeed announces the whole modern world, with its electricity, movies, telephone, gramophones, cars.

What all this tells us is that haunted paradises come to an end just like their pure precursors. There is no hiding from history for long, and we know this from the very first sentence of the book, where we hear of violence before we hear of Eden. "Many years later, as he faced the firing squad, Colonel Aureliano Buendía was to remember that distant afternoon when his father took him to discover ice" [9:11]. *Discover* is *conocer*, to get to know what ice is, to see a piece of ice for the first time, exactly as José Arcadio Buendía discovers that the earth is round. Another name for innocence here is isolation, solitude: not knowing and not having what others know and have. It is a dubious privilege, but even so there is sadness in its cancellation. The *distant afternoon* is the time of the refuge, the tiny settlement and the clear river, and we learn at once that at least one of its inhabitants will find his way to a military rank and a death sentence. Much turbulent Latin American history hovers in that casual mention of the firing squad—in the casualness perhaps even more than in the mention. It is in exactly the same tone that the narrator, describing the founding of the village, alludes to the second civil war before we have heard of the first [28:31].

In this paradise as in others knowledge is the serpent's bait, innocent enough in moderation but only to be had, it seems, in excess. In the early days a band of gypsies is Macondo's single connection to the wide world. They arrive every March, bringing with them what are described as "new inventions" [9:11]—new to Macondo, that is—like magnets, magnifying glasses, instruments of navigation, an alchemy set, false teeth. Their leader is a fat fellow with a beard and sparrow's hands and an "Asiatic look that seemed to know what there was on the other side of things" [13:15]. His name is Melquíades. One March, a fresh set of gypsies appears with the news that Melquíades is dead, and with rather different inventions: a mind-reading monkey, a machine that sews buttons and brings down fever, a poultice for killing time, and the ice Aureliano Buendía discovers in the book's first sentence. José Arcadio Buendía leads his two sons into a tent which is said to have belonged to King Solomon:

there was a giant with a hairy torso and shaven head, with a copper ring in his nose and a heavy iron chain on his ankle, watching over a pirate chest. When it was opened by the giant, the chest gave off a glacial exhalation. Inside there was only an enormous, transparent block with infinite internal needles in which the light of the sunset was broken up into colored stars. [23:25–26]

José Arcadio Buendía touches the ice, "his heart filled with fear and jubilation at the contact with mystery," and solemnly announces, "This is the great invention of our time" [23:26].

José Arcadio Buendía's appetite for inventions is an appetite of the imagination. Even his apparently practical schemes, like finding gold with a magnet or making gold through alchemy, are really dabblings in disinterested science, quests for wonder—the chance of gain a mere mask or excuse for curiosity. And when José Arcadio Buendía and his men go exploring, they are seeking "contact with the great inventions" [16:19], as if they could modernize Eden without damage, as if they could import only wonder. What they find is the Spanish galleon.

There is more than a mild and amusing relativism here. What is new for some is old for others, but the inference points not simply to the variety of human experience but to the vagaries of historical time, and to the special meaning of innocence I mentioned a page or so back. "We do not all inhabit the same time," Ezra Pound said, and García Márquez, later in this book, offers a concise and witty formulation of this theory:

time also stumbled and had accidents, and could therefore splinter and leave an eternalized fragment in a room . . . [303:332]

Certain South American Indians even now live in the Stone Age while we live in the Age of the Concorde. We ourselves have mental equipment, assumptions and values which largely belong to the nineteenth century, as if the twentieth century had not entirely happened to us yet. Terms like the Third World, concepts like backwardness or mental age, rest on the notion of splinterable time, and when, in this novel, the self-taught yet very learned Aureliano Babilonia grows up, he know nothing of his own period, the early twentieth century, but has "the basic knowledge of medieval man" [309:328].

Macondo then is neither benighted nor blessed nor removed from time altogether. It is remote and contemporary, one of time's fragments, a place of temporal solitude. José Arcadio Buendía's wonderment at the ice and his brilliant personal discovery of the earth's roundness are both jokes on him and tributes to him, concrete forms of equivocation, rather like Don Quixote's courage when faced with lions which won't fight him.

The lions are hungry and dangerous, but not in the mood for battle right now, so Quixote's quite genuine courage remains untested: his folly is heroic, but his heroism looks foolish. José Arcadio Buendía's intelligence and imagination are astounding but absurdly situated, and his innocence adds a further twist to the story. He doesn't even know that folly or heroism is in the offing.

Solitudes

The Spanish galleon the settlers find is beached out of its time and out of its element, and it hangs in the mind like an emblem of Macondo and the Buendía family, or rather of the kind of enchantment they suffer and embody:

> Before them, surrounded by ferns and pale trees, white and powdery in the silent morning light, was an enormous Spanish galleon. Tilted slightly to the starboard, it had hanging from its intact masts the dirty rags of its sails in the midst of its rigging, which was adorned with orchids. The hull, covered with an armor of petrified barnacles and soft moss, was firmly fastened into a surface of stones. The whole structure seemed to occupy its own space, one of solitude and oblivion, protected from the blemishes of time and the habits of birds. Inside, where the expeditionaries explored with careful intent, there was nothing but a thick forest of flowers. [18:20–21]

The mood of this vision is oddly attractive and dislocated. Commentators have naturally seized on the sentence beginning "The whole structure seemed to occupy its own space, one of solitude and oblivion . . ," This is, as Jacques Joset remarks in his edition, the first mention of solitude in the book. We have the words *oblivion, forgetting* and *forgetfulness* for *obvido,* but here we really need something like *forgottenness,* a state of abandonment or neglect which is not quite the blankness of oblivion. It is true that the sentence allegorizes the ship, and points to other magical spaces, like Melquíades' room in the Buendía house, the place where time splinters and leaves fragments. But the effect of the image is less logical and discursive than allegory usually is, more like a moment in a dream which trails criss-crossing meanings from waking life. The ship is piracy and conquest, a whole patch of Spanish history. But it is also elegance and magic, a release from the purposes of plunder and voyaging. The rags of sail suggest a disaster, but the orchids look like a carnival.

We are viewing a wonder and a freak, a sight at once ruined and luxurious. It implies a human invasion of nature, and nature's easy incorporation of the man-made. A whole tradition of Latin American fiction is evoked here, in a mixture of homage and mischief—the tradition represented by Rivera's *La Vorágine*, for instance, which ends with the words which Carlos Fuentes has wittily taken as a motto for literature's hitherto losing battle against geography: "The jungle swallowed them," "se los tragó la selva." But then the swallowing here feels curiously benign; the humans have just slipped away, *become* nature, the ship is a landscape. Solitude in this context seems to mean an enviable privacy, and being forgotten might be a kind of historical grace. The "forest of flowers" insists on the sense of what I have called the refuge, the expiry of noise and confusion. If we take these associations back to the Buendías and Macondo, we see some of the attractions of solitude, and something of the immense appeal of this haughty, eccentric and disorderly family; and we have, I think, one of the secrets of the novel's extraordinary success: it beautifully pictures the charm of what we are not ordinarily supposed to find charming.

And yet. The galleon is *only* beautiful, and it is lost. It is stranded, sterile, and has no connection to continuing human life. It is isolated—a word which lacks the proud ring of *solitude*—and being forgotten, like being ignorant, is an equivocal grace. When García Márquez, receiving the Nobel Prize, spoke of the solitude of Latin America—that was the title of his acceptance speech—he meant its difference, its strangeness to others, and the failure of supposedly friendly countries to offer concrete support to its aspirations. It is true that he also took pride in what he saw as the source of this difference, the extravagant unlikeliness of much of life in Latin America, but this is precisely the reverse side of the same coin. Solitude is like progress: one always has too much or too little.

It is worth pausing over the word. *Soledad* is an alluring, mournful, much-used Spanish noun, suggesting both a doom and solace, a flight from love but also from lies, a claim to dignity which is also a submission to neglect. *Loneliness* has some of this flavour, but only some. *Soledad* is part of a culture which calls its streets paradise or bitterness or disenchantment; and gives girls names like Virtues, Sorrows, and Mercies. Soledad is itself a girls' name, and the name of Octavio Paz's Mexican labyrinth. *Soledades* is the title of one of the most famous poems in the Spanish language, Góngora's evocation of a pastoral shipwreck.

The word haunts the book, attaching itself to virtually every character. It is an "air," an appearance which permits all Aureliano's sons to be identified instantly as his [190:204], "a look of solitude that left no doubt as to the relationship" [137:146]. When members of the family are not solitary but gregarious they seem strange, defectors or mutants, and even then we hear of the "bitter solitude" [237:254] of the jolly Aureliano Segundo's revels; and his daughter Meme, a cheerful, sociable girl who hangs out with the newly resident Americans and invites sixty-eight schoolmates and four nuns to stay with her in Macondo over the holidays, finds her own solitude when she is very young. Her lover is shot and crippled for life, and she never speaks again, dying many years later in a convent in Cracow. In her happy days, we are told, she "did not yet show the solitary fate of the family," "no revelaba todavá el sino solitario de la familia" [227:243]—that is, she didn't show any sign of her share in such a fate. The *yet* is cruel and touching, since it knows what she doesn't know, and the *fate* seems horribly accidental. Her lover is injured and their love exposed because he is mistaken for a chicken thief. It is Meme's fate, perhaps, or at least her character, that she should respond to her loss by shutting herself away in silence, but her solitude is only a fragile and disturbing compound of bad luck and stoicism. It is predetermined merely in the sense that it is what the novelist has decided is going to happen to her. García Márquez' use of this kind of textual fate is quite elaborate, and I shall return to it.

There are individual solitudes which are not the mark of the family or of the writer's conspiracy against his characters but responses to particular, troubling experiences: sexual initiation is a "fearful solitude" [31:35]; the possibility of fatherhood makes a man "anxious for solitude" [35:39]. Certain characters, like Aureliano and Amaranta Buendía, actually seem to incarnate solitude, and I shall look at them more closely in later chapters. Incest too, the great family terror and temptation, is an aspect of the theme, a refusal of the world of others, of the outside. But for the moment I want only to insist on the theme's richness and range, and to defend it against a particular simplification, which is that of many critics but also García Márquez' own.

Two instances help here. Rebeca Buendía, after an unhappy love and a tumultuous but contented marriage, becomes a stern and lonely widow, hidden away in her house, and entirely forgotten by Macondo, until someone stumbles on her, as if she were rusty armour or a Spanish galleon. She is said in her later years to have gained "the privileges of solitude," which are contrasted to the "false charms of pity" [194:208—"los privilegios de la soledad/los falsos encantos de la misericordia"]. Better to be alone and uncomplaining then to enjoy the promiscuous pity of others. We recognize a version of Meme's reaction to her grief. There is arrogance in such a posture, of course, but there is also dignity, and much moral authority. The privileges of solitude are not an illusion—and are certainly not to be spirited away by any sort of well-meaning sermon about companionship.

The other instance is even deeper. There is an ancient rivalry between Rebeca and Amaranta. They first fell out, or rather committed themselves to a scarcely spoken but implacable and enduring enmity, over Pietro Crespi, the Italian pianola expert. Amaranta discovers shortly before her death at a fairly advanced age that her feelings have ended neither in hatred nor in love but in "the measureless understanding of solitude," "la comprensión sin medidas de la soledad" [244:260]. Grammatically the phrase could mean that solitude is what is understood, and it is true that the understanding concerns the solitary Rebeca. But the context clearly suggests the measureless understanding which solitude can give, which is the portion, or may be the portion, of those who are truly dedicated to solitude, like the Buendías. It is not an understanding that many of them reach, but the interesting implication lies in the moral possibility: solitude is a way of losing others and the world, but may also be an austere way of finding them. It was in just this sense that Proust spoke of books as the work of solitude and the children of silence.

As I have suggested, García Márquez himself is inclined to moralize this issue in a rather narrow way. "The Buendías," he said in an interview, "were incapable of loving and this is the key to their solitude and their frustration. Solitude, I believe, is the opposite of solidarity." Elsewhere he has insisted that this is "a political concept: solitude considered as the negation of solidarity." It is true that the attraction of solitude, or quietism, is very dangerous, and especially for politically disaffected or despairing Latin Americans. And it is true that the Buendías are a family of monsters. But they are tremendously appealing monsters, and we can't dissipate their appeal by pretending we don't feel it—as García Márquez himself must have felt it. To say that the Buendías are incapable of loving is to travesty all the tenderness and torment and longing that abound in the book, and to muffle all kinds of differences among the characters. The Buendías have a hard time loving anyone. They get tangled in their pride, and they are amazingly stubborn. But this is not a moral or political verdict, or material for a slogan. It is what the novel is made of. García Márquez comments that he is "not very good at these theorizings, which in my case are always *a posteriori*." Or not quite always *a posteriori,* since we also find such theorizings, albeit quite rarely, in the novel itself. These attempts are invariably intelligent and interesting, but generally unavailing. The characters and events slip away, not because they are independent of their author—their place in the plot sees to that—but because they are, in most cases, richer than his formulas for them. This is particularly true, as we shall see, of Colonel Aureliano Buendía. Ideas may slip away too, because they are more complex in their concrete, dramatized form then they are when construed for argument. The Spanish galleon occupies a space of solitude and oblivion, but it is also a material memory, a recall to history, a lingering of the past in the present. It waits in the jungle like a destiny.

Sleep and Forgetting

Paradise can be translated as solitude, and solitude, in this novel, suggests a lapse of memory. But what is forgotten is not necessarily dead, it may not be mislaid or repressed. And even if dead, it may be buried. When the unsettled past is refused by conscious thought, it often returns as a set of spectres—which is one reason for the multiplicity of ghosts in *One Hundred Years of Solitude.* They walk in these pages "like a materialization of a memory" [309:328]—because they *are* a materialization of memory, of a memory which has been denied or distanced, like the Latin language or a lost and found ship. The image is reversed, the ghosts quite plainly made figuratively, when Rebeca is said to have "found peace in that house where memories materialized through the strength of implacable evocation and walked like human beings through the cloistered rooms" [142:152]. The whole novel is an evocation of this kind, since the Buendías are consigned to oblivion *in* the story, but resurrected *by* the story, remembered as often as the story is told.

Of course this story itself could be lost, or not have been told in the first place. We can see with the memory, as Úrsula Buendía does; but there are blindnesses of memory too, and all feats of remembering have to be set against this risk, as lights are held up against an always possible darkness. If there is one thing worse than the traffic of unquiet ghosts, it could well be the entire absence of ghosts, memory's utter abolition. The risk is notably dramatized in an early chapter, where the whole of Macondo finds itself unable to sleep, and consequently unable to remember.

The village has turned into a lively town, with Arab traders and new houses and musical clocks. Two Indians, brother and sister, now work for the Buendías. They have left their home region because of a "plague of insomnia" there [40:44], and this magical disease, reported like everything else in *One Hundred Years of Solitude* as if it were the most natural thing in the world, now smites the family and the town. At first people are quite pleased. They don't sleep but they don't feel tired, and there is plenty to do. "This way we can get more out of life," José Arcadio Buendía happily says [45:50]. But the disease insidiously develops toward "a more critical manifestation: a loss of memory":

When the sick person became used to this waking state, the memories of his childhood began to fade, then the names and notions of things, and finally people's identities and even consciousness of his own being, until he was sunk in a kind of idiocy without a past.[46:50]

The inhabitants of Macondo soon start to long for sleep because they miss their dreams even before they miss their past, and José Arcadio Buendía begins to study the "infinite possibilities of forgetting" [48:53]. Aureliano thinks of a temporary stay against the damage. Every object is marked with its name—table, chair, clock, door, wall, bed, saucepan, cow, goat, pig, hen, banana—and in time with a note about its use—"This is the cow. She needs to be milked every morning so that she will produce milk, and the milk must be boiled in order to be mixed with coffee to make milky coffee . . ." [49:53]. At the entrance to the town a sign says MACONDO, and in the main street a larger sign says GOD EXISTS. Of course these measures will help only as long as people remember the alphabet. "Thus they went on living in a reality that was slipping away, momentarily captured by words, but which would escape irremediably when they forgot the values of the written letters" [49:53]. This sounds like a situation imagined by Borges, but only because Borges has caught so well the spectral, vanishing quality of so much of what is called reality in Latin America. "Only the mist is real," Octavio Paz says in a poem.

Macondo does manage to quarantine itself and to stop the disease from spreading; in an imaginative inversion of the old practice connected with leprosy the town asks visitors to carry a bell signalling that they are healthy. And luckily, before forgetfulness takes over completely, the gypsy Melquíades returns from the dead, recognizes the illness for what it is, and supplies an antidote. The people of Macondo are able to celebrate "the reconquest of memory" [50:55].

Here as elsewhere in *One Hundred Years of Solitude* there is so much deadpan mischief in the writing that any act of interpretation is likely to seem pretty elephantine. I am sure that the chief connection between sleeplessness and forgetting is that there isn't one. Nonsense is precious and should not be recklessly converted into meaning on all occasions. Even so, I can't shake off the feeling of a subtly implied logic here, a sense that confirms rather than quarrels with the nonsense. Sleep is the means of memory, it seems. The past can accumulate only in the apparent forgetfulness of the night. If we were always awake, the time would always be the present. Or more crudely, if we can't forget, we can't remember. This is partly a truism, of course, a mere statement of what the word *remember* means; but it may also be an insight into quite particular fears, a specification of the tightrope that needs to be walked. The *totally* forgotten would not longer be forgotten, it would be nothing, it would have entered oblivion, a meaning the Spanish word *olvido* includes, as we have seen. Macondo is trying to forget history. The galleon and the armour, the Indians, the return of the dead Prudencio Aguilar and the dead Melquíades, are points where the enterprise fortunately fails. The insomnia plague is a figure for the possible and terrible *success* of the enterprise, for what its success would actually mean. There is a forgetting which allows memory to accumulate, unspied on; and there is a forgetting which takes memory away, along with everything else that matters. Time itself is the repository of history; and also an insomnia plague. The final wind which erases Macondo is a materialization of oblivion, the plague's last triumph, mitigated only by the precarious memory game of writing.

Mario Vargas Llosa, "García Márquez: From Aracataca to Macondo," from *Gabriel García Márquez,* edited by Harold Bloom, Modern Critical Views (New York & Philadelphia: Chelsea House, 1989), pp. 5–19. This essay was originally published in *Review,* 70 (1971). © 1971 by the Center for Inter-American Relations, Inc.

In about the middle of 1967, the novel *One Hundred Years of Solitude* was published in Buenos Aires, provoking a literary earthquake throughout Latin America. The critics recognized the book as a masterpiece of the art of fiction and the public endorsed this opinion, systematically exhausting new editions, which, at one point, appeared at the astounding rate of one a week. Overnight, García Márquez became almost as famous a great soccer player or an eminent singer of boleros. The first translations have received an equally enthusiastic response. But the reasons behind the popularity of a book are hard to detect and often extraliterary, and what is especially remarkable in the case of *One Hundred Years of Solitude* is that its thundering fame should be due to virtues which can only be defined as artistic.

What then are the virtues of this book whose existence contradicts the gloomy assertions that the novel is an exhausted genre in the process of extinction? I wish to single out three. First, the fact that this is a "total" novel, in the tradition of those insanely ambitious creations which aspire to compete with reality on an equal basis, confronting it with an image and qualitatively matching it in vitality, vastness and complexity. In the second place, something that we could call its "plural" nature; that is, its capacity for being at one time things which were thought to be opposites: traditional and modern; regional and universal; imaginary and realistic. Yet perhaps the most mysterious of its virtues is the third: its unlimited accessibility; that is, its power to be within anyone's reach, with distinct but abundant rewards for everyone: for the intelligent reader and for the imbecile; for those with a complex mind and for those with a simple one; for the refined who relish prose, contemplate structure and decode the symbols of a story, and for the impatient, who only respond to a crude anecdote. The literary genius of our time is usually hermetical, minoritarian and oppressive; *One Hundred Years of Solitude* is one of the rare instances among major, contemporary literary works that can be read, understood, and enjoyed by all.

The author of this narrative achievement, Gabriel García Márquez, was born in 1928 in a tiny Colombian town of the coastal region overlooking the Caribbean. The town's name is rather like a tongue twister: Aracataca. Founded around the end of the last century, between Barranquilla and Santa Marta, by people who apparently fled the civil wars which decimated Colombia, Aracataca had its golden era between 1915 and 1918, when the banana craze reached its acme, scattering plantations in the region and attracting many people who needed jobs.

United Fruit, an unfortunate famous North American company, established itself in that area and started with a single crop to exploit the land. Many fortunes grew under the shade of banana trees, and popular imagination would later maintain that in those days of prosperity "whores danced the *cumbia* in the nude before magnates who, for them, would use one hundred peso bills instead of candles, to light the candelabra." That was also an era of violent social conflicts: the government repressed a strike of farm workers with the use of machine guns which cut down the lives of hundreds; the bodies were thrown into the sea. At the end of World War I, the banana fever ended, and for Aracataca it was the beginning of an economic collapse, the exodus of its inhabitants, the slow and suffocating death of tropical villages. The town was assaulted by outlaws, decimated by epidemics, ravaged by deluges. At the time when García Márquez was born, however, all that had almost stopped: paradise and hell belonged to the past, and present reality consisted of a limbo make up of poverty, heat and routine. Yet that extinct reality remained alive in the memory and imagination of the people and it was their best weapon against the desolation and emptiness of their present reality. In want of anything better, Aracataca—like so many Latin American towns—lived on remembrances, myths, solitude and nostalgia. García Márquez's entire literary work is built with this material which fed him throughout childhood. When he was born, Aracataca lived off memories; his stories will take life from his memories of Aracataca.

In the neighborhood of the town there was a banana plantation, which, as a child, García Márquez explored many times. It was called Macondo. This will be the name with which he will later baptize the imaginary land where almost all his stories take place, and the "history" of which he will tell, from beginning to end, in *One Hundred Years of Solitude*.

García Márquez was not raised by his parents, but by his grandparents, who were, according to him, his most solid literary influences. They lived in a huge and awesome house, filled with spirits, they were both superstitious and credulous. From the lips of his grandmother, García Márquez heard the legends, fables and prestigious lies with which the popular imagination of Aracataca evoked the ancient splendor of the area, and sometimes he saw his grandmother chatting naturally with ghosts who came to visit her. The elderly woman was an implacable storyteller: she used to tiptoe into her grandson's room at night and wake him to tell stories. Last year, a journalist asked García Márquez about the origin of the fluid, transparent, vital style of his stories, and he answered: "It's my grandmother's." In a certain manner, his grandmother is also the prototype of a whole series of female characters from Macondo: those women who happily converse with dead people, Like Ursula Buendía; or like Fernanda del Carpio de Buendías, who correspond with invisible doctors.

But still more decisive than his grandmother, was the influence exerted on García Márquez by his grandfather, whom García Márquez describes as "the most important figure in my life." The old man had participated in the civil wars, and it was from the memories of that veteran that the grandson relived the most explosive episodes of Colombian violence, as well as the frustration felt by these warriors in their old age, when they discovered that they fought for nothing and that no one even bothered to remember them anymore. The grandfather had a devil who haunted him: he had once killed a man. He would take his grandson to the circus and, quite suddenly, he would stop in the street and exclaim: "Oh! You don't know how much a dead body weighs." In *One Hundred Years of Solitude,* the founding of Macondo will, to a certain extent, be the result of a similar remorse. The first José Arcadio Buendía, founder of the clan whose story intermingles with that of Macondo, kills a man, Prudencio Aguilar, the bloody corpse of the victim harasses him with visions until José Arcadio decides to abandon the heights of Riohacha, crosses the mountain range with twenty-one companions and finds Macondo. The grandfather of García Márquez used to sing: "Mambrú has gone to war / how painful / how painful / how sad." Years later, García Márquez would discover that this song was a Castilianized version of a French song ("Marlborough s'en va-t-enguerre") and that "Mambrú" was in reality "Marlborough." Since the only wars his grandfather had know were the Colombian civil wars, García Márquez decided that a Duke of Marlborough had been a protagonist in the Colombian violence. Hence the phantasmagoric warrior who in five of

García Márquez's books presents himself at the military camp of Colonel Aureliano Buendía, disguised in tiger furs, claws and teeth, turns out to be the Duke of Marlborough. The figure of the grandfather is another of the constant male models in the work of García Márquez: he appears in the first novel *La hojarasca (The Leafstorm)* in the person of the ancient Colonel who defies the wrath of Macondo when be buries the French doctor; he is the hero of García Márquez's second novel *No One Writes to the Colonel*, and appears doubly in *One Hundred Years of Solitude,* magnified in the mythical personality of Colonel Aureliano Buendía, and in that of his friend and companion, Colonel Gerineldo Márques (this time with his own surname).

García Márquez's grandfather died when the writer was eight. "Since then nothing interesting has happened to me," the author asserts. Two books he read through the years contaminated the material he gathered from his grandparents: *The Thousand and One Nights* and *Gargantua and Pantagruel*. Traces of both will appear later in Macondo, not so much in the story, as in the style in which it was written: from the first episodical richness and proliferation as a narrative rule, and from the second, the vocation for excess and exaggeration. All the sources of *One Hundred Years of Solitude* seem already assembled in the mind of García Márquez when he abandoned Aracataca in 1940 to study in a school run by Jesuits in Bogotá. However, many things would have to take place before he could definitely exorcise the devils of his childhood in one great verbal construction.

He claims that since he was eight years old nothing interesting has happened to him, but in reality, many things have. Like almost every Latin American writer, García Márquez undertook the intense study of law; at the end of his secondary education, and also, like most, he soon renounced it. He traded law for journalism. He was a journalist and a writer of editorials for *El Espectador*, a Bogotá paper, in whose literary page his first stories appeared in 1946. In 1950 he lived in Barranquilla, and there, in the café "Colombia," he used to meet Ramón Vinyes, a Catalonian bookseller, as well as three other friends, Alfonso Fuenmayor, Germán Vargas and Alvaro Cepeda, the latter of whom would become a novelist. These people, including Gabriel García Márquez himself, will appear transfigured in the last years of Macondo, when Aureliano Buendía, the hermetist, discovers the prodigious bookstore of the encyclopedical Catalonian scholar,

ONE HUNDRED YEARS OF NOVELISTS

"One Hundred Years of Solitude is the first piece of literature since the Book of Genesis that should be required reading for the entire human race. It takes up not long after Genesis left off and carries through to the air age, reporting on everything that happened in between with more lucidity, wit, wisdom, and poetry than is expected from a hundred years of novelists, let alone one man."

William Kennedy

From "The Yellow Trolley Car in Barcelona: An Interview," in his Riding the Yellow Trolley Car (New York: Viking, 1993), p. 243.

collector of incunabula and seller of Sanskrit manuscripts. In this bookstore Aureliano initiates his friendship with Alvaro, Germán, Alfonso and Gabriel, from whom he learns the art of revelry and with whom he visits the Babilonic, zoological brothel, which, at the age of one hundred and forty-five, Pilar Ternera rules. With these friends Aureliano discovers that literature "is the best toy for making fun of people."

In 1954, *El Espectador* sent García Márquez to Italy to cover the death of Pius XII which was believed to be imminent. But the pontiff died years later, and in the meantime, García Márquez arranged to remain in Europe and from there he sent articles to Bogotá. For a while, he studied at the "Centro Sperimentale Cinematográfico" in Rome and later that year he traveled through Eastern European countries. In 1955, while he froze in the cold weather of Eastern Europe, his Colombian friends discovered inside a drawer of his desk in his office in Bogotá, the manuscript of a novel he had finished just before leaving Colombia but which, due to an exaggerated sense of self-criticism, he had decided not to publish. His friends, *manu militare,* took the manuscript to the printer and so, in 1955, *La hojarasca* appeared. To write a novel is always an attempt at restitution and exorcism; an enterprise by which a man in conflict with reality tries simultaneously to recover from death certain key personal experiences which have remained in his memory and to free himself from those memories which have become tormenting obsessions of "devils." García Márquez's entire work up to the present has been a diligent effort to project into a novel this world, at once real and fantastic, the one which nourished his childhood. The first phase of this enterprise is *La hojarasca* where he describes a period in the history of Macondo between 1903 (the year in which the Colombian civil wars theoretically ceased) and 1928 (the year in which he was born).

In his first novel, Macondo is described in a purely subjective way through the alternate monologues of three characters: a boy of eleven, his mother Isabel, and his grandfather, a gentlemanly and lame old Colonel, appearing before the dead body of a mysterious doctor who hanged himself the night before and whom the people have sworn to leave unburied because they hated him. An odor of putrefaction, a physical, historical and moral decay overwhelms this narrative. Through the story of this anonymous doctor, whom the monologues slowly reveal, appear fragments of the history of Macondo. Who is this doctor? His past, his tragedy are unknown to us. We only know that he arrived in Macondo twenty-five years earlier; that he seemed to be a military man, and that he read French newspapers, which led the people to call him "the Frenchman." He brought with him a letter of recommendation from a certain Colonel Aureliano Buendía, General Governor of the Provinces of the Atlantic Coast. This letter so greatly impresses the Colonel, that he gives him lodging in his own house where the Frenchman will remain for seven years. For a while, he practices medicine, but soon, the banana company falls like a nightmare upon Macondo, dragging with it *La hojarasca* (*The Leafstorm* or human ruins of other settlements) and exploiting the town, making it dizzy with an illusion of prosperity, other doctors settle down in the area and the Frenchman loses patients. But instead of becoming disturbed, in an act of tranquil haughtiness, he abandons his profession and cloisters himself. He first lives closeted up in the Colonel's house but then later he moves to the dwelling across the street, taking with him as his mistress Meme, a maid the Colonel's family has raised. One night—by now the banana company has squeezed Macondo dry and departed, leaving in its wake apparent prosperity and the human refuse which is its monument—Macondo is filled with wounded men brought into the city from a neighborhood battlefield. There are not enough doctors to tend them. The people remember that the cloistered Frenchman is also a doctor and take the wounded to the door of his house, but the foreigner refuses to help. "I have already forgotten all that" he exclaims without deigning to open the door. From that time, the people have sworn revenge. They try to poison him, and the doctor lives in terror, not daring to drink local water for fear that it might poison him. For many years he lives closed up in his cave, by now abandoned by Meme, since she could not stand his determination to destroy himself. Only for one night did he leave his refuge and that was to heal the Colonel when the doctors gave up hope for the old man. In retribution, he asked the Colonel "to throw some earth over his body so the vultures would not eat him" after his death. That is the promise the Colonel has come to fulfill at the beginning of the novel, thus defying the feelings of the people of Macondo, who wish to leave the suicide unburied.

But in this first novel Macondo is still a subjective country, a metaphor of evil. Its reality, the material of fact is that García Márquez had read Faulkner around that time ("When I read Faulkner I discovered I wanted to become a writer," he will later confess), and Macondo bears the metaphysical dew of Yoknapatawpha County. However, the style he chose for the narration is not gratuitous: These intimacies of the three characters presented directly to the reader's experience have as their mission a revelation of Macondo, an exposition of its soul. The characteristic notes of Macondo are, in this instance, frustration, resentment, solitude, wickedness. The voluntary and somewhat incomprehensible seclusion of the doctor symbolizes the seclusion Macondo lives in—a town out of contact with the rest of the world, condemned to fall apart, to rot slowly in broad daylight, just as the people of Macondo like to see the body of the unsociable foreigner rot. The voluntary frustration of the doctor personifies the frustrating lives of all those in Macondo who appear in the novel: of Isabel, the frustrated wife (her husband Martín has abandoned her years before and it is suspected that he only married her out of self-interest: that is, to acquire certain powers and credit from the Colonel); of Meme, who thought that by going to live with the doctor she would escape her condition of a *guajira*, but who, instead when on the first Sunday she shows up for Mass dressed up as a lady, discovered that she had won the hatred of the entire town, which would not forgive her affront to social conventions; of the Colonel himself who, though appearing to be the only upright man and the only one capable of a noble act, is in his own life a victim of the ardent immobility and the prostration of Macondo. What the inhabitants of Macondo hate in the doctor is both the reflection of their own frustration which the foreigner brings them, and his ruin which tragically synthesizes the conditions of total meanness in which Macondo agonizes.

In this first novel, Macondo, like Yoknapatawpha County and Onetti's imaginary port of Santa María, appears as a mental territory, a projection of the guilty conscience of man. On the other hand, the beings inhabiting it and the events which take place there belong to that level of reality which we can call objective or concrete (even though the description of that reality is subjective): everything happens on a rational and probable level. Nevertheless, there already appears here a series of elements which indicate that the unusual also has gained ready acceptance in Macondo. The daughter of the barber is haunted by a male "ghost," which is futilely exorcised by the "Dog," the local parish priest who arrived in Macondo the same day the French doctor did, but who is opposite. Religion is contaminated by madness: the "Dog" delivers sermons which consist of his reading weather forecasts from the Bristol Almanac, rather than teachings from the Gospels. The French doctor practices an unusual diet: he only eats herbs, "those with which asses feed themselves." These are the first traces of the beautiful face of Macondo which will only appear in all its richness in *One Hundred Years of Solitude*.

In the meantime, García Márquez was stranded in Paris, jobless and penniless, because the dictator Rojas Pinilla had shut down the daily newspaper *El Espectador*, which was the author's only source of income. There, in a small hotel on the rue Cujas in the Latin Quarter where he lived on credit, he rewrote eleven times a short and masterful work: *No One Writes to the Colonel*. He worked day and night in a real fury, and one day his typewriter broke down so he had to take it to a repairman. The latter, scratching his head, exclaimed with pity: "Elle est fatiguée, monsieur!" He finished the novel in January 1957, shortly before returning to Latin America, yet he was still unsatisfied: that was not the Macondo he carried in his head. That is probably why, when the book appeared, the location of the novel is only referred to as "the town"; and that is also why Macondo is mentioned in it as a different place. In reality, *No One Writes to the Colonel*, though not the total picture of this imaginary world which obsessed García Márquez, is a revelation which enlarges and enriches what we already knew about it through *La hojarasca*. That world has descended in this book from its psychological clouds to geography and history. That soul now has a body—the Colonel has endowed it with blood, muscles and bones: a landscape, habits, customs and a tradition in which some of the most recurring themes in Latin American regionalism are unexpectedly found but employed in a new sense: not as values, but rather as nonvalues; not as pretexts to exalt local color, but as symbols of frustration. The famous gamecock which, pompous and ruffled passes through the worst Latin American literature like a folkloric apotheosis, metaphorically crosses the pages which describe the moral agony of the Colonel who expects the impossible pension and embodies the provincial sordidness and daily horror of the town. Like the Colonel in *La hojarasca,* like the grandfather of García Márquez, the hero of this novel is a survivor of the civil wars and contemplates a bitter political frustration. For the last fifteen years he has been expecting the government to answer his petition for recognition of services rendered by granting him his pension. Each Friday, he stations himself on the dock to meet the mail boat which will never bring him a letter. He lives with an asthmatic wife, who maintains objectively: "We are rotting alive." Their son Agustín dies nine months before in the cockpit, pierced by gunshots for distributing secret information, and the Colonel inherited from him the gamecock on which he now places all his hope. He hopes to make him compete with a champion cock from a neighboring town. But until the moment of the battle, the cock must be fed, and the Colonel and his wife have no food even for themselves. The people of *La hojarasca* suffered ills which were psychological and moral; the devils which torment these people are physical: violence, the destructive downpours, political oppression, and above all, hunger. Hunger, from which García Márquez suffered in his little hotel room on the rue Cujas while he wrote the book (he claims, in all seriousness, that he boiled chicken bones after chewing them, then placed them on the windowsill and used them over half a dozen times for soup), and the memories of which infected his imaginary world, is perhaps the town's most stinging nightmare. The book opens up with an image of poverty—the Colonel prepares himself coffee by scraping the remains out of a can so that the resulting drink is an infusion of coffee with tin oxide—and concludes with one much worse. The Colonel has decided not to sell the rooster, as his wife suggests, even though there are still forty-five days to go before the fight. "And in the meantime what shall we eat?" she asks. The Colonel answers: "Shit." The entire new face of this world—its corrupt materialism, its abject carnality—is condensed in that ferocious expression which closed the narrative. Also here, as in *La hojarasca,* there is a slovenly parish priest. His name is Father Angel, he has established a code of film censorship based on bell tolls. Twelve tolls means "bad for everyone," and it has been one full year since any film exhibited at the only theater in town has escaped Father Angel's prohibition. But the unusual element is now minimal and is overwhelmed by scrutiny of the most everyday and naturalistic levels of reality: the suspicion and fear inspired by the enactment of martial law, the recent political repression of which only Don Sabas was able to escape—Don Sabas the Colonel's comrade who now is the rich person of the town; the atmosphere of sloth, of boredom and of tedium which the constant rains of October exacerbate. Even the delineation of the characters is naturalistic: the mayor's cheeks swollen by the pain in his molar teeth; Don Sabas's diabetes; the digestive disorders provoked in the Colonel by October; his wife's asthma. The prose in *La hojarasca* has undergone a real process of refinement and technique has been radically simplified. The Faulknerian traces have disappeared. "I have fought them by reading Hemingway," says García Márquez in jest. The style is one of maniacal economy and transparency; the construction of perfect simplicity; the adjustment between the material and the form of the story total. To anyone who might have read in 1957 the then recently finished manuscript (which García Márquez buried, tied with a colored ribbon, in the bottom of a suitcase) the author's decision not to publish it, because he considered the book a failure, would have sounded inconceivable. This novel, *per se,* is a totally successful work. Only later, with the appearance of *One Hundred Years of Solitude,* was it possible to realize that, as a description of Macondo, this excellent narrative could still be surpassed.

In 1957, García Márquez returned stealthily to Colombia to marry a beautiful woman with Egyptian features who had been waiting for him in Barranquilla for four years. Those who wish to know her have only to read *One Hundred Years of Solitude.* She appears in it, with her own name of Mercedes, as a reserved and silent pharmacist "with a thin neck and sleepy eyes," who, to top if off, is engaged to a certain Gabriel. From Colombia he moved to Venezuela, where he lived for a couple of years working for magazines and newspapers, in a Caracas shaken by terrorist attempts: the bullets and bombs with which Pérez Jiménez tortured the people throughout his dictatorship. During these years, García Márquez wrote most of the stories which would make up his third book, *Los funerales de la Mamá Grande,* and which would only be published in 1962. These stories follow the stylistic line of *The Colonel*: a precise, spare language, worked over, stripped of all artifices and without a shade of excessive rhetoric; a lineal structure, freed from complications; short and efficient dialogues. Only the narrative from which the title of the book is taken differentiates itself clearly from the rest by a tone of cunning farce and the rambling cry in which it is written, by the rich and inflated language used. But, though they extend the form of the previous book, these stories offer an image of Macondo in which a new dimension of that world appears, one only vaguely insinuated before: the magic dimension. Macondo is now not only a territory oppressed by evil, mosquitos, the heat, hunger, political violence and inertia: but also a stage for inexplicable and wonderful successes: to a widow who languishes bitterly on a rainy day, "with a white sheet and a comb on her lap and crushing lice with her thumbs," appears the ghost of Mamá Grande, a woman who has been dead for years. Instead of getting frightened the widow asks her "When will I die?" "When your arm starts to hurt you," Mamá Grande answers mysteriously and disappears; there is a strange plague of birds who burst into the houses breaking through the screens on the windows, and dying in the dwellings: the priest is no less original then those of the previous books: his name is Father Antonio Isabel del Santísimo Sacramento del Altar Castañeda y Montero, and, at the age of 94, he has seen the devil on three occasions, and, as if that were not enough, one day he finds the Wandering Jew walking along the streets of Macondo; the funeral of Mamá Grande brings to Macondo figures from the four cardinal points and, among them, the Pope and the President of the Republic, and also a few dead people. Many of the stories in the book are like fragments, chapters of a vaster text, and, in spite of their clean execution, they leave the reader with a certain unsatisfied appetite. That is because these narratives were actually written as episodes of a novel, that novel about Macondo, tried for the third time by García Márquez and for the third time abandoned, in some ways, in the middle.

It was the year 1960 and García Márquez had returned to Bogotá to open there the *Prensa Latina,* an agency founded by Cuba in the year of the revolution. In 1960 this agency sent him to New York as its correspondent, and he remained in this city for a few months until he resigned one day. He then undertook a

Homeric trip through the Deep South "in homage to Faulkner and carrying that author's books under his arms." But as a sign of protest, he did not remain in the South, because, one day, after many of abstinence, he succeeded in borrowing some money and in the best restaurant of New Orleans, ordered *filet mignon,* which they brought "crowned with a peach in syrup." He continued to travel to travel by land, and when he reached Mexico "the sound of the Spanish language and hot food" encouraged him to stay. He spent eight years in the Mexican capital writing subtitles for movies. There, his friends recovered the manuscript of *No One Writes to the Colonel* which by now was becoming moth-eaten in that suitcase and published it in 1961; the following year they arranged to have the stories of *Los funerales de la Mamá Grande* printed. Finally they forced him to enter in a literary contest in Bogotá the manuscript of a new novel written in Mexico, but first they advised him to change the original title, *Este pueblo de mierda* for a less bold one—*La mala hora.* The novel won the contest and was published in 1962. García Márquez had changed the original title; the owners of the press in Madrid, where the sponsors of the competition chose to publish the book, changed the entire text, gave it to an editor who cut all Americanisms and made the inhabitants of Macondo speak in the language of the *Diccionario de la Academia Española.* García Márquez rejected the edition and in the new edition of *La mala hora* placed the following note: "In 1962, when *La mala hora* was first published, a copy-editor gave himself permission to change certain terms and to stiffen the style in the name of the purity of language. On this occasion, the author in his turn has given himself permission to restore the idiomatic inaccuracies and stylistic barbarisms, in the name of his sovereign and arbitrary will." Some time ago a journalist asked García Márquez why he wrote, and the writer replied: "So that my friends will like me." The journalist doubtless thought that it was a good joke, but the truth is that without the obstinacy of his friends, García Márquez would perhaps still today be an unknown writer.

La mala hora does not amplify the view of Macondo as presented in his previous books; rather, it assembles in one novel the different data concerning the imaginary world which was dispersed in the stories and in his two novels. The most immediate effect of the story is one of a detailed and almost entomological realism, but his implacably objective surface hides a fact, which still remains unexplained, perhaps unexplainable. This fact is the appearance of pasquinades stuck on the doors of houses, in which the gossip and slander of the people are described. These lampoons do not invent anything: they repeat what people say in secret, the murmurs, calumnies or forbidden truths which travel in a whisper. Who places the lampoons on the doors? Everyone and no one. The effect is cataclysmic: this collective unfaithfulness revives rivalries, old hatreds, and sows mistrust and enmity. The secret filth of Macondo stands exposed in broad daylight. In a series of static pictures through which pass, one by one, sordid, unusual or picturesque characters, *La mala hora* presents a collective view of the human fauna of Macondo, a social X-ray of their ills.

This novel displeased García Márquez even more than the other; his disappointment resulted in a literary silence which lasted for a few years. He thought that perhaps he would never be able to write the novel of which he dreamed; he decided, in all probability, to forget about Macondo. And suddenly, one day in 1965, the miracle occurred, that is to say, the reward for so many years of faithfulness to what we could call his obsessions. He was traveling by car from Acapulo to Mexico City—he tells us—and suddenly, he "saw" the novel on which mentally he had been working since he was a boy. "I had it so completely formed," he says, "that right there I could have dictated the first chapter word by word to a typist." He immediately closed himself in this office with large supplies of paper and cigarettes and announced to Mercedes that he was going to remain there for about six months and asked her not to disturb him for any reason, least of all with domestic problems. In fact, he stayed walled in that part of his house for a year and six months. When he left that room, euphoric, intoxicated with nicotine and on the verge of a physical breakdown, he had a manuscript of one thousand and three hundred pages (and a household debt of ten thousand dollars). In the wastepaper basket there were some five thousand pages. A few months later *One Hundred Years of Solitude* was published.

One Hundred Years of Solitude extends and magnifies the world erected by his previous books, but also signifies a rupture, a qualitative change within that dry, rough, asphyxiating reality which Macondo was until then. That world, in spite of its coherence and its vitality, suffered a limitation which retrospectively *One Hundred Years of Solitude* revealed: its modesty. Everything in it was struggling to develop and to grow: men, things, dreams suggested more than showed, because a verbal straitjacket restrained their movements and cut them off the moment they were about to come out themselves. The critics used to praise the austerity of García Márquez's prose, his power of synthesis, the parsimony of his stories. All that was true and revealed an original writer who had domesticated his devils and ruled them at his whim. What provoked García Márquez, on that already distant evening, between Acapulco and Mexico City, to open the cages of those devils and let himself be dragged by them into one of the most daring creative adventures of our times? We will probably never know. But we know, on the other hand, and this is what is most important, that thanks to whatever it was, the tight and claustral town of Macondo changed into a universe, a Broceliande of wonders.

In *One Hundred Years of Solitude* we witness a prodigious enrichment. The mathematic, contained and functional prose became a style with volcanic breath, capable of communicating movement and grace to the most audacious creatures of imagination. Fantasy has broken its chains and gallops wild and feverish, permitting itself all excesses, until it has outlined in space and time the life cycle of Macondo, through its most conspicuous inhabitants: the family of the Buendías. The novel does not leave out any of the levels of reality in which the history of Macondo is recorded: it includes the individual and the collective, the legendary and the historical, the daily and the mythical. Restoring a tradition of writing that seemed dead—that of the medieval novels of knighthood—García Márquez rediscovers that the novelist is God, that the limits of literature are those of reality—that it has no limits and that all excesses are permissible to the creator if he has the sufficient verbal power of persuasion to justify them, and that the hero can die and come back to life many times if it is necessary for the perfect realization of the story. In Macondo, as in the enchanted territories where Amadís and Tirant rode, the boundaries separating reality from unreality have gone to pieces. Everything can happen here: excess is a rule, beauty enriches life and it is as truthful as war and hunger: there are flying carpets that take the children of Macondo on rides over the roofs of the town; a plague of insomnia and loss of memory; a gypsy who dies and returns to life "because he is unable to bear loneliness"; a priest who levitates after drinking a cup of chocolate and a

woman who rises to heaven body and soul, escorted by linen
sheets; a man who drifts through life with a halo of yellow butterflies, and a hero, inspired by the knightly crusaders, who pro-
motes thirty-two wars and loses them all. In a chapter of *The
Death of Artemio Cruz*, a novel by Carlos Fuentes, a character,
Colonel Lorenzo Gavilán, gets lost. García Márquez rescues him
and settles him in Macondo, where Gavilán will die swept by
grapeshot in the historical episode of the massacre of the strik-
ers. With the same ease, he gives hospitality in Macondo to Víc-
tor Hugues, a character in a novel by Alego Carpentier, and to
Rocamadour, a character of Julio Cortázar. But this dexterity
could suggest the idea the *One Hundred Years of Solitude* is something like an agreeable and brilliant game. In reality, it is quite
the opposite. It is not about a castle in the air, but about an imaginary construction that has its roots deeply anchored in Latin
American reality, a reality which is reflected through transfigura-
tions and mirages. The landscapes of Macondo contain all the
natural elements of Latin America: its snows, its mountain
ranges, its deserts, its cataclysms. Its dramas also appear
refracted in the political and social life of Macondo: the story of
the banana company and of its president, the haughty Mr.
Brown, who travels in a train of glass and velvet, synthesizes the
drama of colonial exploitation of Latin America and the tragedies
it engenders. Not everything is magic or erotic feast in Macondo:
a clamour of hostilities between the powerful and the miserable
resounds from behind these blazes of fire and sometimes
explodes in orgies of blood. And along the gorges, as in the wil-
derness of the mountain ranges of Macondo, there are, further-
more, those armies which tear each other to pieces while
searching endlessly for each other: a ferocious war which deci-
mates men and frustrates the destiny of the country, as it has
occurred and still occurs in many places in Latin America. But
this is not only an exclusively Latin American reality: it is a spiral
of concentric circles, the first of which would be a family with
characters more or less extravagant, the second the tiny town of
Aracataca with myths and problems, the third Colombia, the
fourth Latin America and the last one, humanity.

In the chronicle of Macondo, living on their own account,
and at the same time valid as symbols, beings, problems, and
myths pass by, symbols which the readers of any country and
language can identify and interpret as their own, because they

are universal and express the condition of humanity. But that universality has been attained by starting from a more concrete reality, deepening it and recreating it from a perspective which is not local, but rather human.

As any novel erected in the image and semblance of reality, *One Hundred Years of Solitude* admits of different readings, because it consists of several levels. The most immediate is that of adventure. The story of the Buendías starts with a crime and ends a century later with the birth of a monster: a child with a tail of a pig. Between both facts that most absurd adventures, the most unusual characters, the most daring phantasies proliferate in an incessant sizzling. But this line of prodigious beings, who want to portray God, who study demonology, who take delight in "creating only to destroy," who engage in improbable wars, or shut themselves up as biblical hermits, are something more than creatures of a pure game of the imagination: they are a testimony to and a metaphor of human experience in its most ample meaning. In the lives of the Buendías (of this tribe where the name of men is always Arcadio or Aureliano and the name of women Úrsula or Amaranta) are described and mingled actions and dreams, what men do and what they wanted to do, what is within reach of their bodies and what only their fantasy and insane dreams allowed them to perform. But in the waking reversals and adventures of the Buendías, their nightmares and torments also reproduce themselves: solitude, which is a hereditary infirmity of the Buendías, alienation which prevents them from communicating (and frustrates them in all their undertakings), inability to adapt to a world they do not understand and to a society in which everything seems possible, except happiness. With the strictest weapons of fiction, *One Hundred Years of Solitude* offers a vast narrative representation of the human reality of our time. Due to the determination, obstinacy and patience of this writer, the anecdotes, fables and lies of a tiny Colombian town lost between marshes and mountains have served in this manner, through reincarnations and changes, as key pieces for the construction of a story in which the men of today find the reflection of their own true selves.

Edwin Williamson, "Magical Realism and the Theme of Incest in *One Hundred Years of Solitude*," from *Gabriel García Márquez: New Readings,*

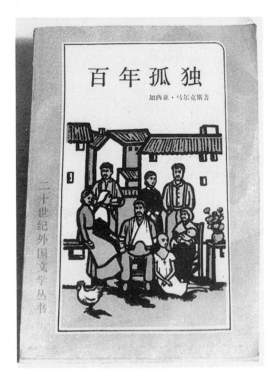

Cover for the edition of *One Hundred Years of Solitude* published in 1972 in the People's Republic of China

edited by Bernard McGuirk and Richard Cardwell (Cambridge: Cambridge University Press, 1987), pp. 45–63.

For all the attention it has received since its publication, *One Hundred Years of Solitude* remains an elusive and enigmatic novel. Although accepted as one of the major examples of Latin America's contribution to modernist writing, the problem of understanding how its highly acclaimed technique of magical realism actually works is still unresolved. At the level of simple definition there can be little disagreement: magical realism is a narrative style which consistently blurs the traditional realist distinction between fantasy and reality. Beyond this, critical opinion is divided as to whether magical realism is entirely self-referring or whether is establishes a new kind of relationship between fiction and reality.[1]

According to the former view, *One Hundred Years of Solitude* is analogous to the *ficciones* of Borges; its fictional world is autarchic, creating through the act of narration special conditions of development and meaning which enable the fictive imagination to achieve a free-floating state of pure self-reference akin to the exhilarated innocence of children at play.[2] The difficulty with such a view is that it cannot explain the political and historical allusions in the novel. To be consistent, it must absorb these also into the realm of ludic autonomy, and it therefore leaves García Márquez open to the charge of having "aestheticized" the history of Latin America.

The other account would have magical realism expand the categories of the real so as to encompass myth, magic and other extraordinary phenomena in Nature or experience which European realism has tended to exclude.[3] This explanation derives from Alejo Carpentier's early ideas about "lo real-maravilloso," and it is especially satisfying because it endows García Márquez's particular brand of modernism with a unique Latin American character.[4] What is more, García Márquez himself has often talked about magical realism in just this way.[5] Nevertheless, this explanation, in so far as it re-introduces a denotative link to an external reality—albeit more inclusive than European realism—produces a very negative, pessimistic reading of the text. The novel ends with the realization of a curse and the fulfilment of prophecy, and so it apparently vindicates the mystical power of a malign fate. As such, it would appear to condemn Latin America to a hopeless condition of historical failure, allowing no scope for change or free human action.[6]

In either account, difficulties arise in reconciling magical realism as a narrative style with the actual movement of the action in the novel. Both accounts regard magical realism as an entirely positive, liberating feature and, in consequence, they are equally hard put to explain the nature of the Buendías' degeneration and the reason for Macondo's destruction.[7] But if one examines how magical realism actually functions in the narrative, it will become clear that there is an intimate connection between it and the degenerative process described in the novel; indeed, magical realism can be shown to be a manifestation of the malaise that causes the decline of the Buendía family.

Magical realism creates its aesthetic impact by fusing terms that are in principle opposed to each other. The effect upon the reader of such a fusion of fact and fantasy or innocence and knowledge is, however, not one of absolute identification with the characters but rather a mixed reaction of sympathy and comic detachment. Let us take as an example José Arcadio Buendía's encounter with ice. In the first instance, the narrator describes the ice in a de-familiarizing way which allows the reader to share in the character's wonderment at the mysterious phenomenon:

> When the giant opened it, the chest let out a chilly breath of air. Inside it there was just an enormous transparent block with countless internal needles which broke up the light of the setting sun into stars of many colours. (p. 22)[8]

And yet, when it comes to *explaining* the mystery, the difference between José Arcadio Buendía's innocent awe and the reader's knowledge is sharply drawn within the text itself, producing an effect of comic irony:

A TOTAL FICTIONAL UNIVERSE

"As best exemplified by *One Hundred Years of Solitude*, García Márquez's ingenious mixture of realism and fantasy has resulted in the creation of a total fictional universe in which the commonplace takes on an aura of magic and the impossible is made believable. His penetrating insights into the ambiguities of human nature are enhanced by a rich vein of anecdotes and leitmotifs he taps from his private mythology. Though he clearly implies moral indignation against brutality, exploitation, and degradation, he delights his readers with his deft fusion of tragedy and comedy and with his seductive powers of language. García Márquez is presently Latin America's most widely known novelist. He is, in addition, one of the truly outstanding literary artists of our time. In its totality his work imparts not only the stark reality of an emerging strife-torn continent but, also, through the humanistic and universalizing elements of myth, imagination, and aesthetic perception, a highly original vision of man and his world."

George R. McMurray

From *Gabriel García Márquez* (New York: Ungar, 1977), p. 162.

Taken aback, yet knowing that his sons expected an immediate explanation, José Arcadio Buendía dared to murmur, "It's the biggest diamond in the world."

"No," the gypsy corrected him, "it's ice." (p. 23)

José Arcadio Buendía's awe at the discovery of ice remains unimpaired—he pronounces it "the greatest invention of our time"—but the reader can no longer share in that response since it is evident that García Márquez intends the gypsy's correction as a signal that the character is touchingly misinterpreting phenomena which the reader is presumed to take for granted in his own experience of the world. The sense of the marvellous afforded us by magical realism is therefore transient, for soon enough García Márquez tips the wink at his reader, as it were, creating a complicity behind the backs of the characters who remain circumscribed by an elemental innocence which charms but is not, of course, meant to convince. Such humorous complicity exists in the more fantastical instances of magical realism, as in, say, Remedious the Beautiful's assumption into heaven in a flurry of white sheets (p. 205). Even though the inhabitants of Macondo might accept this as a true event, as far as the reader is concerned, the fact of its being narrated in the text does not strengthen its claim to literal, historical truth. Rather the opposite, it de-mystifies the phenomenon because of the underlying assumption (as in the ice scene above) that the reader's world-view is at odds with that of the characters.

In spite of its ostensible fusion of fantasy and fact, magical realism is conceived as a wilfully specious discourse that inevitably betrays its hallucinatory character in the very act of its being read by the kind of reader García Márquez is addressing. Were the reader to participate wholly in the perspective of José Arcadio Buendía, there would be no humour in *One Hundred Years of Solitude;* its discourse would be all to solemnly denotative. But García Márquez sets up an ironic interplay between the *identity* of opposites promoted by the magical-real discourse and the inescapable sense of *difference* retained by the reader. The novel is, then, predicated upon a dialectic that opposes the experiences of the world *inside* the fiction to that which lies *outside* it.

The dialectic between identity and difference does nevertheless operate symbolically within the fictional world of Macondo. It is conveyed through the motivation theme of incest. Like magical realism, incest tends towards the fusion of differential categories, and as such constitutes a threat to social organization, since it weakens the vital distinction that underpins cultural order: the difference between self and other. In this sense, incest can be taken as a symbolic equivalent of the solipsism that underlies magical realism. For, when kinship differences are not properly marked, communication or constructive social intercourse are rendered ineffective. The family becomes a focus of centripetal energy, attracting the separate individuals that compose it back into an undifferentiated generic identity.

The fundamental impetus of *One Hundred Years of Solitude* springs from the wish to *avoid* incest. Initially, the Buendías react to the threat of incest in two ways: Úrsula seeks to uphold an ancestral taboo against it, whereas her husband José Arcadio Buendía, having defied this taboo by killing Prudencio Aguilar and forcing intercourse with his wife, looks to establishing a new order. He leaves Riohacha to make contact with "civilization" beyond. The nature of his "civilization" remains vague, but there are indications that it corresponds to that which exists outside the fictional world. In any case, its distinguishing characteristic is scientific knowledge. José Arcadio Buendía in the early stages of the novel is a man in search of science. He undertakes innumerable projects and experiments "with the self-denial of a scientist and even at the risk of his own life" (p. 10); his imagination, we are told, "reached beyond the spirit of nature and even beyond miracle and magic" (p. 9). When his sons see a gypsy and some children fly past the window of his laboratory on a magic carpet, José Arcadio Buendía declares, "Leave them to their dreams. We shall fly better than them with superior scientific resources than that wretched bedspread" (p. 34). Although the humour that characterizes the narrative style of magical realism is not forsaken in the account of José Arcadio Buendía's endearingly perverse quest for useful, scientific knowledge, his efforts are directed, as is indicated above by the last quotation, precisely towards undoing the mentality of magical realism within which he is himself imprisoned. He hopes to move out of the world of the novel, so to speak, and into the world of the reader, where "dreams" such as flying carpets can be successfully distinguished from aeroplanes.

Science, then, would be José Arcadio Buendía's defence against the threat of incest, since its basic concern to discover objective facts about the material world excludes by definition the introverted, solipsistic mental attitudes represented by incest. Úrsula's form of control—through superstitious acquiescence in a taboo—restricts but cannot of itself overcome the problem of introversion and subjectivism; it is essentially a holding operation against incest, reinforced by a suspicion of self-assertion and irrational fears of malign forces beyond the will of man.

José Arcadio Buendía's search for scientific understanding is soon frustrated, not just because his mentor Melquíades is an alchemist whose knowledge is rooted in occultism and medieval learning, but chiefly and decisively because he chooses to abandon it and give way to Úrsula's priorities. Even though an exhaustive exploration of the region convinces him that Macondo is not well placed to make contact with "civilization," he refrains, under pressure from his wife, from moving to a more propitious location. He is, none the less, aware of the consequences: "We shall never get anywhere . . . We'll rot our lives away here without the benefits of science" (p. 19).

José Arcadio Buendía's act of resignation provides the key to the significance of Macondo's decline. It shows that the process of degeneration is set in train by a free human choice, a loss of nerve in fact, and not by some irresistible force of destiny which mysteriously impels the Buendías towards a predetermined end. The unbreakable circle of fate that will appear to enclose the history of the Buendías is, as we shall see, an illusion created by the characters. The founding father's decision not to move on in his quest for "civilization" puts into reverse the rebellious drive against the incest-taboo which had motivated his departure from Riohacha.

There are two main consequences of this reversal. In the first place, it condemns the Buendías to a life without science, to a state of mind, that is, which cannot make firm distinctions between objective fact and the subjective projections of desire. Subsequent generations will find themselves prey to urgent promptings of dream, imagination and memory; their perceptions of the external world will be coloured to such a degree that their hold on reality remains dangerously fragile, leaving them open to delusion or, worse still, deception and exploitation.

Second, the decision deeply affects José Arcadio Buendía's conception of time. Just before his "deep sigh of resignation" we are told that "something occurred inside him; something mysterious and definitive which uprooted him from his actual time and carried him adrift through unexplored regions of memory" (p. 20). Now the ghost of Prudencio Aguilar returns to haunt him, rekindling the fear and guilt associated with his original defiance of the taboo. He begins to neglect his experiments and takes to conversing with ghosts until his communion with the past intensifies to a point at which he smashes up his laboratory and, believing it to be forever a Monday in March, imagines that he has abolished time altogether (pp. 73–74). By abandoning himself to his memories, he shuts out the uncertainties of the future and attempts to bend time back upon itself as if to recover a state of pristine innocence that would spirit away by magic those acts committed in the actual course of his life. This magical escape from history into a kind of cycle of nostalgia will become yet another powerful legacy in the Buendía family.

After José Arcadio Buendía renounces his search for science, the undifferentiated chaos threatened by incest can only be kept at bay by Úrsula's reinstatement of the taboo-mentality. Úrsula's regime provides the basis for a social order of sorts, but it is an order which requires constant vigilance. Úrsula, the lynchpin or axis of this order, is always frantically busy—cleaning the ancestral home, keeping her wayward family in check, defining the legal ties of kinship, overseeing the upbringing of the young, and generally providing a line of continuity from one generation to the next for as long as her energies allow. But for all that, the moral economy of the taboo-regime is repressive, artificial and inefficient. Just as the original observance of the taboo had kept Úrsula and her husband from making love until José Arcadio violently defied it, so too does its re-establishment foster a climate

ONE THOUSAND YEARS OF SOLITUDE?

"To read *One Hundred Years of Solitude* is to dive into a mountain of cotton candy head first and brain last, and endlessly, suffocatingly, sickeningly try to eat one's way out of it. This book that, without false modesty, could call itself *One Thousand Years of Solitude* is repetitious beyond anything but an old-time movie serial, with characters that even a genealogical chart cannot individuate (why should it? since when is the writer's job done by a chart?); the same sticky-sweet mixture of fantasy and social satire stretches on and on. Its mischievousness loses whatever edge it might have through iteration, lip-smacking enjoyment of its own cleverness, and flights into a fancy that seems to me the evasion rather than the extension of truth."

John Simon

From "Incontinent Imagination," *The New Republic*, 192 (4 February 1985) , p. 32.

of sterility and frustration in the family. Úrsula's order cannot eradicate the urge to incest, for it is based on fear rather than understanding and, as such, precludes the possiblity of discriminating between different types of desire. For instance, of her son José Arcadio's prodigious sexual endowment she feels that "it was something as unnatural as the pig's tail her cousin was born with" (p. 29). But equally, her other son Aureliano's desire for knowledge, as evinced by his interest in his father's laboratory, makes her lament her fate, "convinced that these extravagances of her sons were as frightening as a pig's tail" (p. 41).

All desire, therefore, becomes suspect since any one of its manifestations might disguise the dreaded incest-urge. A sinister law regulates Úrsula's taboo-regime. Every true desire, whether incestuous or not, is never fruitfully satisfied. It is either thwarted, displaced or remains sterile. For example, José Arcadio, the first born, satisfied shadowy longings for his mother Úrsula in the arms of Pilar Ternera, who also assuages similar veiled desires in his younger brother Aureliano; she becomes a king of surrogate mother/lover for the two brothers. Pilar, in turn, will find herself the object of her own son Arcadio's desire, but the latter seeks consolation in his wife Santa Sofía de la Piedad. Pilar's other son Aureliano José harbors sexual feelings for his aunt Amaranta, who will eventually inspire a similar obsession in her great-great-nephew José Arcadio. Amaranta herself competes murderously with her putative sister Rebeca for the love of Pietro Crespi but Rebeca is later carried away the blind passion for her putative brother José Arcadio. In another generation, Petra Cotes repeats the role of Pilar Ternera by becoming a surrogate mother/lover to the brothers Aureliano the Second and José Arcadio the

Second. In spite of Úrsula's taboo-ridden anxieties, we find the spectre of incest stalking the family, criss-crossing the generations to form a web of endogamous passion lurking beneath the surface of legal kinship.

Ironically, the family can only perpetuate itself by continually courting the disaster it most fears. Sexual relations become a potential incest-trap, the begetting of offspring a form of tempting fate. Actual procreation is never the result of mutual love but is achieved instead through surrogates, either with an illicit lover who stands in for a desired relative (e.g. José Arcadio, who desires Úrsula but has two sons by Pilar Ternera), or with a legitimate spouse who is a substitute for a desired mistress (e.g. Arcadio who has children by Santa Sofía when he really desires his mother Pilar Ternera, or Aureliano the Second who loves Petra Cotes but has children by his wife Fernanda del Carpio). Genuine desire is not rewarded by legitimate issue; as a rule, children are born either to undesired wives, or to women who have been used vicariously to discharge an unconfessed desire for a family relation. The result is that the legitimacy of the Buendía line is mocked by the emergence of a subsidiary tribe of bastards, mistresses, natural mothers and similar illicit kin that surround the official family and creates in the long run a confusing situation which allows the last two Buendías to commit incest without fully realizing the true nature of their kinship.

The progressive blurring of the distinction between legitimacy and illegitimacy points up the inefficiency of the taboo-regime as a way of controlling the urge of incest. Success is obtained by the repression or displacement of desire, and by a considerable element of sheer luck. In fact, Úrsula's order is purchased at the price of inner devastation of individual lives. Since the Buendías cannot fulfil themselves, they become unhappy with their actual condition and tend to withdraw into a frustrated solitude, repeating the experience of the founding-father. When their initial attempt to assert themselves is frustrated or displaced, they become resigned to a state of sluggish apathy (*desidia*) and live out the rest of their lives either in a self-absorbed nostalgia that disconnects them from historical time, or by distracting themselves in pointless and repetitive activity (*hacer para deschacer*).

In so far as the taboo-regime represses instinct and will, it prevents the characters from realizing a distinctive personality.

Unable to attain to the condition of independent characters who consciously direct their own lives, they are marked instead by generic traits or hereditary vices. This subservience to an impersonal family typology is evidenced by the almost bewildering recurrence of name—José Arcadio, Aureliano, Amaranta, Úrsula, Remedios and combinations thereof—and of psychological characteristics that overwhelm specific motivation: the Aurelianos are clairvoyant, while the José Arcadio are sexually voracious. In the Buendía family tree, analogies and parallels override particular differences; the experiences of the various generations conform to stock pattersn which repeat themselves with such regularity that the linear sequence of historical events appear to be distorted into cycles of time revolving around a still centre of eternity.

And yet, even though the action of *One Hundred Years of Solitude* might appear to express historical time as a series of cyclical recurrences, there is a progressive, linear dynamic to the narrative that belies the typological repetitions generated by the taboo-regime. This dynamic is fuelled by the survival of the founding-father's original desire to rebel against the paralysing fear of the incest-taboo. In every generation there are certain Buendía characters who, albeit confusedly, defy authority in order to break out of the vicious circles of fear that condemn them to conform to type. Struggling to become conscious individuals instead of stock figures, they are prepared to accept the historical present and confront things as they are rather than resign themselves to frustration, solitude and the illusory promise of timelessness afforded by nostalgia.

Let us take the case of that supreme revolutionary leader Colonel Aureliano Buendía. The original motives for his many rebellions are vague. He rebels partly because he is shocked by the deceitfulness of the conservatives (p. 89), and partly because he supports the liberals' wish to accord the same right to natural offspring as to the legitimate (p. 88). But, apart from his nebulous humanitarian sympathies, "Aureliano at that time had very confused ideas about the *differences* between conservatives and liberals" (p. 88; my emphasis). His rebellions are, then, a bid to establish this sort of difference, to assert his independence from an order of things which exacts unthinking conformity to a hereditary set of values. The conservatives, it is said, defend the principle of a divine right to rule, the stability of public order and the morality of the family (p. 88). Nevertheless, Colonel Aureliano's confused assault on the established order stirs up the spectre of incest. For example, his illegitimate son Aureliano José, who burns with passion for his aunt Amaranta, is at one point told by a rebel soldier that the war is being fought "so that one can marry one's own mother" (p. 132). Here one can appreciate the extent to which José Arcadio Buendía's abandonment of his pursuit of scientific knowledge loads the dice against the success of subsequent Buendía rebellions; by simply rebelling against authority, his son Colonel Aureliano assists in the unleashing of incestuous impulses over which he has no control given that he is bereft of the intellectual means to overcome the solipsism that incest represents.

Colonel Aureliano's revolutionary wars, not surprisingly, begin to take on an incestuous quality. The chaotic violence which ravages the county (analogous to the volcanic eruptions of sexual desire that rack his broth José Arcadio) converts the liberals into the mirror-image of their conservative enemies (p. 149); the differences Colonel Aureliano had set out to establish are lost in an all-absorbing, pointless chaos. Faced with failure, Colonel Aureliano now reverts to family type—he "takes refuge in Macondo to feel the warmth of his oldest memories" (p. 147), and experiences the same apathy that came over his father. And yet, even at this low ebb, he shakes himself out of his nostalgic apathy and resolves to put an end to a war which has turned into little more than a naked struggle for power. Once the war is ended, Colonel Aureliano "buried his weapons in the courtyard with the same feeling of repentance as his father when he buried the lance that killed Prudencio Aguilar" (p. 152).

The parallels between Colonel Aureliano's rebellion and that of his father, José Arcadio Buendía, are clear, but a crucial difference can be observed in their respective responses to failure. José Arcadio Buendía withdraws from historical reality and seeks refuge in a form of introverted brooding over the past, whereas his son refuses to resign himself to nostalgia and throws himself instead into the compulsive manufacture of little gold fishes. Defeat may have forced the Colonel into a fruitless solitude, but his *attitude* is the very opposite of resignation. He keeps alive his bitterness at historical failure in a rancorous disaffection from the established order of things; political rebellion is replaced by a permanent psychological rebellion, an unwillingness to escape from history into some magical sphere where the problems of his actual situation can be dissolved. Colonel Aureliano Buendía therefore becomes the most highly individualized member of the family; he remains an isolated, eccentric figure who offers an alternative to the stock Buendía response to the impotence of failure.

The significance of the Colonel's defiant stance emerges when Macondo is suddenly linked to the outside world by the arrival of the railway and finds itself at the mercy of a new wave of outsiders who bring with them the technological inventions of the modern age: the cinema, the telephone, gramophones, and eventually the banana industry. Only the Colonel is capable of perceiving the exploitative use to which they are put. The other inhabitants are confused and seduced by the "intricate hodge-podge of truths and mirages that exasperated the ghost of José Arcadio Buendía under the chestnut tree" (p. 195). These strange artefacts cruelly expose the fatal weakness of the Buendías. Having been deprived of "the benefits of science," they regard such wonders as products of magic and miracle; so much so, that "nobody was able to tell for sure where the limits of reality lay" (p. 195). Technology, not surprisingly, is turned against a defenceless Macondo by the sinister Mr Herbert and his teams of scientific advisers. Even so, the impulse to rebel is not yet extinguished. This time, however, the rebellion must be twofold, not just against the magical-real taboo-regime but also against the foreign exploiters who have been able to take advantage of magical realism to the detriment of Macondo.

The internal rebellion against the taboo is carried out by Meme. When she falls in love with the unsuitable Mauricio Babilonia, she meets with the horrified opposition of Úrsula herself and her own mother Fernanda del Carpio; an arch-conservative prude whose exalted fantasy-life of aristocratic distinction is a grotesquely exaggerated version of Úrsula's preoccupation with the legitimacy of the family. Unerringly, the perverse law that sustains the taboo-regime comes into operation. Any true desire must be repressed, and so Mauricio Babilonia is murdered.

The rebellion against the foreign exploiter falls to José Arcadio the Second, who becomes a ringleader in the strike against the Banana Company. The strike having been put down by a callous massacre of which the only survivor is himself, José Arcadio the Second faces the choice of responding to failure either by emulating José Arcadio Buendía's flight from reality or Colonel Aureliano's stubborn refusal to ignore the facts of history. The existence of that moral choice is conveyed in the narrative through the device of Melquíades's room, which was built for the gypsy mage when he withdrew into an uncommunicative solitude. There he began to write what will turn out to be a prophetic history of the Buendía family. Melquíades's room can be associated with an esoteric and magical interpretation of historical experience. After the gypsy's death the room is sealed off until Aureliano the Second persuades Úrsula to open it up again. It now appears to be bathed in a pure light which keeps it magically free from the dust and cobwebs of time. Still, the state of Melquíades's room varies according to the eye of the beholder. For a character like young Aureliano the Second, who shuts himself up in it and tries to decipher the gypsy's parchments, it is untouched by time, as if it encapsulated that fragment of eternity into which José Arcadio Buendía retired when he resigned his quest for science. By contrast, the unrepentant revolutionary Colonel Aureliano sees it as one would expect it to be, utterly ravaged by the passage of time: "In the air which had been the purest and most luminous in the house there hung an unbearable stench of rotten memories" (p. 209). What is more, after Fernanda del Carpio takes to storing her innumerable golden chamber-pots in that magical retreat, it comes to be known as the "chamber-pot room". For the Colonel, "that was the best name for it because, while the rest of the family were amazed that Melquíades's room should be immune to dust and decay he saw it simply as a dung-heap" (p. 224).

José Arcadio the Second at first vacillates between the historical and the magical conceptions of time. Two images haunt him: a historical one, namely the smile on the face of a man about to be shot during one of Colonel Aureliano's revolutions; and a more nebulous image, that of an old man in a waistcoat wearing a hat shaped like a crow's wings telling marvellous stories next to a dazzling window, which he cannot place in any period of time. The latter image is of Melquíades but it was "an uncertain memory . . . as opposed to the memory of the man before the firing squad which had in fact defined the course of his life" (p. 225).

By joining the strike against the Banana Company, José Arcadio the Second opts for historical action, but after the massacre he takes refuge in Melquíades's room. In that magical sanctuary he is able to raise himself beyond the reach of his enemies; he is invisible to the soldiers who are hunting him and who can see only dust and decay when they search the gypsy's room. Having survived defeat, José Arcadio the Second renounces his allegiance to Colonel Aureliano:

> Years before, Colonel Aureliano Buendía had told him of the fascination of war and had tried to demonstrate it with countless examples from his own experience. But the night when the soldiers looked at him without seeing him, thinking about the tension of recent months, about the miseries of prison life, about the panic in the railway station and the train loaded with dead bodies, José Arcadio the Second came to the conclusion that Colonel Aureliano Buendía had been either a charlatan or an imbecile. He couldn't understand why so many words should be required to explain what one feels in time of war since a single word would suffice: fear. (p. 265)

Immured in the gypsy mage's room, José Arcadio the Second escapes the vicissitudes of history:

> Protected by the supernatural light, by the sound of rain, by the sensation of being invisible, he found the peace he had not enjoyed for a single moment in his previous life, and the only fear that remained was that he might be buried alive. (p. 265)

The peace experienced by José Arcadio the Second is, of course, bought at a price—the last nugget of historical consciousness is absorbed into a magical sphere. The last Buendía rebel thus plays into the hands of his oppressors, who now proceed with impunity to erase the massacre from the history books. Given that José Arcadio the Second abdicates his responsibility as a witness to history, the Buendías lose all vestige of objectivity, and, with it, the capacity to discriminate between elementary differential categories such as truth and falsehood. As a result, the town as a whole suffers the fate that had previously befallen the characters individually. It is completely isolated from the external world by rains which are said to presage its eventual destruction, and it sinks into a state of lethargy as it begins to lose its grip on reality.

In the closing phase of the novel the narrative discourse becomes increasingly self-referring and fantastical; magical realism comes fully into its own as the action moves towards the realization of the wholly implausible incest-curse. The fulfilment of the curse, however, is finally possible, not just because the impulse to rebel has been totally crushed, but principally because Úrsula's taboo-regime breaks down. After the rains have ceased, Úrsula attempts once more to re-impose order by restoring the ancestral home to its pristine condition. Indeed, now that the Banana Company and the other foreigners have departed,

Madcondo appears to have returned to an earlier point in its history. Úrsula is struck by the fact that "time does not pass . . . it just goes round in circles" (p. 285). But this circular sense of historical time soon proves to be an illusion; it is a false renewal, for Úrsula is reaching the limits of her energy, and when she dies shortly afterwards her regime collapses entirely. Neither Fernanda, nor Santa Sofía de la Piedad, nor Amaranta Úrsula can retrieve the ancestral home from the ruin that overwhelms it once Úrsula passes away.

The traditional system of defence against incest having fallen to pieces, the surviving members of the family exist in an ambiguous new freedom which could, on the one hand, provide the means to transcend the taboo-mentality but which, on the other, could leave them helpless before a resurgence of the fatal urge to incest. Both Aureliano Babilonia and Amaranta Úrsula find themselves in a position to overcome the taboo-mentality. Aureliano is originally presented as a potentially messianic figure. He is said by Fernanda to have been discovered in a basket floating in the river like Moses (p. 249), and later, having as a child struck up a friendship with his uncle José Arcadio the Second in Melquíades's room, he is able to relate to the rest of the family the facts of the historic massacre of workers at the railway station, a performance that strikes Fernanda as "a sacrilegious parody of Jesus among the doctors" (p. 295). Together with the occult and supernatural knowledge he learns from José Arcadio the Second, Aureliano gains possession of historical facts that could bring the Buendías back to an objective awareness of the external world. What he needs is a catalyst that would allow him the discriminatory powers to sift the true from the false, the imaginary from the actual. But Amaranta Úrsula's husband Gaston notes that Aureliano "did not buy books for information but to confirm the accuracy of his knowledge" (p. 323).

Amaranta Úrsula, for her part, returns from Europe seemingly unencumbered by superstition and sets about cleaning up the ancestral home: "With the sweep of her broom she put an end to funereal memories, to the piles of useless bric-á-brac, and to all the paraphernalia of superstition that gathered in every corner" (p. 319). But, again, her husband wryly observes that her return to Macondo is due to her having fallen the unwitting victim of "a mirage of nostalgia" (p. 320).

The freedom the last Buendías enjoy after the dissolution of Úrsula's taboo-regime blinds them to the hereditary flaws that lurk within their natures. Amaranta Úrsula's provocatively care-free presence in the ancestral house rouses the latent passions of the hitherto mild and scholarly Aureliano, and so the accumulated momentum of atavistic vices overwhelms the regenerative possibilities of the present. In that disorientating freedom from the taboo, the fundamental law of Úrsula's order is decisively broken; desire is neither displaced nor repressed but contrives at long last to possess its true object.

Caught up in the prolonged frenzy of passion that follows, Amaranta Úrsula watches "the ants devastating the garden, sating their prehistoric hunger on the timbers of the house and she saw the torrent of living lava invade the corridors once more" (p. 341). The order that Úrsula had striven so hard to uphold is now gleefully destroyed in an orgy of erotic release: "It was Amaranta Úrsula who, with her wild imagination and her lyrical voracity, presided over that paradise of disasters as though she had concentrated into love all the indomitable energy that her great-great-grandmother had devoted to the manufacture of little caramel animals" (p. 341). A vortex of mutual passion isolates the incestuous lovers from their surroundings; they become so engrossed in each other that their separate selves seem to fuse into the selfsame identity: "As the pregnancy advanced they started turning into a single being, integrating themselves ever more in the solitude of a house which needed only one last puff to blow it down" (p. 345).

The birth of a child with a pig's tail materializes the curse that haunted Úrsula throughout the novel. This narrative confirmation of superstitious fear is reinforced when Aureliano cracks the code in which Melquíades's chronicles have been written to see revealed before him a prophetic account of the history of the Buendía family. Nevertheless, it is of not little significance that the unveiling of Melquíades's texts coincides absolutely with the devastation of Macondo by a whirlwind. The prophetic consummation of Macondo's history is a form of self-consumption, for as Aureliano reads the parchments, he is enacting the supreme Buendía vice of nostalgia, figured forth as a gathering wind from the past: "Then the wind started—warm, incipient, full of voices from the past, murmurings of ancient geraniums, sighs expressing disappointments that preceded the most tenacious nostalgia"

(p. 350). Aureliano's reading doubles history back upon itself so that the past is not simply left behind by future events but acquires instead a fatal fascination as it creeps up on and eventually devours the present like a cyclone.

One Hundred Years of Solitude sets forth two distinct modes of reading history:[9] that of Aureliano Babilonia and that of the ordinary reader of García Márquez's novel. Each mode is predicated upon a certain type of consciousness. Aureliano's reading might be termed "incestous"; it is devoid of objectively, of reference to an external reality and to linear time. For, as Aureliano deciphers Melquíades's prophetic chronicles, the time narrated moves ever nearer to the time of present experience, and the closer the events Aureliano is reading about get to the time in which he is living, the smaller the gap between the narrative and the history it purports to record. Eventually, Melquíades's text begins to reflect experience with such immediacy that it becomes a "speaking mirror" (p. 350). However, the text as "speaking mirror" is a necessarily transient phenomenon because, if reading is to take place at all, a delay between experience and its narration is inevitable. Aureliano's reflexive reading of his family's history reduces that delay to a point where narrated time and lived time actually meet, and at this point reading becomes impossible because the narrative consumes itself and must disappear. In the last page of the novel one encounters that extraordinary phenomenon of a historical narrative that has become so perfectly self-referring that its sole surviving character reads his own fate while he is in the very process of fulfilling it. The narcissus figure of Aureliano contemplating himself in the "speaking mirror" is thus destined to indulge in the ultimate act of self-regard—auto-cannibalism. It is a fate, as it happens, which lends a piquant, not to say prophetic, quality to the nickname "anthropophagous" which Amaranta Úrsula had given him (p. 319).

However, since One Hundred Years of Solitude can be read, as the ordinary reader is all too obviously aware, García Márquez's version of the Buendía history must be radically different from Melquíades's.[10] Unlike the magical parchments, the novel does not self-destruct; it manages instead to retain what Melquíades's prophetic texts abolish: the necessary delay between events and their narration. The reader of One Hundred Years is, of course, not identical to Aureliano. If Aureliano is an internal reader of the Buendía history who witnesses his own fate in Melquíades's "speaking mirror", the ordinary reader remains outside the narrated events and is therefore capable of an objective, distanced view of that history. How then does García Márquez's version preserve that objectivity which that of Melquíades destroys?

The opening towards a sense of objectivety is, in fact, narrated by García Márquez in his own account of the last days of Macondo. In that late phase of the narrative, after Úrsula's order has broken down, precisely when Macondo as a whole begins to sink into incestuous self-reference, an entirely new set of characters is introduced: a Catalan bibliophile and his young disciples, one of whom is called Gabriel Márquez, the great-grandson of Colonel Aureliano Buendía's comrade-in-arms, Gerineldo Márquez. Aureliano Babilonia befriends Gabriel and also becomes an admirer of the Catalan. Initially, this Catalan appears to be no more than a modest avatar of Melquíades: "When Aureliano met him, he had two boxes full of those motley pages which somehow reminded him of Melquíades's parchments" (p. 336). But the Catalan's attitude to the written word is "a mixture of solemn respect and gossipy irreverence. Not even his own manuscripts were spared this *duality*" (p. 337; my italics). Such duality (as opposed to the obsessive, all-absorbing identification elicited by the "speaking mirror" of Melquíades's parchments) evinces a sense of irony in the Catalan which will prove to be the salvation of Gabriel and his friends from the destruction of Macondo. For when the Catalan returns to his native village he finds that his nostalgia for his birthplace is eventually contradicted by a growing nostalgia for Macondo:

> Confused by two nostalgias confronting each other like two mirrors, he lost his marvellous sense of unreality until he ended up by recommending that they all leave Macondo, that they forget everything he had taught them about the world and the human heart, that they shit on Horace, and that wherever they found themselves they should always remember that the past was a lie, that memory provided no way back, that all the springs they had lived through were irretrievable, and that the most unruly and obsessive love was in any case an ephemeral truth. (p. 339)

Jolted out of a nostalgic frame of mind altogether by the conflicting pulls of two nostalgias, the Catalan becomes an anti-Melquíades figure who suddenly sees through and repudiates the pattern of consciousness fostered in the Buendía family by the gypsy's occultism. Systematically, he condemns the effects of magical realism: the fascination with the past, the escape from history into memory, the longing to recover a pristine innocence, and the surrender to mindless erotic desire.

This ironic awakening comes too late for Aureliano Babilonia. By this time his incestuous passion for Amaranta Úrsula has got the better of him and he has switched his intellectual allegiance back to Melquíades. In doing so, the catalytic effect of his relations with the Catalan, which might have enabled him to salvage the objective truth of the massacre from the welter of nostalgic fantasies he picked up in Melquíades's room, is totally aborted.

By contrast, Aureliano's erstwhile friend Gabriel Márquez takes the Catalan's advice and leaves Macondo. His departure entails a transformation of consciousness from the self-absorbing trammels of magical realism depicted in his visits to the unreal brothel in Macondo to an appreciation of the duality of irony. His journey is from within the fictional world he shared with the Buendías to the world outside the fiction in which the reader of *One Hundred Years* is situated.

Freed from the magical-real consciousness of the Buendías, Gabriel Márquez can look back on his experience and write a history of Macondo to rival the interpretation of Melquíades. Bur since all narrative is an exercise in retrospection, Gabriel must construct his account in such a way as to reflect Macondo's history without himself falling prey to the siron-song of nostalgia. Taking the Catalan's conflict of nostalgias as a

A NEGATIVE VIEW OF *ONE HUNDRED YEARS OF SOLITUDE*

"In Latin America, Gabriel García Márquez has been a household name and face since 1967, when his famous novel *One Hundred Years of Solitude* was first published in Buenos Aires. This novel is said to have sold more than six million copies and to have been translated into more than thirty languages. . . . I thought it quite brilliant and stopped reading it at page 98 (of 383 pages in the paperback edition). A number of intelligent people I know have gone through a similar experience in reading the book. All thought it brilliant, but felt that anywhere from between eighteen to fifty-one years of solitude was sufficient, thank you very much. . . . *One Hundred Years of Solitude* is peculiarly a novel without pace; it is, for its nearly four-hundred pages, all high notes, service aces, twenty-one-gun salutes. In a novel, such nonstop virtuosity tends to pall. To use a simile to describe a novel that its author describes as a metaphor, reading *One Hundred Years* is like watching a circus artist on the trampoline who does only quadruple back somersaults. At first you are amazed to see him do it; then you are astonished that he can keep it up for so long; then you begin to wonder when he is going to be done, frankly you'd like to see something less spectacular, like a heavy-legged woman on an aged elephant."

Joseph Epstein

From "How Good Is Gabriel García Márquez?" *Commentary*, 75 (May 1983), pp. 59–60.

paradigm of liberation from solipsism, Márquez renounces the novelist's traditional allegiance to mimesis and holds up a mirror instead to Melquíades's mirror of the Buendía history. By confronting these two mirrors Gabriel imbues his novel with an ironical duality. The magical realism that informs the consciousness of the Buendías is reproduced in Gabriel's discourse. But it is given the lie by its reflection in the design of the narrative, which orders events in a linear sequence that records the knowledge suppressed by Melquíades's cyclical version of history: the moral capitulation of José Arcadio Buendía, the ravages of Úrsula's regime, the lucid defiance of Colonel Aureliano, the difference between technology and magic, the significance of the massacre at the station, José Arcadio the Second's surrender to fear, and so on. In short, the counterpointing of discourse and narrative design registers the existence of a choice before the characters between resignation to illusion on the one hand, and responsibility to historical truth on the other.

The particular originality of García Márquez's technique lies, however, in his having followed through to its ultimate consequences the logic of his magical-real discourse. As the novel describes Macondo's progressive evasion of history, language slips its insecure moorings in reality and drifts away to a limbo where it can arbitrarily realize its own fantasies until it is finally drawn into the void of pure self-reference. And yet, precisely in the state of limbo, Gabriel narrates the manner of his own flight from Macondo, thereby offering the reader a way back to the historical reality that the discourse of the novel has all but abandoned. What is more, in the last sentence of *One Hundred Years* the duality of the novel is made explicit by an unprecedented authorial intrusion. Macondo is described as "the city of mirrors (or of mirages)." This parenthetical alternative cracks the surface of the "speaking mirror" to reveal the underlying choice between illusion and reality; it invites the reader to question the validity of Melquíades's prophecy and to repudiate the apocalyptic ending inscribed in the discourse as nothing more than a pernicious mirage created by those characters like Aureliano Babilonia who have condemned themselves to magical realism and for whom there is, in consequence, no second chance for other natives of Macondo (like Gabriel Márquez and his friends) who have chosen to leave and who have survived the destructive vortex of incest. On this reading, *One Hundred Years of Solitude* ends, if not exactly on a note of optimism, at least with the sense of relief felt after waking from a nightmare.

Notes

1. For a comprehensive review of critical opinion, see Donald L. Shaw, "Concerning the Interpretation of *Cien años de soledad*," *Ibero-Amerikanisches Archiv*, 3:4 (1977): 318–329.

2. See, for example, Ricardo Gullón, "García Márquez and the Lost Art of Storytelling," *Diacritics*, 1:1 (autumn 1971); Roberto González Echevarría, "With Borges in Macondo," *Diacritics*, 2:1 (1972): 57–60; E. Rodríguez Monegal, *"One Hundred Years of Solitude*: The Last Three Pages," *Books Abroad*, 47:3 (1973): 485–489. A more recent exponent is Regina Janes, *Gabriel García Márquez: Revolutions in Wonderland* (Columbia and London, 1981), pp. 48–69.

3. See, for example, in *Sobre García Márquez*, ed. Pedro Simón Martínez (Montevideo, 1971), the following well-known essays: Mario Vargas Llosa, "El Amadís en América," pp. 106–111; Ernesto Völkening, "Anotado al margen de *Cien años de soledad*," pp. 178–206; *José Miguel Oviedo*, "Macondo: un territorio mágico y americano," pp. 44–53. The fullest study is Vargas Llosa's *García Márquez: Historia de un deicidio* (Barcelona, 1971).

4. See Carpentier's prologue to his novel *El reino de este mundo* (Mexico, 1949). An expanded version appeared in *Tientos y diferencias* (Mexico, 1964).

5. See his remarks in an interview with Plinio Apuleyo Mendoza, *El olor de la guayaba* (Barcelona, 1982), p. 36, where he agrees that the "rationalism" of European readers tends to prevent them accepting that magical realism is inspired in the fact that "everyday life in Latin American shows that reality is full os extraordinary things." Nevertheless, he also observes that "you cannot invent or imagine whatever you like because you run the risk of telling lies . . . Even within what appears to be the utmost arbitrariness, there are laws. You can divest yourself of the fig-leaf of rationality, so long as you do not lapse into chaos, into total irrationality" (p. 31). García Márquez, however, has never explicitly elaborated on the question of the relationship of these "laws" to historical reality, or on the connection between the fantasy-elements in magical realism and "the risk of telling lies."

6. For interpretations that stress the novel's pessimistic fatalism, see James Higgins, *"Cien años de soledad*: historia del hombre occidental," *Cuadernos del Sur*, 11 (1971): 303–14; and Julio Ortega, "Gabriel García Márquez: *Cien años de soledad*," in *Nueve asedios a García Márquez* (Santiago de Chile, 1969), pp. 74–88.

7. Shaw, "Concerning the Interpretation of *Cien años de soledad*," p. 324, observed that no critic had yet convincingly explained "what is, in fact, really wrong with Macondo."

8. I have translated into English all quotations from *Cien años de soledad* (Buenos Aires: Editorial Sudamericana, 1967). Page references to this edition have been incorporated in the text.

9. So far as I am aware, only Roberto González Echevarría, from "*Cien años de soledad*: the Novel as Myth and Archive," *Modern Language Notes*, 99 (1984): 358–380, unequivocally opposes the mythical to the historical elements in the narrative. However, the conclusions he draws from this lead him to a reading which is very different in style and content from my own.

10. Many critics have assumed that the novel is identical to Melquíades's history. For a recent interpretation based on this assumption, see Michael Palencia-Roth, "Los pergaminos de Aureliano Buendía," *Revista Iberoamericana*, 123–124 (1983): 403–417.

Ian Johnston, Lecture delivered on *One Hundred Years of Solitude* in Liberal Studies 402, Malaspina University-College, 28 March 1995.

Introduction

In this lecture I would like to start with an initial question and then suggest some possible directions one might like to explore in answering it. We can all agree, I think, that this novel is amazingly rich, so I don't propose anything like a last word. However, by examining some patterns in the novel, we can perhaps help to shape some potentially illuminating observations.

So I propose to deal with the novel in the following stages:

First, I want to consider *One Hundred Years of Solitude* as an epic, in the traditional sense of the word, and from that consideration to frame an interpretative question.

Second, I propose to look at the complex effects this novel creates: a wonderfully comic sense combined with an overall tragic irony underlying the remarkably energetic and entertaining inventiveness in the plot and the characters.

Thirdly, by way of accounting, at least in part, for these complex effects, I wish to look at three particular aspects: the double sense of time in the novel and the style of magical realism.

Finally, putting all these elements together, I shall address the question posed at the start. I would like to suggest that this novel does, in fact, have something very insightful and important to reveal about the social and political realities of the world it depicts and that this theme may be difficult for North Americans fully to recognize.

One Hundred Years of Solitude As An Epic

It seems clear to me that, in any conventional sense of the literary term, we are dealing here with an epic work: a long narrative fiction with a huge scope which holds up for our inspection a particular cultural moment in the history of a people. The novel is the history of the founding, development, and death of a human settlement, Macondo, and of the most important family in that town, the Buendías. In following the historical narrative of these two elements we are confronted, as we are in any great epic, with a picture of how a moment in human civilization a particular group of people has organized its life (just as we are confronted with the same issue, for example, in the other great epic we have studied, *The Odyssey*).

Like many other epics, this novel has connections with a particular people's historical reality, in this case the development of the Latin American country of Colombia since its independence from Spain in the early nineteenth century (1810 to 1825). The seemingly endless civil war portrayed in the novel one can see as directly based on the civil wars in Columbia from 1885 to 1902, and the character of Colonel Aureliano has many affinities with General Rafael Uribe Uribe, under whom the grandfather of the author fought. Uribe's struggles ended in 1902 with the Treaty of Neerlandia, an event in the novel. The years 1900 to 1928 saw the take over of Colombia by the United Fruit Company of Boston. The ensuing labour trouble culminated on October 7, 1928, in a mass strike of 32,000 workers. The government later sent out the troops to fight the workers, and a massacre took place in Cienaga on December 5, 1928. In addition of course, and most importantly for an understanding of the novel, is the presence in it of the author's family and of the author himself. This point, as I shall argue later, is a key point in understanding what the political point of this epic might be.

I mention this history, not because I think one needs to know the historical facts in order to appreciate the novel, but

THE MULTIFORM MACONDO

"One Hundred Years of Solitude ... seems to me one of the most admirable of South American novels, because, among other reasons, García Márquez understands better than anyone that feelings of autochthony always act as an outlet and not as a limitation. The setting of his book, Macondo, is incredibly Colombian and Latin American *just because it is much more besides;* it is derived from many other things, born of the multiform and, as it were, dazzling presence of literatures differing widely in time and space."

Julio Cortázar

From Rita Guibert, "Julio Cortázar," in *Seven Voices: Seven Latin American Writers Talk to Rita Guibert,* translated by Frances Partridge (New York: Knopf, 1973), p. 301.

simply to point out that *One Hundred Years of Solitude,* like so many other great epics, like *Moby Dick, The Song of Roland,* and *War and Peace,* takes its origin in the history, real or imagined, of a particular people.

Given this epic quality of the novel, the initial question I would like to pose is this: What qualities of life does this novel celebrate? What is the nature of the social-political vision held up here for our inspection? How are we intended to judge the people and the society of Macondo? This, I would claim, is a fairly obvious question which the novel pressures any reader to ask, as a number of critics have pointed out:

> *One Hundred Years of Solitude* . . . can justly lay claim to being, perhaps, the greatest of all Latin American novels, appropriately enough, since the story of the Buendía family is obviously a metaphor for the history of the continent since Independence, that is, for the neocolonial period. More than that, though, it is also, I believe, a narrative about the myths of Latin American history. (Martin 97)

> I do not believe any other novelist has so acutely, so truthfully seen the intimate relationship between the socio political structure of a given country and the behaviour of his characters. (Angle Rama, qu. Martin 107)

So what are meant to derive about the experience of the civilization depicted in the novel?

One possible source of information, the author, has remained stubbornly silent on this question, refusing to debate whether or not there is a political "message" in his novel. His roots with the civilization are obvious enough, for he spent the first eight years of his life in Aracataca, a "steamy banana town not far from the Colombian coast." But he has commented "Nothing interesting has happened to me since." "He also tells the story that his grandmother invented fantasies so that he wouldn't be saddened by the truth of things" (Janes 66). We will be coming back to this latter comment later on. When pressed on the subject of this novel, García Márquez has said that he really wanted to write a book about incest.

If a number of readers have seen considerable political significance in the novel, there has been no agreement about what that political "message" might be. For the novel has attracted all sorts of conflicting political interpretation. One writer has remarked, with good justification, that there is something here for every political view: "[The novel's] appeal is to all ideologies: leftists like its dealing with social struggles and its portraits of imperialism; conservatives are heartened by the corruption and/ or failure of those struggles and with the sustaining role of the family; nihilists and quietists find their pessimism reconfirmed; and the apolitical hedonists find solace in all the sex and swash-buckling" (Bell-Villada 93).

To all of these we might add those readers who decline to see any social-political themes in the novel and who like it because it's a great escapist read. And whatever I might like to claim for its wider implications, *One Hundred Years of Solitude* is certainly a wonderful and popular read, which one can enjoy without having any particular awareness of its historical roots or its political implications. That may be the main reason why it has been such a phenomenally popular book outside Latin America: "The first truly international best-seller in Latin American publishing history" (Martin 98), for which the author received the Nobel Prize for Literature in 1982.

The Magic Realism Of The Novel

By way of explaining my answer to that question I posed about what, if anything, this novel celebrates, I would like to point to two very obvious facts of the novel and then move on to construct some interpretative possibilities from those two facts. In offering this initial interpretative possibility I'm trying to remain true to my experience of reading this novel, an experience which features a curious mixture. On the one hand I find this a wonderfully diverting comic novel, full of the most unexpected and delightful incidents and characters, and thus an extraordinarily uplifting experience. On the other hand, pervading this novel for me there is a strong sense of irony, a powerful undertone of prevailing sadness and a sense of tragic futility. I want, in the following remarks to try to link these emotional reactions to features of the novel.

I suppose one must first observe that here there is an amazingly fecund imagination at work in the characters and incidents of this novel—extraordinary people and intriguing incidents. This novel never loses its capacity to surprise and delight. No matter whom we meet, we quickly learn to expect the unexpected, the colourful, the original—from moments of evocative beauty, like the trail of butterflies, to the satiric, like the priest levitating to chocolate, to erotic scenes of bawdy and prodigious sex, like characters whose farts are so strong they kill all the flowers in the house or a man who runs through the house balancing beer bottles on his penis. The comic energy here is justly famous. The characters, for the most part, may be two-dimensional, and we may meet some of them only for a couple of pages, but there is throughout a sense of vitality and wonder at the world which makes this story hard to put down.

A good deal of this quality comes from the style, the "magic realism," which strikes at our traditional sense of naturalistic fiction. There is something clearly magical about the world of Macondo; it is a state of mind as much as, or even more than, a real geographical place (we learn very little about its actual physical layout, for example). And once in it, we must be prepared to meet whatever the imagination of the author presents to us.

[Note that the term "magic realism" was coined by the German art critic Franz Roh in 1925 to describe "a magic insight into reality. For Roh it was synonymous with the postexpressionist painting (1920–1925) because it revealed the mysterious elements hidden in everyday reality. Magic realism expressed man's astonishment before the wonders of the real world" (Williams 77).]

The intermingling of the fantastic and the factual throughout the novel keeps us always on edge, always in a state of imaginative anticipation, particularly in the story of the Buendía men, whose imaginations are repeatedly going off in various directions, in schemes which are the constant source of amusement, novelty, and delight.

I take it that this quality of the novel is clear to anyone who reads it, so I don't propose to discuss it here. Some readers addicted to psychological naturalism may well find the fantasy interferes with their demands for a more "realistic" engagement with the imagined world of the fiction. As I shall mention before the end of this lecture, however, I think there is an important connection between the fantasy and the reality in the novel; in other words they are not two separate elements. In fact, a particularly important point of this novel is that in many respects the civilization depicted here too often confronts the reality of life with fantasy, because it experiences life as fantasy rather than as historical fact. But more of that later.

Along with all this delight, however, as I mentioned above, I sense a strong underlying irony, a mixture of sadness, anger, and tragic fatality. For this is a story about the failure of the town and the family, which, for all their amazing vitality are finally and irrevocably wiped off the face of the earth. Amid all the delightful fantasy is a great deal of violence, cruelty, and despair—the central ingredient in the "solitude" each of the characters finally becomes immersed in. And this establishes itself as a strong qualification to the comic delight one takes in so much of the novel.

It is important, I think, not to sentimentalize the violence and the despair, as those of us who do not sense these qualities in our own communities are likely to do. In this novel, cruelty, failure, acute despair, and suddenly destructive irrational and inexplicable violence are always present. And however we interpret the story, we need to take those fully into account, and not minimize their impact in order to enjoy the comic inventiveness and the fantasy without any serious ironic qualifications.

Time As Linear History In The Novel

By way of exploring this dual response further, I would like to point to one very marked feature of the novel, the working throughout of two senses of time, linear and circular. The interplay between these two senses creates some of the novel's most important effects.

In the first place, we see that there is a strong sense of a linear development to the history of the town of Macondo. We follow the story from its founding, through various stages up to a flourishing modern town, to its decline and eventual and irrevocable annihilation. In general, the linear history of the town falls into four sections: (a) utopian innocence and social harmony, in which Macondo exists like an early Eden, its inhabitants so innocent that no one has yet died and they don't even have names for things, the world "was so recent that many things lacked names, and in order to indicate them it was necessary to point" (11). This section takes up the first five chapters of the book. The story then moves on to the military struggle in the various civil wars and revolutions (Chapters 6 to 9), then into a period of economic prosperity and spiritual decline (Chapters 10 to 15); and finally to decadence and physical destruction (Chapters 16 to 20).

The narrative is given to us, for the most part, following this linear sense of time, so that we always know roughly where we are in this linear story. And we know because of the nature of the various "invasions" which occur. Usually outsiders arrive bringing the latest in technology or bureaucracy: gypsies, government officials, priests, various military forces, the ubiquitous lawyers, the railway, the American capitalists, the European with the bicycle and the passion for airplanes, and so on.

We repeatedly experience these invasions as something over which the town has no control and no previous warning. And in most cases they have no immediate sense of how to react. Those reactions, from José Arcadio's response to the gypsies to the reaction of the citizens to the telephone and movies, are often amusingly eccentric and unpredictable, but they point to a constant in the world of Macondo: the powerlessness of the people to take charge of the invasions which arrive from outside.

Macondo, you will recall, is founded initially almost by accident. It just happens to be where the Buendía expedition decides to stop. There is no particular reason for stopping there, and no one has a very clear idea of where they are, except that they are in the middle of a number of natural barriers, for all they know cut off from all contact with civilization. And so they found Macondo, the city of mirrors or mirages, an innocent and idyllic community, with no sense of history or no particular political reason for being there. It is an expression of the imaginative desires of José Arcadio, who has sought to flee his past and is incapable, because of his overheated imagination to create a political future for his community.

The development of the Buendía family in a sense underscores this linear sense of time, for they form a series of figures who, in part, symbolize the particular historical period of which they are a part. The patriarch José Arcadio is, in some sense, a Renaissance man of many interests and with pioneering ambitions and energies; his son Aureliano becomes a great military leader, a main participant in the civil wars; in turn, he is succeeded by a bourgeois farmer-entrepreneur, family man, Aureliano Segundo and by the twin José Arcadio Segundo, who works for the American capitalists and becomes the radical labour organizer. And so on. So as we move from generation to generation, we sense a strong linear force, usually imposed from outside, driving events in Macondo.

Italian editions of *One Hundred Years of Solitude*

Time As Circular History

But for all this strong linear sense of history, the response of the people in Macondo, and particularly of the Buendía family, to this linear march creates a second sense of time: history as almost obsessively circular. For all the apparent changes in their main occupations, their personalities constantly repeat the experience of earlier generations.

There's a strong sense of fate about this obsessive repetition. Once a person has been named then the major characteristics of his or her life have been determined and the person is doomed to repeat the events of the lives of their ancestors. As Úrsula remarks:

> While the Aurelianos were withdrawn but with lucid minds, the José Arcadios were impulsive and enterprising, but marked with a tragic sign.

Even their deaths are, in a sense preordained. The José Arcadios suffer as victims of murder or disease; all three Aurelianos die with their eyes open and their mental powers intact. And they all succumb to a self-imposed exile in a solitude which can last for decades.

Out of this sense of repetition, the comic energies which the sexual prowess and the visionary schemes constantly celebrate are always undercut by the irony of "inevitable repetition of probably futile previous actions" (Williams 80), as one of the most important images in the book makes clear:

> There was no mystery in the heart of a Buendía that was impenetrable for [Pilar Ternera] because a century of cards and experience had taught her that the history of the family was a machine with unavoidable repetitions, a turning wheel that would have gone on spilling into eternity were it not for the progressive and irremediable wearing of the axle. (402)

We take great delight in watching the generally erratic spinning of the wheel, but we are increasingly aware of the wearing of the axle and eventually see it snap.

Another way of saying this perhaps is to see that the people of Macondo and the Buendías often have a vital and amusing present, but their lives sooner or later lose meaning because they are incapable of seizing control of their own history. Their past is largely unknown to them, except as nostalgia, their present, if active, is obsessive, and their future non-existent.

The Buendías: Men And Women

The characters in the novel's main family tend to be organized schematically (as in the José Arcadios and the Aurelianos). This is not a psychological novel in the sense that its chief interest does not arise from the inner drama of particular characters (as, say, in Virginia Woolf). We are dealing here, for the most part, with two-dimensional comic creations organized in order to make certain thematic points.

The men, I have observed, are characterized by an obsessive repetitiveness to their lives. Full of amazing energies and intelligence, which generate ambitious projects or passionate sexuality, they are unable to realize any long-term success, and are prone to fits of extreme anger against their earlier projects or else their lives are overtaken by the irrational violence which keeps intruding in their lives.

The women, too, tend to fall into types. The common sense energy and determination of the Úrsulas, particularly of the stern, unmusical matriarchal will of the founding woman, play off against the enduring erotic figures outside the family: Pilar Ternera and Petra Cotes. Those called Remedios remain immature and either die young or disappear.

The women, for the most part, are firmly anchored in daily reality, as obsessed as the men, but with the routines of daily living. Úrsula fights all her life against the incest taboo, and Fernanda devotes her life to imposing the rigorous order of high Spanish Catholicism on an unruly home. They have no interest in speculative imaginative ventures. The centre of their lives is the home or erotic attachments. Simply put, one might observe that in this novel the men suffer from an enduring lack of the reality principle; whereas, the women are encased in it.

What seems to be missing is any consistent ability to find a middle ground between the impossible delusions of weak and unstable men and the down-to-earth home-bound order and stability of the women. And this inability points to what both the men and women seem to lack here, an ability to orient themselves with the wider developing world in which they live and to take some control of their own historical destiny. They are, as residents of Macondo, victims of an illusion in the city of mirages, and the personal constructions they erect in the course of living all fail and plunge them into a cruel and lasting solitude.

In that sense, the "magic realism" of the novel is a good deal more than a stylistic device to lure North American readers tired of naturalism. The fantasy is a central part of the way these people, especially the men, experience their own history, and because such fantasy is no match against outside invaders or the effects of time on such projects, they all fail. And this may, indeed, be one of the main points García Márquez is "celebrating" (if that is the right word) in this epic novel of his people.

So What Is The Novel Saying About Latin America?

As North Americans, we are far more accustomed to thinking of our own history (personal and national) as something of an encounter with destiny: we have confidence that we can take charge of our lives, construct a project-based life, and carry it through, so that in a way the world we have acted in will be transformed from the world into which we are born. The history of our country and often of our families is full of examples of such an authentic life choice undertaken in the confidence that we have a strong sense of a meaningful direction and the means to move there.

But, as many interpreters of García Márquez have pointed out, such may not be the case in Latin America, in whose culture there is

> . . . a haunting theme . . . a familiar and lasting concern of Latin Americans: their fear that they are not quite real people, that their world is not entirely a real world. This is not a metaphysical or epistemological problem, it is not the European anguish of Kafka or Beckett, and it is not the uneasiness of North Americans faced with a fast-changing social and physical landscape. It is an old and intimate feeling, an actor's weariness with a never-ending career, a feeling that what is happening cannot really be happening, that it is all too fantastic or too cruel to be true, that history cannot be the farce it appears to be, that a daily life cannot be merely this losing battle with dust or insects, that this round of diseases, drink, ceremonies, sadness, and sudden death cannot be all there is. (Wood 37)

It is necessary to stress this point, this sense that history is a cruel farce, experienced as fantasy and forgotten quickly, because it may well be the case that, in writing this novel, one of García Márquez's main points is to leave his readers with a strong sense of the tragic futility of such an attitude. We have to remember, close the chapter on Macondo, and get on with constructing a new history for ourselves.

It might be worth remembering that, if we find this attitude too serious and difficult to grasp, that in Buenos Aires last weekend the Mothers of the Plaza de Mayo are still demanding from the authorities an acknowledgment of the thousands of people arbitrarily tortured and killed in the civil wars in Argentina in the 1970's. These people, called "those who have disappeared" have, it seemed, for a long time simply vanished without acknowledgment that anything took place. That they are dead few will dispute. How or why or, in some cases, whether it happened is still under review. In the face of events like this, we might observe that what takes place in the pages of García Márquez's "magic realism" is in many places not so far from the cruel fantasies of killing and forgetfulness still, for example, pictured on the front pages of the *Globe and Mail* (see the edition for Saturday, March 25, 1995, A1).

This point about experiencing one's history as fantasy has been stressed also by Marxist critics, who insist that, since the rules which govern a society are those of the ruling class, those places which have no control over their own destiny live without such rational guidelines. Thus, they argue, García Márquez's novel is not saying that life is a dream but rather that Latin American life is a dream—"the unreality and unauthenticity imposed by almost five hundred years of colonialism—and that when a dream becomes a permanent living nightmare it is probably time to wake up" (Martin 104).

The endless repetition of useless actions are an idologeme for a capitalist society without social or economic vitality. In this sense the colonel's endless battles are the same as his repetitive creation of little gold fish: they both resent a paradigm of action for the sake of action (or production for the sake of production, with no worthwhile return) [note also his production of sons]. Macondo never functions as an authentic participant in the political and economic processes of the nation. It is always marginal at best. Even after establishing his government position in Macondo, Moscote is nothing more than an "ornamental" authority, as he is described in the text. National politics are more a matter of disruption or confusion than an integral part of Macondo's life. After painting and repainting their homes the colors of both the Liberals and the Conservatives, Macondo's citizens eventually have houses of an undefined color, a sign of the failure, in effect, of both traditional parties. (Williams 85)

The same point is emphasized by Gerald Martin:

In *One Hundred Years of Solitude* nothing ever turns out as people expect; everything surprises them; all of them fail; all are frustrated; few achieve communion with others for more than a fleeting moment, and the majority not at all. Most of their actions—at first sight like the structure of the novel as a whole—are circular. . . . Ploughers of the sea, they are unable to make their lives purposive, achieve productiveness, break out of the vicious circle of their fate. In short, they fail to become agents of history for themselves. . . . The only explanation possible is that they are living out their lives in the name of someone else's values. Hence the solitude, central theme (together with the quest) of Latin American history: it is their abandonment in an empty continent, a vast cultural vacuum, marooned thousands of miles away from their true home. Conceived by Spain in the sixteenth century . . . the characters awaken in the late eighteenth-century Enlightenment . . . but are entirely unable to bring themselves into focus in a world they have not made. Influences from outside (the gypsies) are sporadic, piecemeal, throughout the notional hundred years of the novel, which is the span from the Independence era to the early 1960's. . . . Seen in this light, the novel seems less concerned with any "magical" reality than with the general effect of a colonial history upon individual relationships: hence the themes of circularity, irrationality, fatalism, isolation, superstition, fanaticism, corruption, and violence. The judgment as to whether these traits are inherent or produced by history is a much a political as a philosophical or scientific determination. (106)

If one looks briefly at the life of José Arcadio Buendía, the patriarch, one can see these basic points being brought out in the rhythm of the narrative. His story begins with an apparently incestuous marriage and his erotic passions and sense of macho pride, which result in a quick violent murder. This forces him and his wife to move away into the interior. They found Macondo, as I have observed, more or less by accident.

He's a man of great energy, ambition, talent, and imaginative vision, and at first his efforts are remarkable. He wants to find knowledge and make use of it, specifically science, because that will free him from his geographic imprisonment and the town's captivity to magic.

But José Arcadio is incapable of sorting out magic from knowledge. He knows nothing about geography and, although he has a sextant, a compass, and maps, he gets physically lost, defeated by the nature which surrounds them. His imagination is always racing ahead of the business at hand. Thus, he is continually defeated. His desires and talents are huge; he is, however, incapable of directing them purposefully with any firm sense of the reality of his situation.

Thus, he, like so many of his descendants, eventually resigns himself: "We shall never get anywhere. . . . We'll rot our lives away here without the benefits of science" (19). His descendants all inherit the same difficulty, and thus all eventually succumb to the power of nostalgia, to opting out of their historical reality, which they have never really understood clearly. They cope with their failure by an inner withdrawal. This act of resignation, one interpreter has remarked, is the key decision, for "it condemns the Buendías to a life without science, to a state of mind, that is, which cannot make firm distinctions between objective fact and the subjective projections of desire" (Williamson 49). It also leaves him incapable of dealing with time, mired in historical immobility. Initially he becomes haunted with memories (especially of Prudencio Aguilar, the man he killed in the quarrel over his wife), and eventually he smashes his laboratory and abandons himself to his mad nostalgia (just as the Colonel later destroys the revolution for the same reason). The difficulties of his life he finally deals with by opting out of history and settling for the uncertain territory, not of history, but of nostalgic solitude, a "magic" reality in which he might as well be tied up to a tree, because he is wholly alien to anything real in the world.

This pattern is repeated over and over in the novel, especially with the men. They strive for active fulfillment as young men but become frustrated and end up withdrawing. Incapable of dealing with actual conditions effectively, they opt finally for a frustrated solitude:

> Loneliness in Macondo and among the Buendías is not an accidental condition, something that could be alleviated by better communications or more friends, and it is not the metaphysical loneliness of existentialists, a stage shared by all men. It is a particular vocation, a shape of character that is inherited, certainly, but also chosen, a doom that looks inevitable but is freely endorsed. The Buendías seek out their solitude, enclose themselves in it as if it were their shroud. As a result they become yet another emblem of the unreality . . . (Wood 40)

To the extent that Úrsula is the guardian of the family and the constant presence in the house, she embodies a value system that contributes to this self-perpetuation of futility. Her overwhelming concern is the honour of the family and the avoidance of incest. In spite of her concerns, however, incest is always present. Children of the family are produced, not by mutual love but through surrogates—some partner, who may be a wife or someone who is standing in for someone else (especially by Pilar Ternera).

> Genuine desire is not rewarded by legitimate issue; as a rule, children are born either to undesired wives, or to women who have been used vicariously to discharge an unconfessed desire for a family relation. (Williamson 51).

The result is an extraordinarily tangled family tree that leaves the final two able to commit incest without really knowing that they are so closely related. In that sense, the final generation of Buendías indicate that they are so out of touch with their own immediate past that they don't know where they stand in relation to each other, and thus have nothing to oppose to the passionately irrational erotic desires that make them an easy prey for the destructive forces of nature (the ants) that wait always on the edges of the community and the home.

The Conclusion Of The Novel

Taking this line as an interpretative possibility permits us to make some sense of the curious ending of the novel—the fated destruction of the family and the community. Here there are two particular facts I would like to comment upon.

First, the community is fated to end as soon as someone in it fully deciphers Melquíades's manuscript, when, that is, someone fully understands the history of Macondo. For a community and a family that has so committed themselves to solitude is engaged in an enterprise fated to fail and never to be repeated:

> . . . for it was foreseen that the city of mirrors (or mirages) would be wiped out by the wind and exiled from the memory of men at the precise moment when Aureliano Babilonia would finish deciphering the parchments, and that everything written on them was unrepeatable since time immemorial and forever more, because races condemned to one hundred years of solitude did not have a second opportunity on earth. (422)

The town and the family are fated to die because they do not have what is required to continue. Their solitude, their commitment to withdrawal, fantasy, and subjective desires has doomed them.

But the ending is more complex than that because, in a sense, Macondo does survive in this book. It is particularly significant that one of those who takes the advice of the Catalan bookseller to leave the town before its destruction is the author himself, Gabriel García Márquez, descendant of the Márquez who fought alongside Colonel Buendía. Hence, what does survive is a testimony to the life that has been lived there, a story which will remain as a guide to the construction of a better civilization.

If one of the main problems of the Buendías and Macondo was an inability to generate a realistic sense of themselves out of their own history, then this book may help to make sure such a narrative does not happen again. Just as Melquíades, a writer, helped to overcome the plague of insomnia and collective amnesia when that disease infected Macondo from the Indians, so this book, produced by a writer and magician may restore historical memory: the strike and the war will be remembered, as will be the futile fantasies of a civilization which could not incorporate those into its political and historical realities.

It may be significant that, although we learn little about Gabriel García Márquez in the novel, we do know that he escapes Macondo with the complete works of Rabelais (409). The mention here of one of the supremely comic geniuses of world literature may be an important reminder of what the main function of this novel is: to celebrate the tragi-comic history of Macondo in a way that people can learn from it. For if one of the great imaginative purposes of the best comedies, like the *Odyssey*, is, in the words of William Faulkner's Nobel laureate speech, to celebrate the ability of human beings not only to survive but also to prevail, then the comic purposes of *One Hundred Years of Solitude* may well be to make sure that the full educational influences of comedy are delivered to the people.

This point has a certain resonance for me when I reflect upon the fact that one way of looking at the Buendias is to see that, although they are frequently the sources of a hugely vital and erotic sense of fantasy and fun, they are not themselves capable of laughing at themselves, learning from their mistakes, and moving on, so that their characters are educated into a new awareness of what their situation requires. When we discussed the *Odyssey*, we talked about how such a process of transformation is one of the major points of the epic, so that Odysseus is not the same person he was when he first departed from Troy: he has become aware of a new and transforming set of values. Such a development, one might argue, is something the Buendías cannot undergo, and their fate may well be linked to this failure of their comic imaginations.

At any rate, the self-referential quality of the ending of the novel, when it, in effect, writes its own conclusion and points to a world beyond Macondo from which the author, García Márquez, is telling the story, offers a final insight that whatever life is to be lived in Latin America it is not to be the magic but ultimately self-defeating experience of the Buendías and Macondo. In that sense, "the destruction of Macondo, rather than the end of a delightful world of magical realism, points to the foreseeable end of the cultural and ideological heritage of Spain in the New World. The novel is revolutionary in a profound sense" (Incledon 52).

Select Bibliography

Bell-Villada, Gene H. *García Márquez: The Man and His Work*. Chapel Hill: University of North Carolina Press, 1990.

Gonzalez, Anibal. "Translation and Genealogy: *One Hundred Years of Solitude*." In McGuirk and Cardwell, 65–79.

Griffin, Clive. "The Humour of *One Hundred Years of Solitude*." In McGuirk and Cardwell, 81–94.

James, Regina. *Gabriel García Márquez: Revolutions in Wonderland.* Columbia: University of Missouri Press, 1981.

McGuirk, Bernard and Richard Cardwell, eds. *Gabriel Garcia Marquez: New Readings.* Cambridge: Cambridge University Press, 1987).

Martin, Gerald. "On 'Magical' and Social Realism in García Márquez." In McGuirk and Cardwell, 95–116.

Williams, Raymond L. *Gabriel García Márquez.* Boston: Twayne, 1984.

Williamson, Edwin. "Magical Realism and the Theme of Incest in *One Hundred Years of Solitude.*" In McGuirk and Cardwell. 45–63.

Wood, Michael. "Review of *One Hundred Years of Solitude.*" In *Critical Essays on Gabriel García Márquez.* McMurray, George R., ed. Boston: G. K. Hall, 1987.

APPROACHES OF THE CRITICS

Although his book is brief and focuses only on *One Hundred Years of Solitude,* Michael Wood is the critic who succeeds in placing García Márquez in the widest context. He places the author in both history and literary history and offers a variety of interpretations of this novel. The mythic, the biblical, the feminist, the historical—all these approaches may be found in his small book.

Wood suggests that *One Hundred Years of Solitude* is "the story of a place, the human geography of the family's fortunes,"[27] that it draws on wider contexts. He also suggests that the story of Macondo can be viewed as "the history of paradise."[28]

Some critics have approached *One Hundred Years of Solitude* from a feminist point of view, arguing that in assigning women one set of characteristics and men another, he is participating in an anachronistic sexism. Luis Harss is one of those critics:

In García Márquez men are flighty creatures, governed by whim, fanciful dreamers given to impressible delusions, capable of moments of haughty grandeur, but basically weak and unstable. Women, on the other hand, are solid, sensible, unvarying and down to earth, paragons of order and stability. They seem to be more at home in the world, more deeply rooted in their nature, closer to the center of gravity, therefore better equipped to face up to circumstances.[29]

Indeed, Úrsula Iguarán holds the family together, and is "solid" and "sensible," as is Santa Sofía de la Piedad, who does the family chores without uttering a word of complaint. Pilar Ternera, mother of the first children of both José Arcadio and Colonel Aureliano Buendía, is another of those figures. García Márquez himself has tried to defuse feminist criticism, by asserting that his "women are masculine,"[30] that in fact they enjoy the qualities conventionally assigned to men. Nonetheless, as Bell-Villada puts it, Úrsula Iguarán de Buendía remains, "the classic figure of the mother."[31]

Several critics have discussed Gabriel García Márquez in the light of his own admiration for the novels of William Faulkner, noting a certain affinity between the two. He told Luis Harss, "When I first read Faulkner . . . I thought: 'I must become a writer.'"[32] In "The Presence of Faulkner in the Writings of García Márquez," Harley D. Oberhelman notes that both writers depict "the struggle of human beings against social and material decadence, the common lot dealt to all in Yoknapatawpha County and Macondo."[33]

Oberhelman points out that "García Márquez's use of Macondo as a microcosm for the study of a whole society was also the technique used by Faulkner when he created his own locale in which to reexamine the South, its great tragedy, and its system of traditional values . . . in *Cien años*, the development of the Buendía family through five generations parallels Faulkner's creations."[34] Even the plots are similar: "The primeval paradise of Yoknapatawpha as undeveloped Indian territory and of Macondo in its earliest years is lost when human exploiters come to violate the innocence of nature. Later intruders—carpetbaggers and the banana company—arrive to accentuate the decline through the exploitation of the 'fruit' of the land."[35]

In his essay, "Teaching *One Hundred Years of Solitude* with *The Sound and the Fury*," Mark Frisch offers a similar perspective. Frisch compares the themes of "the land and the family" in both writers and concludes that "both novelists define themselves as literary artists by defining in turn their relatively new cultures."[36] Like *The Sound and the Fury*, *One Hundred Years of Solitude* "has no main character," and in both the theme of incest "serves as a unifying plot device."[37] Jason Compson is like the Buendía brothers in experiencing "life as a battle for individual survival against threatening, outside forces."[38]

In his 1976 essay "The Faulkner Relation," William Plummer notes that "the 'relation' between García Márquez and Faulkner is unavoidable."[39] Yet, he calls García Márquez "not a *modern*, but a *post-modern*. He is not interested in being 'difficult,' formally difficult, the way Joyce, Eliot and Faulkner were." In writing *One Hundred Years of Solitude*, however, he had "to replicate Faulkner's model, the paradigm D. H.

THE GREATEST JOY OF A WRITER

"I think it's fun when you start to control your book. There isn't anything more wonderful than writing when you truly have the book in your grip. That is what I call inspiration. There is a definite state of mind that exists when one is writing that is called inspiration. But that state of mind is not a divine whisper, as the romantics thought. What it is is the perfect correspondence between you and the subject you're working on. When that happens, everything starts to flow by itself. That is the greatest joy one can have, the best moment."

García Márquez

From Claudia Dreifus, "*Playboy* Interview: Gabriel García Márquez," *Playboy*, 30 (February 1983), p. 174.

Lawrence located in 'The Leatherstocking Tales,' and called the American myth."[40]

Plummer also notes that from a thematic point of view, "García Márquez is engrossed by the same spectacle as Faulkner: that of innocence confronting the inscrutable artifacts and attitudes of the contemporary world, and of the innocent's always awesome, often farcical attempt to make sense of them."[41]

Another approach to studying García Márquez's fiction is through examination of his embroidering incidents of magic realism into the texture of *One Hundred Years of Solitude*. In "Magical Romance/Magical Realism: Ghosts in U.S. and Latin American Fiction," Lois Parkinson Zamora places the work of García Márquez in a wider context of magic realist fiction.

She considers García Márquez together with the Argentine writer Borges. In her discussion of *One Hundred Years of Solitude*, Zamora focuses on the "archetypalizing intent" of García Márquez, suggesting that "the Buendías are more significantly connected to prior human patterns than to prior individuals." Genealogy, the family tree, becomes irrelevant since "one José Arcadio is in some sense all José Arcadios, one Aureliano all the rest."[42]

Zamora concludes that the "shifting relation of individual to archetype" in *One Hundred Years of Solitude* "attends the psychological of magical realist characters" in general, and that there are "the offspring of Jung, not Freud. The Buendías are ciphers of a collective unconscious, related to each other less by family history than by mythic paradigm."[43]

Focusing as well on the nature of magic realism as an approach to *One Hundred Years of Solitude*, Edwin Williamson in "Magical Realism and the Theme of Incest in *One Hundred Years of Solitude*," pauses to examine the origins of the term *magical realism* and connects the technique to the substance of the novel. "Magical realism," Williamson suggests, "can be shown to be a manifestation of the malaise that causes the decline of the Buendía family."[44]

Marrying a study of the technique of magical realism to an examination of the political perspective in the novel, Gerald Martin in "On

'Magical' and Social Realism in García Márquez" provides a much needed corrective to the approaches to the novel through magic realism alone. Martin sees *One Hundred Years of Solitude,* as "a metaphor for the history of the continent since Independence . . . for the neocolonial period." For Martin, the novel is "a narrative about the *myths* of Latin American history," and "this is where its true importance lies."[45]

Martin also summarizes what for him have been the "three basic errors" that have infected criticism of the work of García Márquez:

(1) Critics have failed to perceive that history is not only devoured by myth, as is so frequently claimed, but that every myth also has its history. This novel is not about "history-and-myth," but about the myths of history and their demystification.

(2) They fail to differentiate correctly between the perspective of the novelist and that of his characters, an elementary distinction with infinitely complex ramifications in this most subtle yet apparently straightforward text.

(3) They largely ignore the context, historical and literary, in which the novel was written and published.[46]

Martin considers both the realist perspective and the magic realist qualities of *One Hundred Years of Solitude.* In this novel, he believes, "García Márquez's apparent underlying tragic vision is not *necessarily* in contradiction with a revolutionary standpoint on Latin American development."[47] He goes on to place García Márquez among the cultural movements of his time, and from this vantage, to locate how he uses magic realism. He discusses how the solitude of Macondo is related to its being a neocolonial society and how this solitude necessarily leads to a yearning toward nostalgia.

For Martin, the strike against the banana company and the ensuing massacre are "the central shaping episode of the entire novel."[48] His conclusion, as he juxtaposes the magic realism of the novel against its social reality, is that "the novel seems less concerned with any 'magical' reality than with the general effect of a colonial history upon individual relationships."[49]

Scholars have combined various critical approaches. In "*Cien años de soledad:* The Novel as Myth and Archive," Echevarría examines the co-presence of myth and history in *One Hundred Years of Solitude.* Echevarría argues that the wellspring of modern Latin American novels such as *One Hundred Years of Solitude* is anthropological. According to

Echevarría, "the modern Latin American novel transforms Latin American history into originary myth in order to see itself as other. The theogonic Buendía family in *Cien años de soledad* owes its organization to this phenomenon."[50] Echevarría makes a strong case for the importance of myth in *One Hundred Years of Solitude:*

> (1) there are stories that resemble classical or biblical myths, most notably the Flood, but also Paradise, the Seven Plagues, Apocalypse, and the proliferation of the family, with its complicated genealogy, has an Old Testament ring to it; (2) there are characters who are reminiscent of mythical heroes: José Arcadio Buendía, who is a sort of Moses, Rebeca, who is like a female Perseus, Remedios, who ascends in a flutter of white sheets in a scene that is suggestive not just of the Ascension of the Virgin, but more specifically of the popular renditions of the event in religious prints; (3) certain stories have a general mythic character in that they contain supernatural elements, as in the case just mentioned, and also when José Arcadio's blood returns to Úrsula; (4) the beginning of the whole story, which is found, as in myth, in a tale of violence and incest.[51]

Echevarría concludes that "the blend of mythic elements and Latin American history in *Cien años de soledad* reveals a desire to found an American myth."[52]

Other critics have focused on the nature of García Márquez's storytelling technique. In "Gabriel García Márquez and the Lost Art of Storytelling," Richard Gullon examines how the author creates a world similar to our own, and yet radically different. Gullon concludes that it is the narrator's tone, never allowing himself to indulge either in "interjection or amazement," which accomplishes this feat. Gullon points to "the circular structure of the novel" that "leads the reader from the chaos and void where creation occurs to the chaos and void where all ends and is resolved," a circularity that reinforces the narrative's universality. Gullon also examines the relationship between the narrative's tone and its rhythm.[53]

Still another approach to studying *One Hundred Years of Solitude* is through considering García Márquez's use of history and politics. In "Liberals, Conservatives, and Bananas: Colombian Politics in the Fictions of Gabriel García Márquez," Regina Janes aids the reader of *One Hundred Years of Solitude* in understanding how García Márquez has integrated the political "with everything else." She traces the history of the conflicts between Liberals and Conservatives, quoting Hernandez Rodríguez to the effect that the political parties were "similar to two races which live side by side but hate each other eternally."[54]

Janes compares, in particular, the details of the banana strike in the novel with the actual historical event upon which it is based, locating the episode in *One Hundred Years of Solitude* in terms of its actual context:

> The period was a boom period, but the position of the workers was not altogether advantageous. Workers were paid on a piece-work system by the number of bunches of bananas cut or the amount of land cleared. For the most part, they were not employed directly by the company or by individual growers, but worked under foremen-contractors and migrated from one plantation to another. Part of their wages were paid in scrip for exchange at the company's commissaries, kept stocked by the ships of the banana fleet that must otherwise have returned empty from New Orleans. The system of contract labor allowed both native growers and United Fruit to evade the provisions of Colombian law intended to protect the workers by requiring employers to provide medical care, sanitary dwellings, collective and accident insurance. Since the contractors lacked capital, they were not legally required to provide those benefits; since the growers did not employ the workers directly, neither were they. In 1918, the workers of the region had exerted enough pressure on the company to persuade it to promise to consult its Boston home office on the complaints raised by the workers, principally demands for wage increases and the elimination of scrip payments, as well as fulfillment of the company's obligations under the labor laws for workers' conditions. Ten years later, the workers raised their demands again, and the company refused to bargain but again promised to consult."[55]

Janes goes on to compare the version of the banana massacre offered by the commander of the army troops, General Cortés Vargas, with that of García Márquez in *One Hundred Years of Solitude*. She points to one of García Márquez's omissions: "In Cortés Vargas's account, the principal reason the people did not disperse when ordered was that the people were confident that the soldiers, common people like themselves, would not act against them but would throw down their arms and join them."[56]

Still another approach to studying *One Hundred Years of Solitude* is offered by Floyd Merrell. Noting that "the novel can be construed as symbolic of Colombia (the socio-political level), Latin America (the mythico-cultural level), Christianity (the mystico-religious level), the world (the historical/archetypical levels), or the universe (the cyclical/ entropic levels)," Merrell examines José Arcadio Buendía's experiments and inventions, approaching the novel by comparing the "scientific paradigms of José Arcadio Buendía with "the structural history of scientific philosophy in the Western World."[57] José Arcadio Buendía's model of nature is materialistic, as birds in cages are replaced by clocks. His project is to exercise his "dominion over the 'metals,' or nature." His experiments chronicle the history of scientific thought.[58]

Aníbal González examines *One Hundred Years of Solitude* in the light of "the role of translation in literary history and in the constitution of the novel as a genre."[59] Gonzalez notes that the "text of *One Hundred Years of Solitude* abounds with 'scenes of translation' and references to learning and speaking foreign languages."[60]

Near the end of his life Melquíades speaks "in a complex hodge-podge of languages" (77), and García Márquez also takes note of the differences between Rebeca's speaking the Guajiro language and others speaking Spanish. González offers a plethora of examples where the problem of language is pushed to the foreground of the novel, not least during the episode when José Arcadio Buendía goes mad and speaks no longer Spanish but "a high-sounding and fluent but completely incomprehensible language"(85) that turns out to be Latin.

The theme of deciphering the manuscript of Melquíades, which runs through the entire novel, is related, González suggests, to García Márquez's raising epistemological questions that confront the dilemma of the relationship of all novels to truth. The final Aureliano, Aureliano Babilonia, González points out, is a translator, even as "the apparently parallel lines of genealogy and translation in the novel converge: Melquíades's code, as we learn in the last pages of the novel and as the manuscripts' epigraph suggests, is the language of kinship itself: '*The first of the line is tied to a tree and the last is being eaten by the ants.*'"[61] González also notes that the repeated references in the novel to the issue of language and translation invoke Cervantes, and the origin of the novel as a genre in *Don Quixote*.

González concludes that "Aureliano Babilonia's tragic discovery that he, too, is a translation, far from being an assertion of Latin America's perpetual 'dependence' on some foreign original or 'sacred' text, is García Márquez's way of calling attention to *all* literature's origins in translation, in the transport—through violence or exchange—of meaning from other texts and other languages into the literary text."[62]

A corrective to many of the critical approaches has been the effort of some writers to explore *One Hundred Years of Solitude* as a comic novel. Cervantes was considered a comic writer, and as his worthiest successor, García Márquez, according to Clive Griffin in "The Humour of *One Hundred Years of Solitude*," might "be examined with profit first and foremost as a humorist."[63] Its popularity for many readers unfamiliar with either Colombian history or recent Latin American literature is "largely due," Griffin suggests, "to the wide range of different types of humour employed by the author."[64]

Among the types of humor Griffin identifies in the novel are "'eternal comic situations like beatings, disguises, mistaken identity, wit, buffoonery and indecency.'"[65] There is humor connected with sexuality and bodily functions. Amaranta as a virgin beyond her time is nonetheless "the object of incestuous fantasies for generations of Buendías."[66]

Humor also helps García Márquez, according to Griffin, to avoid becoming "over-sentimental." Humor may even be linguistic, as in unlikely figures of speech such as "the eggplant-patch of her memories." There is also a good deal of irony, as in the Liberal soldier's claim that "we're waging this war against the priests so that we can marry our own mothers."[67]

Many critics have commented on the relationship between *Don Quixote* and *One Hundred Years of Solitude* with respect to references to the novel as manuscript. Griffin puts the point succinctly: "In *Don Quixote* Cervantes had invented a certain Cide Hamete Benengeli who, he playfully told the reader was the 'author' of the work, the original version of which was written in Arabic; in *One Hundred Years* García Márquez equates his novel with the manuscripts written in Sanskrit by one of its characters, Melquíades. Just as Cide Hamete is at the same time both 'a most truthful historian' and a 'lying Moor,' so Melquíades is said to be 'an honest man' . . . but, as we realize from the very first page, is a gypsy and a charlatan. . . ."[68]

For Griffin, "the final joke" of the novel "comically deflates not just an episode or a character, but the whole novel":

> At the end of the last chapter Aureliano Babilonia discovers that Melquíades's manuscripts are an account of the history of Macondo including the moment at which Aureliano Babilonia discovers this fact. . . . The implication is that the reader should ask himself how serious a work can be which is written by a liar, which is a self-confessed piece of fiction— Macondo is constructed of "mirrors (or reflections)" . . . and

its characters suspect that they are unreal . . .—and whose rightful destiny is to be stored away like the manuscripts among disused chamber-pots."[69]

Griffin concludes by remarking that the "over-earnest reader or critic" of *One Hundred Years of Solitude* is "the final butt of the author's jokes." Equating Aureliano Babilonia, misguidedly, with the author, he quotes the line about that character's discovering that "literature was the best toy which had ever been invented to pull people's legs."[70]

From the perspective of literary history, the most frequent approach to a novel has been the biographical, exploring the author's life as the source of the themes and style of his work. There has not yet been a full-length English-language biography of García Márquez. The most influential work about this author, the Spanish-language *Historia de un Deicidio* by Vargas Llosa, does compare the work of García Márquez up to 1971 with the life and the historical and cultural context from which he emerged.

Vargas Llosa titles his first chapter, "La Realidad Como Anécdota" (Reality as Anecdote). In biographical fashion, he begins his story with the life of García Márquez's father, Gabriel Eligio García, who at the age of twenty left Since, the town in the department of Bolivar where he was born, to go to the university in Cartagena.

Lacking money, García had to leave school, and he became the telegraph operator in Aracataca, where he found not fortune, but love. From the account of the courtship of García Márquez's parents, Vargas Llosa moves on to tell the story of the grandfather and grandmother who raised him, focusing on the military career of Colonel Nicolás Márquez, and of the community in the banana zone where they settled.

Vargas Llosa points out that García Márquez was already five or six years old when he met his mother for the first time, and it was only then that he learned that he had siblings (García Márquez is the oldest of sixteen children). Writing biography in a novelistic style, Vargas Llosa brings to life the early years and landscape from which García Márquez would create his fiction.

Vargas Llosa discusses the influence of the storytelling style of García Márquez's maternal grandmother on the author's narrative voice. Vargas Llosa also reveals how García Márquez transformed the experiences of his grandfather in the plot of *One Hundred Years of Solitude*:

Gracia a los recuerdos de este veterano, el nieto revivió los episodios más explosivos, los heroismos y padecimientos de esta guerra, y ese material le serviría para elaborar, en las historia de Macondo, las treintaidós guerras civiles que inicia y pierde el coronel Aureliano Buendía.[71]

(Thanks to the memories of this veteran, the grandson relived the most explosive episodes, the heroics and the suffering of this war, and that material would serve him to elaborate the history of Macondo, the thirty-two civil wars that Colonel Aureliano Buendía began and lost.)

From the perspective of critical biography, there is no substitute for this exhaustive and splendid effort by Vargas Llosa. His comprehensive approach includes García Márquez's brief membership in the Communist Party of Colombia. In 1955 the party made contact with him, and he used some information that it supplied him for his journalistic articles. It was a brief relationship in part because the Party did not appreciate his less than realistic fictional style:

Su breve militancia consistió casi exclusivamente en discusiones políticas e intelectuales. Sus companeros consideraban que el estilo "artístico" en quite estaba escrita "La hojarasca" no era el adecuado para describir los problemas más urgentes de la realidad colombiana. . . .[72]

(His brief militancy consisted almost exclusively in political and intellectual discussions. His comrades thought that the artistic style in which he had written *Leaf Storm* was not one adequate to describe the urgent problems facing Colombia. . . .)

In *García Márquez: The Man And His Work*, Gene H. Bell-Villada provides an introduction to the author that draws on anecdotes from his life, and in the absence of a more comprehensive work in English, does offer some biographical material. Bell-Villada offers material about Colombia, as a nation with a particular culture that sets it apart from other Latin American countries. He briefly places García Márquez in his political context, describes the impact of *One Hundred Years of Solitude* on Latin America in general, and attempts to offer a profile of the author by drawing on examples from his early journalism.

A much more valuable and individualistic critical approach is that employed by José Donoso in *The Boom in Spanish American Literature*. Donoso places García Márquez in literary history, by connecting him to the "boom" of Latin American writers between 1962 and 1968, when a dozen superb novels appeared. These include *La muerte de Artemio Cruz* (1962; translated as *The Death Of Artemio Cruz,* 1964) by Carlos Fuentes,

Rayuela (1963; translated as *Hopscotch,* 1966) by Julio Cortázar, and *La ciudad y los perros* (1963; translated as *The Time Of The Hero,* 1966) by Vargas Llosa, as well as *One Hundred Years of Solitude.* Donoso suggests that it might be more fruitful to study these authors, not with earlier generations of Spanish American novelists, or contemporary surrealists, but with the modernists who influenced them all: Joyce, Proust, Woolf, Kafka, Faulkner, and Thomas Mann.

The Latin American novelists of the "Boom" embody a distinct set of characteristics: they share a skepticism about realism and defy traditions of social realism. They believe that, as Carlos Fuentes asserted in 1962 at the Congress of Intellectuals at the University of Concepcion in Chile, Latin American politics and literature are inseparable.[73] Most of these novelists demonstrated their support for the Cuban revolution, just as most would protest against the imprisonment of poet Herberto Padilla in Cuba in 1971.

These writers have also shared the experience of exile; for example, García Márquez spent years living in Paris, Mexico City, and later Barcelona, and also traveled through Eastern Europe. As a result, they share qualities of cosmopolitanism and internationalism. Guillermo Cabrera Infante in a 1970 interview downplayed this phenomenon of the Latin American writer as exile by pointing out that most of the exiles, unlike himself, have been free to return home:

> . . . technically speaking, I am the only exile. Perhaps the other writers feel themselves somewhat exiled in spirit, but the only one who cannot return to his country is also the only one who never so much as dreamed of leaving Havana. In fact, I am the *only* one of them all who would find myself in serious trouble if I ever thought of returning to my country.[74]

Donoso's point remains valid: the styles of many of these writers, García Márquez included, have grown more complex as their reading public has extended beyond their own countries. As Donoso notes:

> It was the appearance of this mature, continental, and international public that so radically changed our world in the mid '60s. Now the audience proposed to the novelist was not limited to that writer's own country but, instead, was the entire Spanish-speaking world. It was now clear that this public was interested in literature as such and not merely as an extension of pedagogy, patriotism, or history.[75]

Speaking of "The Boom," Cabrera Infante agrees with Donoso's assessment and points out that "the fact that the novel exists in Spanish America at the present time is due to the rise to power—to wealth, which is a form of power—of the Latin American middle classes in big cities such as Mexico City, Buenos Aires, Caracas, Lima, Bogotá, Montevideo, and San Juan. These are the great buyers of novels—although buyers and readers do not always coincide."[76] The rise of the novel in Latin America parallels the evolution of the genre in England in the eighteenth century with the growth of a middle-class reading public there.

In his study of "The Boom" Donoso also raises the question of how literary history is written. The Boom seemed to have been dominated by "the supposed Mafia bosses: Julio Cortázar, Carlos Fuentes, Gabriel García Márquez and Mario Vargas Llosa. The public suspects that they are inseparable friends with identical literary tastes, with similar political positions, each one the master of a particular court which will follow him until death, all living in great comfort in foreign capitals and rubbing elbows with 'the cream of the intellectuals'. . . ."[77]

Donoso adds that other writers might equally be placed in the "Boom" were it not that they belong to the right of the spectrum politically, among them Borges with his "reactionary political positions"[78] and Cabrera Infante with his determinedly anti-Castro position.

It might be added as well that since Donoso wrote his book in 1972, Fuentes and Vargas Llosa have grown apart politically, with Fuentes considered to be on the left, and Vargas Llosa far to the right. García Márquez and Vargas Llosa are certainly not as close as they were at the time that Vargas Llosa wrote *Historia de un Deicidio*. Donoso's book is important as an essay on the question of how literary reputations are nurtured: Donoso reveals the means by which the politics within a movement may influence how an author is perceived from the vantage of literary history.

Other writers identified with the "Boom" have commented skeptically on the so-called literary movement. The Argentine novelist Cortázar, in an interview with Rita Guibert, speaks from a skeptical point of view:

> . . . when I was in Prague, chatting with the editors of the review *Listy*, I said that if one of the airplanes taking our best novelists to international congresses and gatherings were to crash, it would be revealed all of a sudden that Latin American literature was much more precarious and less rich than was supposed. Of course this teasing remark was aimed at García

Márquez and Carlos Fuentes, who accompanied me on their visit to Czech writers and whose well-known horror of losing contact with the ground made them look noticeably green. But behind this crack of mine lay a truth, that the so-called boom in our literature was in no way comparable to the great periods in the literature of the world, such as the Renaissance in Italy, France and England, the Golden Age in Spain, or the second half of the nineteenth century Western Europe. We lack a base, a cultural and spiritual foundation (which depends of course on economic and social conditions), and although during the last fifteen years we can congratulate ourselves on a sort of self-conquest in the field of letters (writers who end by working as Latin Americans and not as mere adaptors of foreign aesthetics to regional folklore, and readers who read their own writers and support them, thanks to a dialectic of challenge and response that was nonexistent until very recently), it is only necessary to study a good map, read a good magazine, and take stock of the precarious situation of our economy, sovereignty, and historical destiny, to understand that the reality is considerably less important than it is supposed to be by temporary patriots and foreign critics. . . .[79]

Passionately, Cortázar defends those fellow Latin Americans, who, like himself, chose at least partial exile. He argues that far from having lost a sense of their native ground, they have placed the countries into a wider context.

An approach to *One Hundred Years of Solitude* from the perspective of Colombian history sheds considerable light on this novel. As Janes notes, García Márquez himself "once remarked that the reader of *Cien años de soledad* who was not familiar with the history of his country, Colombia, might appreciate the novel as a good novel, but much of what happens in it would make no sense to him."[80] Although no single work has completely placed *One Hundred Years of Solitude* in its historical perspective, several critics have drawn upon this critical approach, including Janes, Wood, and Bell-Villada.

ONE HUNDRED YEARS OF SOLITUDE CRITICALLY ANALYZED

García Márquez has stated that he is a "socialist realist," and only an interpretation that includes his larger political perspective does justice to *One Hundred Years of Solitude*. "Many people believe that I'm a writer of fantastic fiction," he has said, "when actually I'm a very realistic person and write what I believe is the true socialist realism."[81] As for a psychoanalytic interpretation, which critics might choose, given the theme of incest in the work, as well as the image of the umbilical cord as a thread of blood linking son to mother even in death, García Márquez has discouraged this approach.

He has noted that at a meeting of psychoanalysts in Buenos Aires where *One Hundred Years of Solitude* was discussed, the group "came to the conclusion that it represented a well-sublimated Oedipus complex" and that "the characters were perfectly coherent from a psychoanalytic point of view, they seemed almost like case histories." But what interested the author "was that the aunt should go to bed with her nephew, not the psychoanalytic origins of this event."[82] Of this psychoanalytic approach, he has said "I don't have much admiration for that. Nothing I do is consciously that way. I understand that literary work, especially fiction, exists on the edge of the unconscious, but when somebody tries to explain that unconscious part of my work, I don't read it."[83]

In fact, no one critical approach can do justice to so encyclopedic a novel, a work that is so psychologically acute, that rises to mythic proportions, and that features all the Jungian archetypes. In *One Hundred Years of Solitude* García Márquez has offered a history of the world, not excluding its possible future. Science and war, politics and love are present from the moment of their origins, and the very notion of history is called into question as immediately García Márquez describes both how human life has evolved and how it has been depicted. He begins when "the world [was] so recent that many things lacked names" (1) and concludes at the apocalypse.

The failures in José Arcadio Buendía's laboratory, despite the verve and flair of the inventions brought by the gypsies, suggest that science will contribute little to humanity's survival. It may not be the fault of science, however; it is José Arcadio who wants to use the magnifying glass with which he has become fascinated as a weapon of war. Out of an irrationality that is a constant obstacle to social and personal peace, the Buendías make all the wrong decisions.

The social harmony of Macondo precedes politics and foreign exploitation: "It was a truly happy village where no one was over thirty years of age and where no one had died" (10). Macondo begins as a socialist democracy. José Arcadio Buendía even lays out the streets and the location of new houses so that is equal: "no house got more sun than another during the hot itme of day" (9). The land is distributed equitably. No government is required; the town was not founded "so that the first

Cover for the Romanian edition (1971) of *One Hundred Years of Solitude*

upstart who came along would tell them what to do" (62).

García Márquez suggests that had there been no outside interference, from the invention-bearing gypsies, from "pirates" like Sir Francis Drake, from politics-bearing magistrates like Don Apolinar Moscote, and from the most dangerous enemy to human happiness of all, the North American banana company, Macondo might have remained a "happy village." Even seemingly innocent outsiders bring trouble. Pietro Crespi creates a life-long animosity between Amaranta and Rebeca and meets an untimely end; Gaston, the husband of Amaranta Úrsula, invites in the Germans, who immediately lay claim to their share of the national wealth by setting up the national airline.

The Buendías and the other founders of Macondo scarcely have time to create their community before they are ravaged from outside. The first to arrive is Don Apolinar Moscote who takes power by force: "six barefoot and ragged soldiers, armed with shotguns" (62). His absurd insistence that the fronts of houses be painted Conservative blue is the first salvo in the century of civil wars to follow. Macondo's failure to break out of the cycle of civil wars in which both sides actually represent the same thing—the perpetuation of the power of the oligarchy—leaves the community vulnerable to the incursion of the banana company that comes in the second half of the novel.

However, Úrsula Iguarán, the practical, sane, best side of the Buendía family, herself contributes to the fall of democracy in Macondo. She supports the creation of an oligarchy in the town, one that matches the one which dominates the country. For guests to her grand party she invites only "the descendants of the founders" (67), adding only the family of Pilar Ternera since she has borne children from among them. The daughters of Don Apolinar Moscote are not invited.

One Hundred Years of Solitude is also unique in literary history in revealing how the political and the psychological coincide. Having exhausted his spirit in war, Colonel Aureliano Buendía, the hero of the novel, who is not always heroic, becomes incapable of loving, and his failures in humanity also make the community vulnerable to exploitation from outside. His heroism comes in his self-knowledge, no less than his realization that he had to go on fighting. First, however, he realizes that he has been fighting "because of pride" rather than principle.

Through the character of General José Raquel Moncada, a Conservative, whose name echoes the revolution in Cuba led by Fidel Castro, García Márquez presents his own point of view. He chooses the general as his spokesman to make it clear that he supports neither the Liberal nor the Conservative side.

It is General José Raquel Moncado who is "an antimilitarist," who knows that military men are all too often "unprincipled loafers, ambitious plotters, experts in facing down civilians in order to prosper during times of disorder." The tragedy of the novel is that Colonel Aureliano Buendía has him murdered; it is the tragedy of the colonel personally that he does so.

As does any satirist who exposes the foibles of mankind and the means by which society defeats itself, for example, British author Jonathan Swift in *A Modest Proposal* (1729), García Márquez includes several passages that reveal how things ought to be. The strongest of these describes the friendship between General Moncada and Colonel Aureliano Buendía:

> There were pauses with a certain festive atmosphere, which General Moncada took advantage of to teach Colonel Aureliano Buendía how to play chess. They became great friends. They even came to think about the possibility of coordinating the popular elements of both parties, doing away with the influence of the military men and professional politicians, and setting up a humanitarian regime that would take the best from each doctrine. (160)

When the colonel goes off "sneaking about through the narrow trails of permanent subversion" (160), General Moncada becomes a beneficent magistrate:

> He wore civilian clothes, replaced the soldiers with unarmed policemen, enforced the amnesty laws, and helped a few families of Liberals who had been killed in the war. He succeeded in having Macondo raised to the status of a municipality and he was therefore its first mayor, and he created an atmosphere of confi-

dence that made people think of the war as an absurd nightmare of the past. (160–161)

The rationality of the rule by General Moncada is in sharp contrast to the persistent irrationality of the wars, and García Márquez's insistence in the novel that, finally, the distinction between Liberals and Conservatives is meaningless. The futility and the stupidity of that conflict is expressed in the dialogue between Aureliano José and a fellow Liberal soldier. "Can a person marry his own aunt?" (163) Aureliano José asks. As he is saturated with desire for Amaranta, the theme of incest, the personal, coalesces with the political. "He not only can do that," a soldier tells him, "but we're fighting this war against the priests so that a person can marry his own mother" (163). As Griffin has observed, historically, one of the things for which the Liberals were fighting was the recognition of the legitimacy of civil marriages; this remark is an example of García Márquez's "employment of a *reductio ad absurdum* of local political issues." Clearly, the soldier does not really know why he is fighting. It is not long before Colonel Aureliano Buendía himself remarks, in despair, "the only difference today between Liberals and Conservatives is that the Liberals go to mass at five o'clock and the Conservatives at eight" (261).

Úrsula is correct in warning that the Buendía family will meet disaster, symbolized by the birth of a child with a pig's tail, should the family succumb to incest. But just as men cannot find their way out of war and devastation, individuals and families cannot organize themselves within the boundaries of harmony and good sense.

Finally, General Moncada tells Colonel Aureliano Buendía that he has become what he has hated most: "What worries me is that out of so much hatred for the military, out of fighting them so much and thinking about them so much, you've ended up as bad as they are" (174). Even hearing these words, the colonel cannot break out of the cycle of self-destruction, and he allows his order that General Moncada be executed to stand.

García Márquez does not let the colonel off lightly. He is forced to witness everything for which he has fought turned into a sham, as "the Liberal landowners, who had supported the revolution in the beginning, had made secret alliances with the Conservative landowners in order to stop the revision of property titles" (178). Amid this debacle, Colonel Aureliano Buendía loses his capacity to love and his capacity to be human. He is calmed only when his bodyguards have ransacked the house of General Moncada's widow.

"Watch out for your heart, Aureliano" (179), his friend Colonel Gerineldo Márquez warns him. It is too late.

Rendered politically impotent by the life he has led, Colonel Aureliano Buendía now listens complacently to the news, brought by one of the soldiers guarding him, of the anarchy that has befallen the land:

> That the Conservative government. . . . with the backing of the Liberals, was reforming the calendar so that every president could remain in power for a hundred years. That the concordat with the Holy See had finally been signed and a cardinal had come from Rome with a crown of diamonds and a throne of solid gold, and that the Liberal ministers had had their pictures taken on their knees in the act of kissing his ring. That the leading lady of a Spanish company passing through the capital had been kidnapped by a band of masked highwaymen and on the following Sunday she had danced in the nude at the summer house of the president of the republic. (215)

"Don't talk to me about politics," Colonel Aureliano Buendía replies. It is only when the gringos come and take over the community with a brutality hitherto unknown does the Colonel realize that it was a mistake not to continue his wars. In fury he shouts, "One of these days, I'm going to arm my boys so we can get rid of these shitty gringos!" (257) Agents of the government, in the pay of the banana company, hunt down his seventeen illegitimate sons, and they are all murdered.

One Hundred Years of Solitude then begins its downward spiral. Time moves not in a circle but with a moral trajectory. Úrsula perceives that time is breaking down progressively: "she shuddered with the evidence that time was not passing . . . but that it was turning in a circle" (361), she notices. As an extremely old woman, speaking for the author, Úrsula comes to believe that Colonel Aureliano Buendía "had not lost his love for the family because he had been hardened by the war," but, rather, that "he had never loved anyone" (267). She realizes that he had fought out of "pure and sinful pride" (267). He had been, the author passes his final and most cruel judgment, "Simply a man incapable of love" (267).

The coldness afflicting Colonel Aureliano Buendía in the last years of his life is one of the warning messages that this novel delivers. It is a coldness to the bone: "he had learned to think coldly so that inescapable memories would not touch any feeling" (286). It is the coldness of a living death.

Like García Márquez, who never ceases to love his characters, who sympathizes with them all, Úrsula feels compassion for the son who wept in her womb. She realizes as well, as the author means for the reader to understand, that Amaranta ruined the lives of Pietro Crespi, of Colonel Gerineldo Márquez, and of herself, out of "a mortal struggle between a measureless love and an invincible cowardice, and that the irrational fear that Amaranta had always had of her own tormented heart had triumphed in the end" (268).

In such didactic passages García Márquez makes direct statements to the reader. He issues his message by setting an example. As he forgives his people, his readers might do well to forgive each other.

The failure and death of Colonel Aureliano Buendía, and the death of Úrsula, who heroically remains alive as long as she can, permit the self-destruction of Macondo, and that of the Buendía family, to proceed unimpeded. The ending, the mad passion of Amaranta Úrsula and her nephew Aureliano, is a return to a primeval slime: "They saw themselves in the lost paradise of the deluge, splashing in the puddles in the courtyard" (439). As Amaranta Úrsula's "pregnancy advanced, they were becoming a single being" (440), with all human differentiation obliterated. The foundations of the Buendía house collapse as their world comes to an end. They are "living like cannibals" (441), divorced from human society and condemned to the insularity of the Buendía history.

At first it seems as if the last Aureliano will change the course of history. He seems to have been born with all the best qualities of the José Arcadios and the Aurelianos; he seems "predisposed to begin the race again from the beginning and cleanse it of its pernicious vices and solitary calling." He of all the Buendías is "the only one in a century who had been engendered with love." When he is turned over, the tail of a pig is revealed. It is too late.

Only when Aureliano sees the corpse of his baby, devoured by the red ants, does he perceive the meaning of the parchments: "*The first of the line is tied to a tree and the last is being eaten by the ants*" (446). The magical manuscripts are "the history of the family" and were written "one hundred years ahead of time" (446), suggesting that had the Buendías been able to overcome their solitude, history could have been reversed. The episodes "coexisted in one instant" (446), implying that their order was reversible. History is neither cyclical nor predetermined.

At the last the fall of the Buendías becomes a good thing. It is salutary that everything written on the parchments is "unrepeatable," that history need not repeat itself. The novel becomes a warning to mankind:

"races condemned to *One Hundred Years of Solitude* did not have a second opportunity on earth" (448).

NOTES

1. Mario Vargas Llosa, *García Márquez: Historia de un Deicidio* (Barcelona: Breve Biblioteca de Respuesta: Barral Editores, 1971), p. 20.

2. Vargas Llosa, *Historia de un Deicidio,* p. 24.

3. Ibid., p. 59.

4. Ibid., p. 85.

5. Ibid., pp. 87–88.

6. Michael Wood, *Gabriel García Márquez: One Hundred Years of Solitude* (Cambridge: Cambridge University Press, 1990), p. 6.

7. Ibid., p. 7.

8. Ibid., p. 15.

9. Ibid., p. 49.

10. Ibid., p. 57.

11. Ibid., p. 58.

12. Gene H. Bell-Villada, *García Márquez: The Man and His Work* (Chapel Hill: University of North Carolina Press, 1990) p. 19.

13. Ibid., p. 21.

14. Ibid.

15. Edwin Williamson, "Magical Realism and the Theme of Incest in *One Hundred Years of Solitude,*" in *Gabriel García Márquez,* edited by Harold Bloom, Modern Critical Views (New York & Philadelphia: Chelsea House, 1989) p. 48.

16. Gerald Martin, "On 'Magical' and Social Realism in García Márquez," in *Gabriel García Márquez,* edited by Bloom, p. 97.

17. Ibid., pp. 98–99.

18. Ibid., p. 101.

19. Ibid., p. 105.

20. Regina Janes, "Liberals, Conservatives, and Bananas: Colombian Politics in the Fictions of Gabriel García Márquez," in *Gabriel García Márquez,* edited by Bloom, p. 128.

21. Ibid, p. 130.

22. Ibid., p. 146.

23. Roberto González Echevarría, "*Cien años de soledad:* The Novel as Myth and Archive," in *Gabriel García Márquez,* edited by Bloom, p. 108.

24. Ibid., p. 111.

25. Ibid., p. 115.

26. Floyd Merrell, "José Arcadio Buendía's Scientific Paradigms: Man in Search of Himself," in *Gabriel García Márquez,* edited by Bloom, p. 28.

27. Wood, *Gabriel García Márquez,* p. 24.

28. Ibid., p. 49.

29. Quoted in Bell-Villada, *The Man And His Work,* p. 100.

30. Luis Harss and Barbara Dohmann, p. 327.

31. Bell-Villada, *The Man And His Work,* p. 101.

32. Harss and Dohmann, p. 322.

33. Harley D. Oberhelman, "The Presence of Faulkner in the Writings of García Márquez," *Graduate Studies at Texas Tech University,* 11 (August 1980): 27.

34. Ibid., p. 34

35. Ibid.

36. Mark Frisch, "Teaching *One Hundred Years of Solitude* with *The Sound and the Fury,*" Center for Faulkner Studies, Southeast Missouri State University, *Teaching Faulkner Newsletter.* Available online at http://www2.semo.edu/cfs/frisch.html

37. Ibid., p. 4.

38. Ibid., p. 5.

39. Plummer, "The Faulkner Relation,"in *Gabriel García Márquez,* edited by Bloom, pp. 33–34.

40. Ibid., p. 38.

41. Ibid., p. 39.

42. Lois Parkinson Zamora, "Magical Romance/Magical Realism: Ghosts in U.S. and Latin American Fiction," in *Magical Realism: Theory, History, Community,* edited by Zamora and Wendy B. Faris (Durham, N.C.: Duke University Press, 1995), p. 502.

43. Ibid.

44. Williamson, "Magical Realism and the Theme of Incest," p. 46.

45. Martin, "On 'Magical' and Social Realism," p. 97.

46. Ibid., p. 99.

47. Ibid.

48. Ibid., p. 107.

49. Ibid., p. 106.

50. Echevarría, "The Novel as Myth and Archive," p. 111.

51. Ibid., p. 114.

52. Ibid., p. 115.

53. Richard Gullon, "Gabriel García Márquez and the Lost Art of Storytelling," *Diacritics,* 1, no. 1 (1971): 27–32).

54. Janes, "Liberals, Conservatives, and Bananas," p. 129.

55. Ibid., p. 141.

56. Ibid., p. 144.

57. Merrell, "José Arcadio Buendía's Scientific Paradigms," p. 21.

58. Ibid., p. 26.

59. Aníbal González, "Translation and Genealogy: *One Hundred Years of Solitude*," in *Gabriel García Márquez: New Readings*, edited by Bernard McGuirk and Richard Cardwell (Cambridge: Cambridge University Press, 1987), p. 65.

60. Ibid., p. 66.

61. Ibid., p. 74.

62. Ibid., p. 77.

63. Clyde Griffin, "The Humour of *One Hundred Years of Solitude*," in *Gabriel García Márquez: New Readings*, edited by McGuirk and Cardwell, p. 81.

64. Ibid., p. 82.

65. Ibid., p. 83.

66. Ibid., p. 90.

67. Ibid., p. 88.

68. Ibid., p. 90.

69. Ibid., p. 93.

70. Ibid., p. 94.

71. Vargas Llosa, *Historia de un Deicidio*, p. 27.

72. Ibid., p. 45.

73. José Donoso, *The Boom in Spanish American Literature*, translated by Gregory Kolvakos (New York: Columbia University Press/Center for Inter-American Relations, 1977), p. 48.

74. Rita Guibert, "Guilermo Cabrera Infante," in *Seven Voices: Seven Latin American Writers Talk to Rita Guibert*, translated by Frances Partridge (New York: Knopf, 1973), p. 343.

75. Donoso, *The Boom*, p. 79.

76. Guibert, *Seven Voices*, p. 424.

77. Donoso, *The Boom*, p. 110.

78. Ibid., p. 111.

79. Guibert, "Julio Cortázar," in *Seven Voices*, p. 296.

80. Ibid., p. 301.

81. Janes, "Liberals, Conservatives, and Bananas," p. 125.

82. Guibert, *Seven Voices*, p. 315.

83. Claudia Dreifus, "*Playboy* Interview: Gabriel García Márquez," *Playboy*, 30 (February 1983): 176.

84. Griffin, "The Humour of *One Hundred Years of Solitude*," p. 88.

ONE HUNDRED YEARS OF SOLITUDE
IN HISTORY

PUBLIC RESPONSE

One Hundred Years of Solitude (1967) was greeted with acclaim simultaneously by the reading public, fellow novelists of García Márquez, and the reviewers. In keeping with his custom of showing his works in progress to a handful of selected friends, García Márquez showed the first three chapters of *One Hundred Years of Solitude* to Mexican novelist Carlos Fuentes. In a Mexican magazine, Fuentes described his ecstatic response:

> I have just finished reading the first seventy-five pages of *Cien años de soledad.* They are absolutely magisterial . . . all "fictional" history coexists with "real" history, what is dreamed with what is documented, and thanks to the legends, the lies, the exaggerations, the myths . . . Macondo is made into a universal territory, in a story almost biblical in its foundations, its generations and degenerations, in a story of the origin and destiny of human time and of the dreams and desires by which men are saved or destroyed.[1]

A few months later, excerpts from the novel began to appear in magazines—*Eco* in Bogotá, *Mundo Nuevo* in Paris, *Dialogos* in Mexico, and *Amaru* in Lima. They provoked a response similar to Fuentes's. At the beginning of 1966 García Márquez received a letter from a Buenos Aires publishing company called Editorial Sudamericana, proposing to him that they republish his early books. Instead, he offered them the novel that he was working on—*One Hundred Years of Solitude.*

Its success was instantaneous. The early editions all sold out in a few days. In three and a half years the novel had sold half a million copies. Within a few months García Márquez had contracts for foreign translations from the United States, France, Italy, Finland, Brazil, Sweden, Germany, Russia, Norway, Holland, Poland, Rumania, Czechoslovakia, Yugoslavia, England, Denmark, Japan, and Hungary.

Cover for the twenty-ninth printing of a Brazilian edition of *One Hundred Years of Solitude*

From being a writer whose reputation was "skimpy," as José Donoso put it in *The Boom in Spanish American Literature*, García Márquez with *One Hundred Years of Solitude* inspired a worldwide fascination with Latin American writing:

MAGIC REALISM AND IMPOSSIBLE REALITY

"I was born and raised in the Caribbean. I know it country by country, isle by isle, and perhaps the source of my frustration is this: nothing has ever occurred to me, nor have I been able to do anything, that is more awesome than reality itself. The most I've been able to do has been to alter that reality with poetic devices, but there's not a single line in any of my books that doesn't have its origin in actual fact. One of those alterations is the stigma of the pig's tail that so troubled the Buendía family in *One Hundred Years of Solitude.* I could have chosen any number of images, but I thought giving birth to a son with a pig's tail was least likely to coincide with reality. However, as soon as the novel became known, confessions cropped up, in different parts of the Americas, from men and women who had something resembling a pig's tail. In Barranquilla, one youth exhibited himself in the newspapers. His explanation was even more surprising than his tail: he had been born with the tail, but he had never revealed it until he read *One Hundred Years of Solitude.* 'I never wanted to tell anyone that I had it because I was ashamed,' he said. 'But now, having read the novel and listened to people who have read it, I realize it's a natural thing.'"

García Márquez

From "Latin America's Impossible Reality," translated by Eleria Brunet, *Harper's,* 270 (January 1985): 15.

It has to be asserted that the Boom—noisy and vulgar and tarnished with the flattery and envy by which it is known today—gave a reason for publishers to pull hair from their beards in frustration for having rejected such-and-such a manuscript in which they did not know how to recognize quality; and it gave a reason, too, for the novelists—but only a few—to be able at last to impose modest conditions by means of literary agents, who soon began to collect Latin Americans. All of this begins with *One Hundred Years of Solitude.*[2]

Mario Vargas Llosa echoed his colleagues. The publication of *One Hundred Years of Solitude* in Buenos Aires came as "a literary earthquake throughout Latin America. The critics recognized the book as a masterpiece of the art of fiction and the public endorsed this opinion, systematically exhausting new editions, which, at one point, appeared at the astounding rate of one a week."[3]

The reading public, including even uneducated readers, immediately embraced *One Hundred Years of Solitude,* confirming the truth of García Márquez's contention that the book was simple reading. Fuentes reported that his cook in his Mexico City house read García Márquez. An Argentine maid refused to return to work until she had finished what she called "the last page of the history of Macondo," García Márquez learned. He has also recounted the story of an incident in rural Cuba in the early 1970s:

A group of peasants inquired what he did for a living.

"I write," García Márquez said, modestly.

"What do you write?"

"I wrote a book called *Cien años de soledad.*"

"Macondo!" one of the peasants cried out.[4]

The response was enthusiastic almost throughout the continent. North American writer Ron Arias recalls a conversation with his fellow bus passengers one afternoon in Caracas:

I remember riding a crowded bus one day in Caracas, and two women who looked like secretaries on their lunch break were laughing over certain episodes they'd read in *Cien años de soledad.* I joined in; then it seemed half the bus did. This was in 1969 and it was the year's best seller. Everyone who had read it was bringing up his or her favorite character, and we were all howling together. The book as a whole had struck a common chord with us all, since historically we had all come from Macondo . . . we all had a tío [uncle]or more in a revolution, and I'm sure there were people in our lives chasing more than butterflies.[5]

The life of García Márquez was at once transformed by the overwhelming public response to *One Hundred Years of Solitude.* He himself has described this phenomenon:

It's changed my whole life. I was once asked . . . how my life differed before and after that book, and I said that after it "there are four hundred more people." That's to say before the book I had my friends, but now there are enormous numbers of people who want to see me and talk to me—journalists, academics, readers. It's strange . . . most of my readers aren't interested in asking questions, they only want to talk about the book. That's very flattering if you consider case by case, but added up they begin to be a problem in one's life. I would like to please them all, but as that's impossible I have to act meanly . . . you see? For instance, by saying I'm leaving a town when all I'm really doing is changing my hotel. . . . [6]

He found himself forever meeting people who were reading *One Hundred Years of Solitude:* "readers seem to emerge from caves like ants."[7] To his surprise, he found that his book was read by educated and uneducated readers alike:

I know of readers, people without intellectual training, who have passed straight from "comics" to that book and have read it with the same interest as the other things they have been given, because they underestimated it intellectually. It's the publishers who, underestimating the public, publish books of a very low literary value; and the curious thing is that that level also consumes books like *One Hundred Years of Solitude.* . . . [8]

SUBSTANTIAL SALES

"Outside of García Márquez with his fabulous *One Hundred Years of Solitude*, I do not believe that the author's rights of any Latin American writer can justifiably be called 'substantial'. On the contrary, the life of the Boom writers is and has been rather difficult and their greatest struggle is to steal a few hours for writing from the work that grants them a modest subsistence. The very same García Márquez, who barely survived by writing film scripts in Mexico, left work when *One Hundred Years of Solitude* had ripened inside him and he was ready to write, knowing that he and his family would experience poverty. Thanks to the money lent to him by such friends as the Colombian poet Álvaro Mutis, he was able to go into seclusion to write the most talked-about novel in Spanish that I can remember. *One Hundred Years of Solitude* was published in 1967. From then on, certainly the triumph at the level of commotion and scandal of García Márquez' novel—and I must clarify that 'scandal' is a product, above all, of how unbearable it is to some people that a book of such literary quality can also be an unprecedented success—has made it the only [Latin American] novel whose sales may justifiably be called 'substantial'."

José Donoso

From his *The Boom in Spanish American Literature*, translated by Gregory Kolovakos (New York: Columbia University Press/Center for Inter-American Relations, 1977), p. 56.

Speaking at a university in Lima, as Vargas Llosa puts it, "su llegada provocó una verdadera conmocion en el ambito intelectual y universitario" (his arrival provoked a veritable commotion on intellectual and academic circuits).[9] At home so many journalists called that he could no longer answer his telephone:

No hay día en que no llaman dos o tres editores y otros tantos periodistas. Cuando mi mujer contesta al teléfono, tiene que decir que no estoy. Si éstas es la gloria, lo demas debe ser una porquería (No: mejor no ponga eso, porque esa vaina escrita, es ridícula). Pero es la verdad. Ya uno no sabe ni quiénes son sus amigos.[10]

(There isn't a day when two or three editors and other journalists don't call. When my wife answers the telephone, she has to say that I'm not at home. If one offers praise, the rest is probably worthless. [No: better not write that because a vain writer is ridiculous.] But it's the truth. One no longer knows who his friends are.)

In vain has García Márquez argued that should anyone want to know what he thinks, they can read his works: "El que quiera saber qué opino, que lea mis libros. En *Cien años de soledad* hay 350 páginas de opiniones."[11] (If anyone wants to know my opinion, they can read my books. In *One Hundred Years of Solitude* there are three hundred and fifty pages of opinions.)

His sense of humor, so abundant in his fiction, has seen him through. When an editor came proposing that he write the prologue to the diary of Che Guevara in the Sierra Maestra, García Márquez told him that he would do it with great pleasure, but that it would take him eight years to complete it because he wanted to deliver "una cosa bien hecha" (a well-made product).

Magdalena River in the 1940s, when García Márquez frequently traveled on it

---

One Hundred Years of Solitude has sold twenty million copies since its publication, more copies than any book in Spanish since *Don Quixote* (1605); admiration for this work has been constant. Its author moved to Barcelona where, free of financial concerns, he was able to devote himself entirely to his writing.

HISTORICAL REFLECTIONS

Even the first reviews recognized the historical importance of this work. The *Antioch Review* wrote that *One Hundred Years of Solitude* signaled that "Latin American literature will change from being the exotic interest of a few to essential reading and that Latin America itself will be looked on less as a crazy subculture and more as a fruitful, alternative way of life."[12] In *Books Abroad*, Klaus Müller-Bergh called this novel "an earthquake, a maelstrom."[13] Several of the reviewers were themselves Latin American artists of distinction. Chilean poet Pablo Neruda was quoted in *Time* magazine as calling the book "the greatest revelation in the Spanish language since the *Don Quixote* of Cervantes."[14]

The importance of the work for many critics rests in the broad range of its thematic structure, that it leaps from the particular, the story

THE FATE OF ARACATACA

"A Bogotá journalist went to Aracataca in 1969 and found that the home of García's ancestors was being eaten by red ants, just as García had predicted the dust storm that would bury the Buendía house and the town forever. The journalist found ruins and solitude in the town, no doubt what he went to find, and which would always exist everywhere if you look closely. But the fading of Aracataca was not the consequence of a cursed, fateful prophecy. It had been predicted by García Márquez not because he had chosen it to be that way in his godlike role as novelist, but because—like the gypsy Melquíades, who in *Cien Años* had written in the coded parchments that 'The first of the line is tied to a tree and the last is being eaten by ants'—he deciphered the key to history, and he knew that events occurred because they had to, that the turn of time was cyclical and that the vital, bloody warmth of every life held in itself not only its own dusty eventuality, but the seeds of regeneration as well."

William Kennedy

From "The Yellow Trolley Car in Barcelona: An Interview," in his *Riding the Yellow Trolley Car* (New York: Viking, 1993), p. 267.

of the Buendía family over one hundred years, to the general, responding to all of Latin America and even all human experience.

Robert G. Mead Jr. in the *Saturday Review* made a similar observation, pointing out that "Macondo may be regarded as a microcosm of the development of much of the Latin American continent."[15] Although, Mead argues, the novel is "first and always a story," it also "has value as a social and historical document."

Some critics have described the importance of the novel in terms of the influence of William Faulkner; just as Faulkner based his legendary Yoknapatawpha County on the area around Oxford, Mississippi, where he was born, García Márquez converts Aracataca into Macondo.

Other critics have been wary of comparing *One Hundred Years of Solitude* with Faulkner's works. García Márquez has warned readers against too close a relationship between himself and Faulkner:

I'm not sure whether I had already read Faulkner or not, but I know now that only a technique like Faulkner's could have enabled me to write down what I was seeing. The atmosphere, the decadence, the heat in the village were roughly the same as what I had felt in Faulkner. It was a banana plantation region inhabited by a lot of Americans from the fruit companies which gave it the same sort of atmosphere I had found in the writer of the Deep South. Critics have spoken of the literary influence of Faulkner, but I see it as a coincidence: I had simply found material that had to be dealt with in the same way that Faulkner had treated similar material.[16]

In an interview with Rita Guibert, García Márquez goes further in explaining the relationship between *One Hundred Years of Solitude* and his reading of the works of William Faulkner:

All the critics have mentioned Faulkner's influence. I accept that, but not in the sense they think when they see me as an author who read Faulkner, assimilated him, was impressed by him and, consciously or unconsciously, tries to write like him. That is more or less, roughly, what I understand by an influence. What I owe to Faulkner is something entirely different. I was born in Aracataca, the banana-growing country where the United Fruit Company was established. It was in this region, where the Fruit Company was building towns and hospitals and draining some zones, that I grew up and received my first impressions. Then, many years later, I read Faulkner and found that his whole world—the world of the southern United States which he writes about—was very like my world, that it was created by the same people. And also, when later I traveled in the southern states, I found evidence—on those hot, dusty roads, with the same vegetation, trees, and great houses—of the similarity between our two worlds. One mustn't forget that Faulkner is in a way

Cover for the Israeli edition of *One Hundred Years of Solitude*, published in Tel Aviv in 1976

a Latin American writer. His world is that of the Gulf of Mexico. What I found in him was affinities between our experiences, which were not as different as might appear at first sight. Well, this sort of influence of course exists, but it's very different from what the critics pointed out.[17]

Thor Vihjalmsson has said in his *Books Abroad* review: "García Márquez does not fail to deal with the dark forces, or give the impression that the life of human beings, one by one, should be ultimately tragic"; yet, simultaneously, "he also shows every moment pregnant with images and color and scent which ask to be arranged into patterns of meaning and significance while the moment lasts."[18]

Remarkably, given García Márquez's avowed Marxism and his definition of himself as a revolutionary socialist, North American critics have embraced his work and acknowledged the historical importance of *One Hundred Years of Solitude*.

In his study of García Márquez, George R. McMurray suggests that reports of the death of the novel have been greatly exaggerated, that García Márquez single-handedly provides "evidence that the genre is still thriving."[19]

Nearly universally, García Márquez has been acknowledged from the time of the publication of *One Hundred Years of Solitude* as the master of fiction of the second half of the twentieth century. Gregory Rabassa, his translator, compares García Márquez to Miguel de Cervantes in the enormous range of his vision:

> García Márquez has brought breadth to the telling of tales as we have known the art in our culture, new dimensions that give a hint of stellar time and the anachronic coincidences that make up our false sense of once-ness as far as the heavens, and other areas, are concerned. The limits of our own time become clear toward the end of *One Hundred Years of Solitude* as Aureliano Babilonia (Whore of Babylon?), who is also reading the book, finds out that time, the hundred years, the time of his dynasty, will come to an end with the end of the book . . . he has returned to the roots of reality, which are the roots of the novel as it was conceived by Cervantes, but he has gone even deeper and given us the Roc once more that is the nature of his ancient art.[20]

The reputation of *One Hundred Years of Solitude* has remained constant since its publication in 1967. Gabriel García Márquez won the Nobel Prize in literature in 1982, reaffirming both the stature of his masterpiece and his preeminence as an artist.

ADAPTATIONS

Although other of his works have been adapted for movies and for television, García Márquez has consistently refused to sell the rights of *One Hundred Years of Solitude* to the movies. His concern has been that the reader might be cheated because "the film viewer sees a face that he may not have imagined."[21]

"In movies, the image is so definite that the spectator can no longer imagine the character as he wants to, only as the screen imposes it on him,"[22] García Márquez has added. He prefers that the readers be free to translate the characters into their own experiences:

. . . film does not allow for that. The face of the actor, of Gregory Peck, becomes the face of the character. It cannot be your uncle, unless your uncle looks like Gregory Peck.[23]

García Márquez has remarked that he "can't think of any one film that improved on a good novel, but I can think of many good films that came from very bad novels." Originally he thought that the visual impact of the cinema was greater than that of literature. But he changed his mind:

. . . but then I realized the limitations of the cinema. That very visual aspect puts it at a disadvantage compared to literature. It's so immediate, so forceful, that it's difficult for the viewer to go beyond it. In literature one can go much further and at the same time create an impact that is visual, auditory, or of any other sort.[24]

"When I studied the way movies were made," García Márquez has observed, "I realized that there are limitations in the form that do not exist in literature. I've become convinced that the novelist's work is the freest work that exists. You are totally your own master." He illustrates that point with a comparison between the absolute freedom of the novelist and the situation of the writer who provides but one element in the cinematic totality, which is always a communal effort: "If I shut myself in my room I can write exactly what I want to. I don't have to put up with an editor saying, 'Get rid of that character or incident and put in another.'"[25]

To discourage movie offers, he told his agent to set a price of one million dollars. When offers came in at that price, she raised it first to two, and then to three million dollars. "I prefer that it remain a private relationship between the reader and the book,"[26] García Márquez has said.

NOTES

1. William Kennedy, "The Yellow Trolley Car in Barcelona: An Interview," in *Riding The Yellow Trolley Car* (New York: Viking, 1993), p. 258.

2. José Donoso, *The Boom in Spanish American Literature*, translated by Gregory Kolvakos (New York: Columbia University Press/Center for Inter-American Relations, 1977), p. 89.

3. Mario Vargas Llosa, "García Márquez: From Aracataca to Macondo," in *Gabriel García Márquez*, edited by Harold Bloom (New York & Philadelphia: Chelsea House, 1989), p. 5.

4. Quoted in Gene H. Bell-Villada, *García Márquez: The Man and His Work* (Chapel Hill & London: University of North Carolina Press, 1990), p. 5.

5. Ibid.

6. Rita Guibert, *Seven Voices: Seven Latin American Writers Talk to Rita Guibert,* translated by Frances Partridge (New York: Knopf, 1973), p. 310.

7. Ibid., p. 312.

8. Ibid., p. 322.

9. Vargas Llosa, *García Márquez: Historia de un Deicidio* (Barcelona: Breve Biblioteca de Respuesta: Barral Editores, 1971), p. 82.

10. Ibid., pp. 82–83.

11. Ibid., p. 83.

12. *Antioch Review* (Winter 1991): 154.

13. Klaus Müller-Bergh, "*Relato de un naufrago:* García Márquez's Tale of Shipwreck and Survival at Sea," *Books Abroad,* 47 (Summer 1973): 460.

14. Quoted in "Magic, Matter, and Money: Pioneers Who Have Explored Four Aspects of Reality," *Time,* 120 (1 November 1982): 88.

15. Robert G. Mead Jr., "*One Hundred Years of Solitude,*" *Saturday Review* (7 March 1970): 34–35.

16. Peter Stone, "Gabriel García Márquez," in *Writers at Work: The Paris Review Interviews—Sixth Series,* edited by George Plimpton (New York: Viking, 1984), p. 321.

17. Guibert, *Seven Voices,* p. 327.

18. Thor Vilhjalmsson, "Presentation of Gabriel García Márquez," *Books Abroad,* 47, no. 1 (1973): 10–11.

19. George R. McMurray, *Gabriel García Márquez* (New York: Ungar, 1977), p. 6.

20. Gregory Rabassa, "Beyond Magic Realism: Thoughts on the Art of Gabriel García Márquez," *Books Abroad,* 47, no. 3 (Summer 1973): 449.

21. Stone, *Writers at Work,* p. 338.

22. Claudia Driefus, "*Playboy* Interview: Gabriel García Márquez," *Playboy,* 30, no. 3 (1983): 174.

23. Marlise Simons, "The Best Years of His Life: An Interview with Gabriel García Márquez," *New York Times Book Review* (10 April 1988).

24. Guibert, *Seven Voices,* p. 321.

25. Driefus, "*Playboy* Interview": 174.

26. Stone, *Writers at Work,* p. 338.

ONE HUNDRED YEARS OF SOLITUDE
AS STUDIED

WORKS FREQUENTLY STUDIED WITH *ONE HUNDRED YEARS OF SOLITUDE*

SIMILAR BY GENRE: Works that include elements similar to those of magic realism are José Donoso's *Obsceno pajarode la noche* (1970; translated as *The Obscene Bird of Night*, 1973), Toni Morrison's *Beloved* (1987), Isabel Allende's *La casa de los espíritus* (1982; translated as *The House of the Spirits*, 1985), and Salman Rushdie's *Midnight's Children* (1981). Pierre Menard, in Jorge Luis Borges's *Ficciones* (1956; translated as *Fictions*, 1962), obviously reflects the character of Melquíades in *One Hundred Years of Solitude,* and García Márquez has frequently been studied with Argentine writer Borges, in particular with "The Aleph" (1949).

Other works based on magic realism with which García Márquez can be studied include two works by Alejo Carpentier, *El reino de este mundo* (1949; translated as *The Kingdom of This World,* 1957) and *Los pasos perdidos* (1953; translated as *The Lost Steps,* 1956). As Raymond L. Williams has pointed out, both were published "precisely during García Márquez's period of literary apprenticeship."[1]

One Hundred Years of Solitude can also be studied with works by Guy de Maupassant, Henry James, and Edgar Allan Poe that treat the supernatural.

From an historical perspective, Williams lists four novels that pointed to a new direction for the "Spanish-American" novel and paved the way for the writers of the Boom to follow: *El Señor Presidente* (1946; translated as *The President,* 1963) by Miguel Ángel Asturias, another Nobel laureate; *Al filo del agua* (1947; translated as *The Edge of the Storm,* 1963) by Agustin Yáñez of Mexico; *Adan Buenosayres* (1948) by Argentine Leopoldo Marechal; and *El reino de este mundo* by Carpentier.[2]

Williams also places García Márquez as a novelist in his Colombian tradition, beginning in the 1920s with José Eustacio Rivera's *La vor-*

Cover for the first Greek edition (1979) of *One Hundred Years of Solitude*

agine (1924; translated as *The Vortex,* 1935), José Felix Fuenmayor's *Cosme* (1927), and *Una triste aventura de 14 sabios* (A Sad Adventure of 14 Wise Men, 1928). These writers were innovators, and in 1950, according to Williams, García Márquez praised the work of Fuenmayor. Not least, García Márquez's *One Hundred Years of Solitude* can be studied with other literature set in coastal Colombia, including Álvaro Cepeda Samudio's *La casa grande* (1962; translated as *The Big House,* 1991) and Hector Rojas Herazo's *Respirando el verano* (Breathing the Summer, 1962).³

WORKS RELATED TO THE EPIC: Possible choices of epics to study with *One Hundred Years of Solitude* are the *Iliad,* the *Odyssey,* and *The Book of Genesis.*

WORKS THAT INCLUDE TRAGIC ELEMENTS: Sophocles' *Antigone* and *Oedipus Rex,* both of which García Márquez has said have influenced his fiction are possible works to study with *One Hundred Years of Solitude.*

WORKS THAT RAISE THE ISSUES OF LANGUAGE AND TRANSLATION: One such novel is Alejo Carpentier's *El siglo de las luces* (1962; translated as *Explosion in a Cathedral,* 1963), in which, as Aníbal González points out, "one of the protagonists, Esteban, translates the Declaration of the Rights of Man and other documents of the French Revolution into Spanish."⁴ Other novels that deal with language as an issue include Guillermo Cabrera Infante's *Tres tristes tigres* (1967; translated as *Three Trapped Tigers,* 1971) and Julio Cortázar's *Rayuela* (1963; translated as *Hopscotch,* 1967). These novels, along with *La muerte de Artemio Cruz* (1962; translated as *The Death of Artemio Cruz,* 1964) by Carlos Fuentes, are also studied together as part of the Boom in Latin American literature in the 1960s.

The novel from which all novels began, the greatest novel in the Spanish language before *One Hundred Years of Solitude,* Miguel de Cervantes' *Don Quixote* (1605), is also frequently studied with García Márquez's work. In particular, critics have stressed similarities in modes of narration, in the emphasis on the relationship between the manuscript and truth (for García Márquez, an ambiguity), and in the epic scope of both works.

ON READING

"Until you're about the age of twenty . . . you read everything, and you like it simply because you are reading it. Then between twenty and thirty you pick what you want, and you read the best, you read all the great works. After that you sit and wait for them to be written. But you know, the least known, the least famous writers, they are the better ones."

García Márquez

From William Kennedy, "The Yellow Trolley Car in Barcelona: An Interview," in his *Riding the Yellow Trolley Car* (New York: Viking, 1993), p. 261.

THE BEST READER OF *ONE HUNDRED YEARS OF SOLITUDE*

"A Russian friend met a lady, a very old lady, who was copying the whole book out by hand, right to the last line. My friend asked her why she was doing it and the lady replied, 'Because I want to find out who is really mad, the author or me, and the only way to find out is to re-write the book.' I find it hard to imagine a better reader than that lady."

García Márquez

From García Márquez and Plinio Apuleyo Mendoza, *The Fragrance of Guava,* translated by Ann Wright (London: Verso, 1983), p.78.

SIMILAR BY LITERARY MOVEMENT: There is some dispute among critics about whether García Márquez belongs to the modernist or to the postmodernist movement. He himself has pointed to the influence of modernist writers such as James Joyce, Virginia Woolf, and Franz Kafka on his writing. *One Hundred Years of Solitude* has been studied with Kafka's *The Metamorphosis* (1915), a seminal work in the development of García Márquez. Woolf's *Mrs. Dalloway* (1925) is another influence, particularly on García Márquez's handling of time. Kafka's *The Metamorphosis* was a major influence on García Márquez, introducing him to the fantastic as a technique.

One Hundred Years of Solitude is most often studied with other great works of Latin American literature, as well as with works of the Boom of the 1960s. Walter D. Mignolo at the University of Michigan teaches the novel along with works by lesser known writers such as Rigoberta Menchu, who wrote *Me Llamo Rigoberta, Mechu y asi nacio me concienca* (1983; translated as *I Rigoberta Mechu, An Indian Woman in Guatemala,* 1984), and Rudolfo Anaya, author of *Bless Me, Ultima* (1972). Menchu, Mignolo points out, "considers the opposition between her own Quiche culture and the Spanish tradition." He contrasts oral and written narratives and considers the question of "under what conditions does a narrative become a novel?"[5] and draws on the approaches of Mikhail Bakhtin and Ortega y Gasset.

His course raises larger questions, such as "why a writer in Latin America is compelled to take over the task of the historian, whether to narrate specific events of modern and contemporary history (dictatorship novels), of the colonial period, or an overview of the general history of Latin America, as is the case in *One Hundred Years.*"[6]

SIMILAR BY THEME: García Márquez's friend Álvaro Cepuda Samudio wrote a novel titled *La casa grande* about the banana strike against United Fruit in Colombia in 1928. This novel comes closest of any work to using the historical materials used in *One Hundred Years of Solitude.*

Hanna Geldrich-Leffman of Loyola College has designed an honors seminar titled "Visions of Reality," in which *One Hundred Years of Sol-*

itude is taught along with works in a variety of genres: in fiction, Kafka's *The Trial* (1925), Borges's *Ficciones,* and Juan Rulfo's *El llano en llamas* (1953, *The Burning Plain*), but also Jean-Paul Sartre's play *No Exit* (1946), Eugene Ionesco's play *Rhinoceros* (1959), and poetry by Paul Celan. Geldrich-Leffman points out, however, that despite the general theme of the course, "visions of reality," *One Hundred Years of Solitude* is studied along with "a presentation on the Latin American situation or a more specific discussion of Colombia, the economic involvement of the United States in the 'banana republic. . . . '"[7]

Lois Parkinson Zamora of the University of Houston has chosen to group North and South American authors in a course titled "Communal Identities in the Americas (A Comparative Survey of American Literary Relations)," a comparative literature approach. *One Hundred Years of Solitude* appears in a unit titled "American Myths, American Memory," along with William Faulkner's *Absalom, Absalom!* (1936) and *What's Bred in the Bone* (1985) by Canadian novelist Robertson Davies. The works by García Márquez and Faulkner both raise questions "about cultural and national identity," and she recommends these works as "essential points of departure." (The course also includes works by Octavio Paz, Alejo Carpentier, Carlos Fuentes, Manuel Puig, Jorge Luis Borges, Julio Cortázar, and José Donoso.) Zamora points out that "teaching a comparative course in American literature makes sense only when United States students think of *America* as including Latin America, Canada and the Caribbean."[8]

In another course, Zamora teaches "The Caribbean Context (Modern American Fiction)" and includes again *One Hundred Years of Solitude* and *Absalom, Absalom!* but also other North American works—*The Confessions of Nat Turner* (1967) by William Styron, *Beloved* by Toni Morrison, and *The House of Breath* (1951) by William Goyen. Her theme is "cultural, racial, and literary mixing—and the way in which writers have described and dealt with challenges of cultural and racial pluralism." She points out, as have many critics, García Márquez's own description of "his affinity for Faulkner's world view": "Yoknapatawpha County has Caribbean shores; thus, in some sense Faulkner is a Caribbean writer, in some sense a Latin American writer."[9]

Zamora suggests as well a course largely devoted to modernists—"In Search of History: Time and Memory in Modern Narrative." She explores *One Hundred Years of Solitude* in "its historical perspective: its circular and linear temporal patterns, its mythic history of the New World that coexists with the specifics of Colombian history, its sweeping narrative perspective" and moves on to study Marcel Proust's *Swann's Way* (1913), Virginia Woolf's *Orlando* (1928) or *To The Lighthouse* (1927), Thomas Mann's *The Magic Mountain* (1924), and other works.

The sixteenth-century fortress of Cartagena des Indios on the Caribbean coast of Colombia, a frequent setting in the fiction of García Márquez

Although she excludes James Joyce's *Ulysses* (1922) because of its "length and complexity," it could easily be added to this syllabus. But it is with *One Hundred Years of Solitude* that she begins the course:

> Melquíades's narrative situation connects the subject of history to the problem of its telling. We are witnesses to the genesis and the apocalypse of Macondo through the eyes of Melquíades, an errant gypsy who defies his own temporal limits—he comes back from the dead—to write the hundred-year history of the Buendía family in a room where, we are told, it is always March and always Monday.[10]

Finally, Zamora poses a more predictable course in "Magical Realism in Contemporary Narrative." Once more she begins with *One Hundred Years of Solitude,* which is followed by *The Tin Drum* (1959), by Günter Grass; *Midnight's Children,* by Salman Rushdie; *The House of the Spirits,* by Isabel Allende; *Beloved,* by Toni Morrison; *Casa de campo* (1978, *House in the Country*), by José Donoso; and other works. Her focus is on authors such as García Márquez who "have often used fantastic events and characters to address the abuses of contemporary political and social institutions."[11]

Other teachers, such as Chester S. Halka of Randolph Macon Woman's College, have taught *One Hundred Years of Solitude* in courses devoted not to other works of literature but to history and politics. Halka points out that several critics "see Colombian and Latin American history, especially the critique of historical understanding," as the main theme of *One Hundred Years of Solitude*." Halka notes that with his treatment of the civil wars and the banana company massacre "García Márquez follows Colombian history to a degree that can surprise those students whose first impression of the novel is rooted primarily in a response to the more obvious magical realism of the work, rather than to the equally pervasive—through perhaps less obvious—social realism it contains."[12]

Another thematic approach to *One Hundred Years of Solitude* can well be in terms of the image of women in this novel, what qualities they share and how they differ from the men. The novel can then be studied in relation to the present situation and status of women in Colombia and in Latin America in general. As María Elena de Valdés points out in an essay titled "*One Hundred Years of Solitude* in Women's Studies Courses":

> only by re-creating what Fernand Braudel calls the history of everyday life can we appreciate and examine the novel's ideology of identity. García Márquez is not a feminist, nor is the novel a text for women about women. But it is a subversion of the patriarchal belief system that both church and state maintain in Latin America as the ideological apology for the status quo that ensures their control of political power.[13]

De Valdés studies social myths in the novel, among them "the myth of good and evil" as "of vital importance for the study of women."[14]

Yet, another focus places *One Hundred Years of Solitude* in interdisciplinary courses. Sandra M. Broschetto of Michigan Technological University suggests that the novel "offers its readers the opportunity to explore problems pertaining to Third World development, history, political ideology, and ethics, as well as issues relating to industrialization in low-technology cultures."[15]

An understanding of how García Márquez treats Colombian history in *One Hundred Years of Solitude* must begin with the two volumes of *La Violencia en Colombia: Estudio de un Proceso Social* (1963, 1968, The Violence in Colombia: Study of a Social Process), by Germán Guzmán, Orlando Fals Borda, and Eduardo Umaña Luna. The images of the actual events of "la violencia" described find an echo in *One Hundred Years of Solitude*.

THE WEIGHT OF SUCCESS

"For a long time, of course, things did not work out for me—almost the first 40 years of my life. I had financial problems; I had work problems. I had not made it as a writer or as anything else. It was a difficult time emotionally and psychologically; I had the idea that I was like an extra, that I did not count anywhere. And then, with "One Hundred Years of Solitude," things turned. Now all this is going on without my being dependent on anyone. Still, I have to do all sorts of things. I have to sit on a bicycle in the morning. I an on on an eternal diet. Half my life I couldn't eat what I wanted because I couldn't afford to, the other half because I have to diet."

García Márquez

From "Gabriel Márquez on Love, Plagues and Politics," by Marlise Simons, who translated the interview, *The New York Times*, 21 February 1988.

Other works that aid in an understanding of how *One Hundred Years of Solitude* reflects Colombian society include *Sociedad y Religion en Colombia* (1965), by Benjamin E. Haddox, and, for basic facts, the most recent *Area Handbook for Colombia* (1964), available from the Superintendent of Documents, U.S. Government Printing Office, Washington, D.C. Classic works on Colombian society include *The Church and the Latin American Revolution* (1965), by Francois Houtart and Emile Jean Pin; *Ideológias politicas y agrárias en Colombia* (Political and Agrarian Ideologies in Columbia, 1973), by Oscar Delgado; and *Elites in Latin America* (1967), by Seymour Martin Lipset and Aldo Solari. See also the more recent *Colombia, guerra en el fin de siglo* (Colombia, War at the End of the Century, 1998), by Alfredo Rangel Suárez.

Such a context places into its historical situation the murder of the seventeen illegitimate sons of Colonel Aureliano Buendía and suggests why García Márquez felt justified in making the death toll of the banana strike not hundreds of victims, as was probably the case, but three thousand. An important critical approach might involve a comparison between the current crisis facing Colombian society, in which the government is involved in dividing up the country with the ascendant guerrilla movements, with the events of *One Hundred Years of Solitude*.

This approach might begin with a study of the increasing disintegration of Colombian society, which seems today like the Macondo collapsing at the end of *One Hundred Years of Solitude*.

SIMILAR BY TYPE OF NOVEL: *One Hundred Years of Solitude* may be considered an "imaginary biography . . . a tradition which can be traced from the Bible to the Renaissance."[16] Williams suggests that a modern example is Woolf's *Orlando*. Other examples include Borges's *Historia universal de la infamia* (1935; translated as *A Universal History of Infamy*, 1972) and Marcel Schwob's *Vies imaginaires* (1896; translated as *Imaginary Lives*, 1924).

As a novel that is a "collective story," as Williams suggests, *One Hundred Years of Solitude* can be compared to Daniel Defoe's *A Journal of the Plague Year* (1722), the novel García Márquez took with him when he went to Europe in the mid 1950s. Another example is Faulkner's *Absalom, Absalom!* Among family chronicles that may be used for comparison are Thomas Mann's *Buddenbrooks* (1900), John Galsworthy's *The Forsyte Saga* (1906–1921, three novels and two interludes published as a single book in 1922), and Émile Zola's *Les Rougon-Macquart* (1867–1893, a twenty-volume series).

In his study of García Márquez, Mario Vargas Llosa suggests that the act of writing novels is itself an act of rebellion, "contra la realidad, contra Dios, contra la creacion de Dios que es realidad"[17] (against reality, against God, against the creation of God which is reality). In this sense, because García Márquez creates a unique reality in *One Hundred Years of Solitude,* his work can even be studied with utopian or dystopian novels, such as George Orwell's *1984* (1949) or Aldous Huxley's *Brave New World* (1932).

NOTES

1. Raymond L. Williams, *Gabriel García Márquez* (Boston: Twayne, 1984), p. 82.

2. Ibid., p. 2.

3. Ibid., p. 5.

4. Aníbal González, "Translation and Geanealogy: *One Hundred Years of Solitude,*" in *Gabriel García Márquez: New Readings,* edited by Bernard McGuirk and Richard Cardwell (Cambridge: Cambridge University Press, 1987), p. 77.

5. Walter D. Mignolo, "*One Hundred Years of Solitude* in Latin American Literature Courses," in *Approaches to Teaching García Márquez's One Hundred Years of Solitude,* edited by Maria Elena de Valdés and Mario J. Valdés (New York: Modern Language Association, 1990), p. 71.

6. Ibid., p. 75.

7. Hanna Geldrich-Leffman, "*One Hundred Years of Solitude* in Humanities Courses," in *Approaches to Teaching García Márquez's One Hundred Years of Solitude,* pp. 16–17.

8. Lois Parkinson Zamora, "*One Hundred Years of Solitude* in Comparative Literature Courses," in *Magical Realism: Theory, History, Community,* edited by Zamora and Wendy B. Faris (Durham, N.C.: Duke University Press, 1995), p. 23, 25.

9. Ibid., pp. 27, 28.

10. Ibid., p. 29.

11. Ibid., p. 30.

12. Chester S. Halka, "*One Hundred Years of Solitude* in History, Politics, and Civilization Courses," in *Approaches to Teaching García Marquez's One Hundred Years of Solitude,* pp. 33, 35–36.

13. Maria Elena de Valdés, "*One Hundred Years of Solitude* in Women's Studies Courses," in *Approaches to Teaching One Hundred Years of Solitude,* p. 47.

14. Ibid., p. 51.

15. Sandra M. Broschetto, "*One Hundred Years of Solitude* in Interdisciplinary Courses," in *Approaches to Teaching One Hundred Years of Solitude,* p. 58.

16. Williams, p. 81.

17. Mario Vargas Llosa, *García Márquez: Historia de un deicidio* (Barcelona: Biblioteca de Respuesta, Barral Editores, 1971), p. 85.

RESOURCES FOR STUDY OF
ONE HUNDRED YEARS OF SOLITUDE

STUDY QUESTIONS

1. Describe three examples of magic realism in *One Hundred Years of Solitude* and show how they contribute to the work as a whole.

2. Discuss the treatment of time in *One Hundred Years of Solitude*. What techniques does García Márquez use to suggest that, although events are constantly occurring, time is standing still?

3. Analyze the opinion expressed by some critics that in *One Hundred Years of Solitude* the views of García Márquez are sexist because women are awarded one separate and distinct set of personal characteristics and the men another. Consider García Márquez's reply that "my women are masculine." Are they? Why or why not? In responding, compare the variety of women characters in this novel: the matriarch, Úrsula, her daughter Amaranta, Rebeca, Pilar Ternera, Remedios the Beauty, and the last woman figure in the Buendía family, Amaranta Úrsula.

4. Read an epic work—the *Iliad* or the *Odyssey*—and then examine in what sense *One Hundred Years of Solitude* might also be considered an "epic." Begin by developing a definition of the "epic."

5. Read either William Faulkner's *The Sound and the Fury* or *Absalom, Absalom!* and compare Faulkner's novel with *One Hundred Years of Solitude*. Consider what similarities might exist between García Márquez and Faulkner, in terms of the authors' respective backgrounds, as well as what similarities of setting, character, tone, and style may be found in their works. Include in your answer an analysis of García Márquez's own description of the way in which he was influenced by Faulkner's fiction, quoted in the chapter "*One Hundred Years of Solitude* in History."

6. Some critics have termed Gabriel García Márquez a "modernist," while others have called him a "postmodernist." Define these terms, and then consider whether García Márquez is a modernist or a post-

modernist, using examples from *One Hundred Years of Solitude* as the basis for your argument.

7. Discuss the character of Melquíades in *One Hundred Years of Solitude*. Is he an archetypal figure? If so, what archetype do you think he represents? What characteristics does he embody and with what other archetypal figures in literature might he be compared?

8. Discuss the ways in which the war fought by Colonel Aureliano Buendía might reflect "La violencia" of the twentieth century much more than the civil wars of the nineteenth. Research newspaper and magazine articles about the political situation in Colombia since the 1940s for information to support your argument.

9. Analyze the reiteration of motifs in *One Hundred Years of Solitude*—for example, the several mentions of the red ants or of ice. What role does this repetition of images play in the overall structure of *One Hundred Years of Solitude*?

10. What reflections are there in Macondo of the Caribbean coast culture of García Márquez's birthplace? Write a geographical comparison of the fictional Macondo with the real Colombian towns of Riohacha, Aracataca, and the larger cities of Barranquilla, Santa Marta, and Cartagena de Indias.

11. Is critic Michael Wood correct in viewing Colonel Aureliano Buendía as the "dark conscience" of *One Hundred Years of Solitude*? Describe how the colonel functions as the "conscience" of the novel.

12. Describe the narrator of *One Hundred Years of Solitude*. Can you discern his particular sympathies or political perspective? Does he admire some characters more than others? What techniques does García Márquez employ to inform the reader of the places where he agrees with his narrator?

13. In what sense can Úrsula Iguarán de Buendía be perceived as the traditional "earth mother?" How does she function within the novel? What role does she play within the Buendía family and within the town? Why do you think she lives as long as she does?

14. What does García Márquez mean by "solitude," and how does it figure in *One Hundred Years of Solitude*? Is there more than one kind of solitude?

15. Why in *One Hundred Years of Solitude* is nostalgia almost as great a danger as solitude? What do the two states of being have in com-

mon? What are the attractions and benefits of nostalgia? Is nostalgia inevitable?

16. How does the worldview of García Márquez emerge from the moments of magic realism in *One Hundred Years of Solitude?* In what ways is the social realism of the novel indispensable to the moments of magic realism?

17. Compare the treatment of magic realism in *One Hundred Years of Solitude* with that in a novel by another author, choosing your example from these novelists: José Donoso, Salman Rushdie, Toni Morrison, or Isabel Allende.

18. What does Carlos Fuentes mean when he argues that in the case of *One Hundred Years of Solitude,* "all 'fictional' history coexists with 'real' history, what is dreamed with what is documented. . . . "? Discuss how memory and references to remembering people and events recur through the novel. What role does history play in the novel?

19. Discuss how, as Regina Janes argues in *García Márquez: Revolutions in Wonderland, One Hundred Years of Solitude* is a "total novel," which treats Latin America "socially, historically, politically, mythically and epically." What specific examples of each of these elements can you find in the novel?

20. Discuss the structure of the plot of *One Hundred Years of Solitude.* What effect does García Márquez create by his use of flashbacks, flash-forwards, and digressions? Frequently, the narrator seems to imply something that never actually happens, as in the first line of the novel: "Many years later, as he faced the firing squad, Colonel Aureliano Buendía was to remember . . . ," which implies that the colonel will be shot, although he actually dies of old age. What effect do such "miscues" have on the reader? Is García Márquez just being playful, or do you think he is trying to make a deeper point about how we see the world?

21. García Márquez has asserted that there is not a single conscious symbol in *One Hundred Years of Solitude.* Are there symbols in the novel that may be present whether or not he was aware of having created them?

22. Compare the labor unrest and the banana strike of 1928 as depicted in *One Hundred Years of Solitude* with the details of the historical events upon which it is based. How has García Márquez altered the historical facts? Why? In what ways does the fictionalized account remain "true"?

23. What does *One Hundred Years of Solitude* contribute to an understanding of Colombia, its history, its present crisis, and its future? Is García Márquez conveying a message to his fellow Colombians in this novel? What message, or messages, might he be conveying?

24. Compare the political events of *One Hundred Years of Solitude*—in particular the wars fought by Colonel Aureliano Buendía—with the current decomposition of Colombia: the division of the country and the renewed ascendancy of the guerrilla movements.

25. García Márquez has indicated that his first four books were preparation for *One Hundred Years of Solitude,* and he has referred to *One Hundred Years of Solitude* as his first book. Read his first published work, *Leaf Storm,* and/or other examples of García Márquez's early work, and compare them to *One Hundred Years of Solitude* in terms of plot, character, style, and setting.

26. What evidence is there in *One Hundred Years of Solitude* of the fascination of García Márquez with the profession of journalism and for his long and continuing career as a reporter? What elements of the novel seem as though they could be part of news reports? What is there about García Márquez's writing style in the novel that seems journalistic?

27. Why does love not bring happiness to any of the Buendías? Describe the various ways in which love fails to bring happiness or brings unhappiness into the characters' lives.

GLOSSARY OF LITERARY TERMS

Archetype: a literary term borrowed from the teachings of psychoanalyst Carl Jung that refers to universal or primordial images shared by all human beings over all time. Archetypal figures or characters and events refer to universal human experiences. Studies of fairy tales and myths reveal that societies in different times and places invent stories that include the same basic archetypes. According to Jung, archetypes come from the collective unconscious, the part of the mind that includes the shared images and ideas of the entire human race. The six principal figures in the Jungian system of archetypes are the shadow, the anima-animus, the mother, the child, the maiden, and the wise old man.

According to Robert L. Sims in "Archetypal Approaches," there are four characters in *One Hundred Years of Solitude* who can be analyzed in relation to archetypal figures: José Arcadio Buendía (the patriarch), Úrsula Iguarán (the great mother), Colonel Aureliano Buendía (the warrior), and Melquíades (the wise old man). Other archetypes include the virgin (Amaranta and Remedios the Beauty) and the witch (Pilar Ternera and Petra Cotes). The novel also includes "the archetypal motifs of creation, circular time, paradise, the quest myth, the family, and the biblical pattern from Genesis to Apocalypse and the idea of Macondo as the seat of time and myth." (*See* Maria Elena de Valdés and Mario J. Valdés, eds., *Approaches to Teaching Gabriel García Márquez's One Hundred Years of Solitude.*)

The Boom: the resurgence of Latin American novelists and poets in the 1960s and 1970s. Among these writers are are Gabriel García Márquez, Carlos Fuentes, Mario Vargas Llosa, and Julio Cortázar. (*See* Michael Wood, *Gabriel García Márquez: One Hundred Years of Solitude.*)

Epic: a story that chronicles the daring exploits of heroes and the fate of the society and community in which they act.

Episodic: an adjective applied to a work that is structured loosely according to the random accumulation of scenes and events. Such works do not follow the classic Aristotelian model, which begins with exposition, has a middle characterized by rising action and climax, and ends with resolution of the action.

Genre: a category of literary expression. The term, which comes from the French for "type," is used loosely to designate works that have some common characteristic. Some consider genre to designate subject matter. These users would call romance fiction and mystery fiction genres. Other traditional critics use the term to designate broad types of fiction: novel, poem, and short story. There are also subgenres of the novel such as the romance, the satire, the confession, the thriller, science fiction, the detective story, and the horror story. So wide is the scope of *One Hundred*

Years of Solitude that it encompasses several of these subgenres: the romance, the satire, the horror story, the fantasy, and science fiction.

Imagery: the figurative language employed in a work of literature. Images may connect emotional, political, or psychological themes with sensory comparisons. The scent of bitter almond and almond trees form persistent images in the work of García Márquez, particularly in *One Hundred Years of Solitude* and *Love in the Time of Cholera*.

Irony: a technique frequently employed by García Márquez. Verbal irony means saying one thing and meaning another. In dramatic irony, events prove contradictory to what had been accepted as received wisdom. An example of irony in *One Hundred Years of Solitude* is that Remedios the Beauty is so lovely and inspires so much love that she herself is unable to find love in this world.

Magic Realism: the mixture of fantasy, or the unreal, with the traditional social realism of the novel. Cuban novelist Alejo Carpentier's term for this technique was *lo real maravilloso Americano* (the American marvelous real). According to the *Dictionary of Twentieth-Century Culture: Hispanic Culture of South America*, "magic realism" involves "fiction that does not distinguish between realistic and non-realistic events, fiction in which the supernatural, the mythical or the implausible are assimilated to the cognitive structure of reality without a perceptive break in the narrator's or characters' consciousness. Magic realism is a style associated with Latin American Fiction especially in the 1960's and after."

As Michael Wood explains the term in his book on García Márquez, "distortion stumbles on a truth." Wood describes *One Hundred Years of Solitude* as presenting "a world where the imaginary and the figurative are seriously entertained and not visibly discriminated against."

Edwin Williamson in "Magical Realism and the Theme of Incest in *One Hundred Years of Solitude*," puts it this way: "magical realism is a narrative style which consistently blurs the traditional realist distinction between fantasy and reality." Magic realism "creates its aesthetic impact by fusing terms that are in principle opposed to each other."

Metaphor: a figure of speech that indirectly compares two unlike elements. In *One Hundred Years of Solitude* "Children and adults sucked with delight on the delicious little green roosters of insomnia, the exquisite pink fish of insomnia, and the tender yellow ponies of insomnia." The state of being unable to sleep is compared to roosters, fish, and ponies—a typical flight of García Márquez's fertile imagination. (Compare **simile**.)

Modernism: a literary movement flowering in the 1920s that rejected the conventions of realism prevalent in the nineteenth century. Modernist fiction writers sought to focus on the inner lives of characters, on psychic reality. Novelists such as James Joyce (in *Ulysses* and *Finnegans Wake*) and Virginia Woolf (in *Mrs. Dalloway* and *To The Lighthouse*) broke up narrative continuity and developed techniques such as the stream-of-consciousness interior monologue.

The modernists relied on symbolism and irony to the exclusion of the conventional well-developed plot. Their worldview was more pessimistic than that of writers prior to World War I. Influenced by Sigmund Freud, Karl Marx, and Friedrich Nietzsche, they questioned religious and political certainties. Rejecting the notion of the stable, unified character knowable to himself and others, they even suggested that identity was dependent upon the observer. Focusing on subjectivity, they offered little substantive conflict between their characters and the world in which they moved.

Myth: a story that becomes symbolic of large forces and issues. Traditional myths present supernatural episodes to explain the origins of man and human society, nature, or the universe. A myth generally relates to the experiences of a group rather than of individuals. There is a mythic quality to *One Hundred Years of Solitude,* which chronicles not only experiences of the Buendía family but of all Latin America.

Naturalism: a form of realism, in which particular is paid attention to the raw physical details of life. Naturalistic characters are viewed as creatures of nature, animal in their needs and desires, and in the strictest sense of the term, *naturalism* is used to describe fiction in which a being's every thought and action is determined by hereditary and environmental factors. There are moments of raw realism or naturalism in *One Hundred Years of Solitude*—for example, the details of the death in childbirth of Remedios, the wife of Colonel Aureliano Buendía.

Narrator: the teller of a tale. A novel or story may be told either by a first-person narrator, usually a character in the story, or by a third-person narrator, who is sometimes omniscient, able to see into the minds of all the characters, and sometimes limited, able to see events from the viewpoint of one character (or one character at a time). An omniscient narrator may intrude into the narrative to comment on the action or the characters. García Márquez uses a quasi-omniscient narrator, who surprises the reader by using the first person ("I" or "We" or "Our"), thus defining himself as a member of the community about which he is writing.

Picaresque Novel: an episodic work of fiction that chronicles a series of adventures and daring escapades of a roguish character known as a picaro, or knave, who is generally mischievous, sly, and crafty rascal. Both the Spanish novels that influenced García

Márquez, the anonymous *Lazarillo de Tormes* (1554) and Miguel de Cervantes' *Don Quixote* (1605), are picaresque novels.

Plot: the sequence of events in a story, linked, usually but not always, through causal connections. It is the action of a novel or what happens.

Postmodernism: a literary movement that developed after World War II, which involved a rejection of modernist norms. Disillusioned by the totalitarianism of the twentieth century, the senselessness of the atomic bomb, and the self-destruction of Soviet Communism, postmodernist authors view the world as absurd, random, and unintelligible. Yet, they differ from the modernists in accepting the arbitrary nature of the world; hence, they reject the pessimism of writers who, despite their disenchantment, still entertain hopes of change and an amelioration of human suffering. In fiction they reject the idea of the work of art as an organic whole. In so doing, they reject the very notions of "character" or "plot" as valid. Subjectivity becomes one more delusion; psychology, one more arbitrary construct.

Postmodernists reject even meaning itself as a hopeless delusion and imply that trying to understand the world is not worth the effort; some even suggest that there is no such thing as "the world" to be understood. Their universe is one of increasing fragmentation, of human powerlessness. They consider the literary experiments of modernism to be conventional and substitute an inverted fascination with language and self-reference, and an obsession with words for their own sake. Politically, they accept the status quo as unchangeable. Authors such as John Barth, Thomas Pynchon, Donald Barthelme, Don DeLillo, and Paul Auster are generally regarded as postmodernists.

Realism: the major tradition in the novel, which began as a form of entertainment for the middle classes. It demands verisimilitude of the action, a resemblance to everyday life as the reader knows it; the behavior of the characters in a realist work is causally connected, and action in the present can be traced to causes in the past. Realism minimizes the use of coincidence or accident: it is no accident, for example, that all seventeen of the Aurelianos meet the same catastrophic fate.

Setting: the background of the story or novel, not only the room or the weather or the streets, but also the historical and cultural context of the work of fiction. The settings of García Márquez's novels figure importantly in both plot and characterization. Sometimes the setting even becomes a character in its own right, particularly Macondo of *One Hundred Years of Solitude.* Macondo stands simultaneously for Caribbean Colombia, for Colombia in general, and even for the entire Latin American continent and its history since independence from Spain.

Simile: a figure of speech that draws a direct comparison between two entities, generally using *like* or *as.* In *One Hundred Years of Solitude,* the letters in indecipherable manuscripts "looked like clothes hung out to dry on a line," a simile. (Compare **metaphor.**)

Symbol: something in a literary work that is not only itself but also stands for something else. A symbol speaks in concrete terms of the abstract. García Márquez told Claudia Dreyfus, an interviewer for *Playboy,* that there was not a single conscious symbol in *One Hundred Years of Solitude.*

GLOSSARY OF REFERENCES IN
ONE HUNDRED YEARS
OF SOLITUDE

Alchemy: a medieval chemical philosophy whose practicioners had the major aims of finding a way to transmute base metals into gold and of discovering an elixir for longetivity. Alchemy can also refer to any seemingly magical power.

Collective unconscious: based on the view of the psychoanalyst Carl Jung, the theory that the entire human species shares a set of primal beliefs and emotional responses that emerge most lucidly in dreams.

Equinox: The words "equinox, equinox" are chanted by Melquíades. An equinox is either of two points on the celestial sphere where the ecliptic intersects the celestial equator. The more common meaning is either of the two times during a year when the Sun crosses the celestial equator and when the length of the day and night are approximately equal. The vernal equinox is 21 March and the autumnal equinox is 21 September.

Fluorescence: the emission of electromagnetic radiation, especially of visible light, resulting from the absorption of incident radiation and persisting only as long as the stimulating radiation is continued. "Fluorescence" also refers to the radiation so emitted.

Hermetic: completely sealed, as in being impervious to outside interference or influence; cloistered (retreated to the hermetic confines of his room). Another meaning has to do with works on the occult sciences and magic, particularly those ascribed to Hermes Trismegistos.

Alexander von Humboldt: a name uttered by Melquíades in his last days. Friedrich Alexander von Humboldt (1769–1859) was a German naturalist, statesman, and explorer of South America and Asia.

Incunabula: specifically, books printed from movable type before 1501; the term can mean an artifact from an early period.

Necromancy: the art that professes to conjure up the spirits of the dead and commune with them in order to predict the future. "Necromancy" also can refer to black magic or sorcery in general or to magical qualities.

Nostradamus: the Latinized name of Michel de Notre-Dame or Nostredame (1503–1566). He was a French astrologer and physician and the author of a collection of prophecies—the "keys"—that are phrased in so obscure a fashion that they are susceptible to a variety of interpretations. Interest in Nostradamus revived in the 1930s when many people thought his writings prophesied the rise of Adolf Hitler and the events of World War II.

Saracen: a member of a pre-Islamic nomadic people of the Syrian-Arabian deserts. It can also mean any Muslim, especially of the time of the Crusades.

Solipsism: the theory that the self is the only thing that can be known and verified; or, the theory or point of view that the self is the only reality. This perspective is anathema to Gabriel García Márquez.

Theogonic: the adjective related to theogony: a recitation of the origin and genealogy of the gods, especially as in ancient epic poetry.

Velocipede: an old-fashioned bicycle with the front wheel much larger than the rear. A velocipede is an early form of the bicycle propelled by pushing the feet along the ground while straddling the vehicle. It also refers to any early bicycles having pedals attached to the front wheel.

Wandering Jew: a term out of an anti-Semitic Christian legend about a Jew who was doomed to wander over the earth until the Second Coming because he joined in the mocking of Jesus at the time of the Crucifixion. This figure has appeared in literary contexts.

HISTORICAL EVENTS, PEOPLE, AND PLACES

Banana Strike Massacre: In 1928 the Conservative government in Bogotá sent General Cortés Vargas to suppress a strike of banana workers who were employed by the American United Fruit Company under untenable conditions. Although in *One Hundred Years of Solitude,* Gabriel García Márquez says 3,000 workers were killed, he has admitted that he exaggerated; historians put the actual figure much lower.

As Mario Vargas Llosa has put it in "From Aracataca to Macondo," after the banana plantations of United Fruit were gone, "the town was assaulted by outlaws, decimated by epidemics, ravaged by deluges." The banana company stimulated material needs never before felt in Colombia, even as they brought "progress," not least, the first railroad connecting the coast of Colombia with the interior.

Bogotázo: This name was given to the outpouring of rage and the rioting following the murder of Jorge Eliécer Gaitán. The rioting following the assassination was a profound experience for the young García Márquez, who was still a student at the National University.

Sir Francis Drake: Drake (1540–1596) was the first Englishman to sail around the world. The English pirate, known in Western European history as an "explorer," was given to attacks on the Spanish Fleet. As even the benign *World Book Encyclopedia* notes, Drake "was as much a pirate as any leader of a cutthroat crew that

ever flew the skull-and-crossbones flag." García Márquez calls him a "pirate" as well.

Drake attacked Riohacha, a city neighboring Aracataca, in 1568. In 1580 aboard his ship *Golden Hind* he was knighted by Queen Elizabeth I. Sir Francis Drake is frequently invoked by García Márquez as the symbol of economic exploitation of his native land.

Jorge Eliécer Gaitán: Gaitán became the leader of the Liberal Party of Colombia in the 1940s. He had gone to Cienaga to investigate the banana company massacre, and after he was elected to Congress in 1929 he denounced the government for both its part in the massacre and the subsequent cover-up. On 9 April 1948 Gaitán was assassinated during lunch hour on the streets of Bogotá; his death set off riots and violence that became known as the Bogotázo.

Before long the entire country was overtaken by "La Violencia," twenty years of murder and mayhem between Conservatives and Liberals. Gaitán had been in favor of radical reform; his progressive views split the Liberal Party and allowed the Conservatives to win in the election of 1946. Gaitán restrained his followers from a violent uprising, but strikes and police repression grew.

Che Guevara: Guevara was a medical doctor and revolutionary born in Argentina who became one of the leaders of the Cuban Revolution against Batista in 1959. Guevara and Fidel Castro became inspirations to revolutionaries in other countries of Latin America seeking to accomplish what they had done in Cuba.

Liberals and Conservatives: From the moment of Colombia's independence from Spain, the colonial elites argued among themselves about whether or not the national government should be federalist, resembling the United States, or centralist and more authoritarian. The federalists and centralists immediately formed rival groups, which are the antecedents of the later political parties, the Liberals and the Conservatives.

The separation of church and state was a deciding issue. The federalist leader was Camilo Torres; the Centralist leader was Antonio Nariño. Civil war loomed before the independent country was even established. In 1811 a congress was installed, in the federalist mode, with the army subordinate to Bogotá.

The Liberals were anticolonial. Those who joined were from the new merchant class and included artisans, manufacturers, and small farmers. The Liberal Party also included slaves seeking their freedom. They favored less power for the president, separation of church and state, freedom of the press, freedom of religion, and even elimination of the death penalty. Colonel Aureliano Buendía was of this party.

The Conservatives favored preserving the colonial legacy brought by Spain and the colonial institutions that the Spanish had established. They wanted to uphold the alliance between church and state and to continue slavery. They preferred an authoritarian government, which would eliminate what they perceived as the excesses of freedom. Over the years they sought to curtail the independence of the press.

La Violencia: Throughout Colombia, Liberals murdered Conservatives; and Conservatives, Liberals. Entire villages were wiped out. Unspeakable acts of mutilation were committed. La Violencia lasted until the mid 1960s with the growth in the Colombian countryside of guerrilla groups determined to overthrow the oligarchy that had ruled the country since 1820 when Simon Bolívar accomplished its liberation from Spanish rule.

BIBLIOGRAPHY

Adams, Robert M. "Big Little Book," *New York Review of Books,* 14 April 1983, p. 3.

Anderson, Jon Lee. The Power of García Márquez, *New Yorker* (27 September 1999): 57–71.

Barnard, Timothy, and Peter Rist, eds. *South American Cinema: A Critical Filmography, 1915–1994.* Austin: University of Texas Press, 1996.

Barroa, Rei. *Literature of the Americas.* College Park: University of Maryland Press, 1990.

Bell, Michael. *Gabriel García Márquez: Solitude and Solidarity.* New York: St. Martin's Press, 1993.

Bell-Villada, Gene H. *García Márquez: The Man And His Work.* Chapel Hill & London: University of North Carolina Press, 1990. A comprehensive and illuminating introduction to Gabriel García Márquez with many quotations from interviews and a strong biographical approach.

Bloom, Harold, ed. *Gabriel García Márquez.* New York & Philadelphia: Chelsea House, 1989. This is a good collection of eighteen essays. Two deal with the influence of William Faulkner on García Márquez. Colombian politics is discussed in Regina Janes's essay, "Liberals, Conservatives, and Bananas: Colombian Politics in the Fictions of García Márquez," as well as in "The Autumn of the Patriarch," by critic Raymond Williams.

Brink, André. "Making and Unmaking: Gabriel García Márquez: *One Hundred Years of Solitude,*" in his *The Novel: Language and Narrative from Cervantes to Calvino.* New York: New York University Press, 1998. A South African novelist, Brink has used many of the techniques of magic realism in his own work, particularly in the novels *Imaginings of Sand* (1997) and *Devil's Valley* (1999).

Brotherston, Gordon. *The Emergence of the Latin American Novel.* Cambridge: Cambridge University Press, 1977.

Buford, Bill. "Haughty Falconry and Collective Guilt," *TLS: Times Literary Supplement* (London), 10 September 1982, p. 965.

Bushnell, David. *The Making of Modern Colombia: A Nation in Spite of Itself.* Berkeley: University of California Press, 1993.

Conversations with Latin American Writers: Gabriel García Márquez, interviewed by Silvia Lemus, 44 mins., Films For The Humanities & Sciences, 1998, video. Lemus, the interviewer, is the wife of Mexican novelist Carlos Fuentes. She interviews García Márquez in Cartagena, the setting for *Love in the Time of Cholera.* The discussion ranges from autobiographical sources of the novel to García Márquez's reflections on the art of fiction.

Delgado Oscar, ed. *Ideologías políticas y agrarias en Colombia.* Bogotá: Tercer Mundo, 1973.

Detjens, Wilma Else. *Home as Creation: The Influence of Early Childhood Experience in the Literary Creation of Gabriel García Márquez, Agustín Yáñez, and Juan Rulfo.* New York: Lang, 1993.

Dolan, Sean. *Gabriel García Márquez.* New York: Chelsea House, 1994.

Donoso, José. *The Boom in Spanish American Literature,* translated by Gregory Kolovakos. New York: Columbia University Press / Center for Inter-American Relations, 1977. This superb and personal book chronicling Donoso's own career places García Márquez in the literature of the era and of his continent. There are personal glimpses of García Márquez and other writers such as Carlos Fuentes and of course Donoso himself.

Dreifus, Claudia. "*Playboy* Interview: Gabriel García Márquez," *Playboy,* 30, no. 3 (February 1983): 65–77, 172–178. The political naiveté of the interviewer mars this interview. When García Márquez asks her playfully whether, like other North American journalists, she is going to ask him whether he is a communist, she becomes flustered, and lacking any knowledge of Colombian politics, goes ahead and does it.

Epstein, Joseph, "How Good Is Gabriel Garcia Marquez?" *Commentary,* 75 (May 1983) : 59–65.

Fau, Margaret Eustella. *Gabriel García Márquez: An Annotated Bibliography, 1947–1979.* Westport, Conn.: Greenwood Press, 1980.

Fau and Nelly Sfeir de González. *Bibliographic Guide to Gabriel García Márquez, 1979–1985.* Westport, Conn.: Greenwood Press, 1986.

Fiddian, Robin, ed. *García Márquez, Modern Literatures in Perspective.* London & New York: Longman, 1995.

Foster, David William. *Handbook of Latin American Literature.* New York: Garland, 1987.

Frisch, Mark. "Teaching *One Hundred Years of Solitude* with *The Sound and the Fury.*" On-line document. http://www.2.semo.edu/cfs/frisch.html.

Fuentes, Carlos. *Gabriel García Márquez and the Invention of America,* E. Allison Peers Lectures, no. 2. Liverpool: Liverpool University Press, 1987.

Gabriel García Márquez: Magic and Reality, written, directed, and produced by Ana Cristina Navarro, 60 minutes, Films For the Humanities & Sciences, 1981, video. Available in both Spanish and English, this documentary offers interviews with the author as well as several of his friends and critics, among them Alfonso Fuenmayor, who appears as a character in *One Hundred Years of Solitude.* Especially interesting is the footage of the Bogotázo, the riots following the assassination of Liberal leader Jorge Eliecer Gaitan, and old photographs and rare footage as well of the Santa Marta railroad built by the banana company and of the strike described in *One Hundred Years of Solitude;* survivors of the massacre are interviewed.

Gallagher, D. P. *Modern Latin American Literature.* New York: Oxford University Press, 1973.

Gonzalez, Nelly Sfeir de. *Bibliographic Guide to Gabriel García Márquez, 1986–1992.* Westport, Conn.: Greenwood Press, 1994.

Guibert, Rita. *Seven Voices: Seven Latin American Writers Talk to Rita Guibert.* Translated by Frances Partridge. New York: Knopf, 1973. This book is an excellent introduction to García Márquez and easily the most comprehensive interview with this author. He discusses his work process and his techniques fully. See also in this volume a rare interview with Guillermo Cabrera Infante, who offers some remarks about García Márquez.

Gullon, Ricardo. "Gabriel García Márquez and the Lost Art of Storytelling," *Diacritics* (1971): 27–32.

Guzmán Campos, Gérman. *Camilo Torres.* New York: Sheed & Ward, 1969.

Guzmán Campos, Orlando Fals Borda, and Eduardo Umana Luna. *La Violencia en Colombia: Estudio de un Proceso Social,* volume 1. Bogota: Ediciones Tercer Mundo, 1963. This book, although only available in Spanish, is indispensable for any understanding of Colombia and the historical culture from which García Márquez emerged.

Haddox, Benjamín. *Sociedad y religión en colombia: Estudio de las institutiones religiosas colombianas.* Bogotá: Ediciones Tercer Mundo, 1965.

Harss, Luis, and Barbara Dohmann. *Into the Mainstream: Conversations with Latin American Writers.* New York: Harper & Row, 1967.

Houtart, François, and Émile Jean Pin. *The Church and the Latin American Revolution,* translated by Gilbert Barth. New York: Sheed & Ward, 1965.

Janes, Regina, *Gabriel García Márquez: Revolutions in Wonderland.* Columbia: University of Missouri Press, 1981.

Janes. *One Hundred Years of Solitude: Modes of Reading.* Boston: Twayne, 1991.

Kakutani, Michiko. "*García Márquez* Novel Covers Love and Time," *New York Times,* 6 April 1988, C21.

Kennedy, William. "All of Life, Sense and Nonsense, Fills an Argentine's Daring Fable," *National Observer,* 9 (20 April 1970): 23.

Kennedy. "The Yellow Trolley Car in Barcelona and Other Visions: A Profile of Gabriel García Márquez," *Atlantic,* 231, no. 1 (January 1973): 50–58. Republished in *Riding the Yellow Trolley Car: Selected Nonfiction.* New York: Viking, 1993, pp. 243–267. Despite Kennedy's knowledge of Spanish, and the generous offering of his time by García Márquez, this interview adds little to the existing literature. This was the first biographical interview widely available to readers in the United States and England.

Kline, Harvey F. *Colombia: Democracy under Assault.* Boulder Colo.: Westview, 1995.

Lipset, Seymour Martin and Aldo Solari, eds. *Elites in Latin America.* New York: Oxford University Press, 1967.

Luis, William, ed. *Dictionary of Literary Biography, 113: Modern Latin-American Writers,* Detroit: Gale Research, 1992.

"Magic, Matter, and Money: Pioneers Who Have Explored Four Aspects of Reality," *Time,* 120 (1 November 1982): 88–89.

Mano, D. Keith. "A Death Foretold," *National Review,* 10 June 1983, pp. 699–700.

McGuirk, Bernard, and Richard Cardwell, eds. *Gabriel García Márquez: New Readings.* Cambridge: Cambridge University Press, 1987. This anthology is superior to Bloom's and more scholarly in approach. There are twelve essays, including Robin Fiddian's "A Prospective Post-script: Apropos of *Love in the Time of Cholera,*" which offers a somewhat dissenting view regarding the treatment of women in the works of García Márquez. "On 'Magical' and Social Realism in García Márquez" by Gerald Martin is particularly helpful.

McMurray, George R. *Gabriel García Márquez.* New York: Ungar, 1983.

McNerney, Kathleen. *Understanding Gabriel García Márquez.* Columbia: University of South Carolina Press, 1989.

Mead, Robert G., Jr. Review of *One Hundred Years of Solitude, Saturday Review,* 7 March 1970, pp. 34–35.

Minta, Stephen. *García Márquez, Writer of Colombia.* New York : Harper & Row, 1987.

Müller-Bergh, Klaus. "*Relato de un náufrago:* García Márquez's Tale of Shipwreck and Survival at Sea," *Books*

Abroad, 47, no. 3 (Summer 1973): 460–466.

Oberhelman, Harley D. *The Presence of Faulkner in the Writings of García Márquez,* Graduate Studies Texas Tech University, no. 22 (Lubbock: Texas Tech Press, 1980).

Ortega, Julio, and Claudia Elliott, eds. *Gabriel García Márquez and the Powers of Fiction.* Austin : University of Texas Press, 1988. This collection of essays includes "Exchange System in *One Hundred Years of Solitude,* " by Ortega; "The Ends of the Text, Journalism in the Fiction of Gabriel García Márquez," by Aníbal González; and a translation of "The Solitude of Latin America," García Márquez's 1982 Nobel lecture.

Pearce, Jenny. *Colombia, Inside the Labyrinth.* London: Latin America Bureau (Research and Action)/New York: Monthly Review Press, 1990.

Pynchon, Thomas. "The Heart's Eternal Vow," *New York Times Book Review,* 10 April 1988, pp. 48–49.

Rabassa, Gregory. "Beyond Magic Realism: Thoughts on the Art of Gabriel García Márquez," *Books Abroad,* 47, no. 3 (Summer 1973): 449.

Rangel Suárez, Alfredo. *Colombia, guerra en el fin de siglo.* Bogotá: TM Editores / Universidad de los Andes, Facultad de Ciencias Sociales, 1998.

Riding, Alan. "Revolution and the Intellectual in Latin America," *New York Times,* 13 March 1983.

Rodman, Selden. "Gabriel García Márquez," in *Tongues of Fallen Angels: Conversations.* New York: New Directions, 1974.

Simon, John, "Incontinent Imagination," *New Republic,* 192 (4 February 1985): 32–35.

Simons, Marlise. "The Best Years of His Life: An Interview with Gabriel García Márquez," *New York Times Book Review,* 10 April 1988. Simons is a journalist and not a scholar, but there are some interesting moments here.

Simons. "Love and Age: A Talk with García Márquez," *New York Times Book Review,* 7 April 1985. This interview appeared at the time of the publication of *Love in the Time of Cholera* and is excellent.

Simons. "A Talk With Gabriel García Márquez," *New York Times Book Review,* 5 December 1982.

Sims, Robert Lewis. *The Evolution of Myth in García Márquez from La hojarasca to Cien años de soledad.* Miami: Ediciones Universal, 1981.

Stone, Peter. "Gabriel García Márquez," in *Writers At Work: The Paris Review Interviews—Sixth Series,* edited by George Plimpton. New York: Viking, 1984, pp. 313–339.

Streitfield, David. "The Intricate Solitude of Gabriel García Márquez," *Washington Post,* 10 April 1994, pp. F1, F4.

Valdes, Maria Elena de and Mario J. Valdes, eds. *Approaches to Teaching García Márquez's One Hundred Years of Solitude.* New York: Modern Language Association of America, 1990.

Vargas, Gérman. "Autor de una obra que hará ruido," *Bogotá Encuentra liberal,* 29 April 1967.

Vargas Llosa, Mario. *García Márquez: Historia de un Deicidio.* Barcelona: Breve Biblioteca de Respuesta: Barral Editores, 1971. Written at a time when Vargas Llosa and García Márquez were still friends, this book is an affectionate and comprehensive critical biography. Especially useful are the discussions of the youth of García Márquez as a *costeño.*

Williams, Raymond L. *Gabriel García Márquez.* Boston: Twayne, 1984.

Wood, Michael. *Gabriel García Márquez: One Hundred Years of Solitude.* Cambridge & New York: Cambridge University Press, 1990. This personal, yet brilliant and accessible, study of García Márquez is the most measured piece of writing about this author. The chronology is particularly useful and includes historical material as well as the details of the life of García Márquez.

Zamora, Lois Parkinson and Wendy B. Faris, eds. *Magical Realism: Theory, History, Community.* Durham: Duke University Press, 1995. This comprehensive volume is a must for penetrating the nuances of "magical realism" from its beginnings to the present and including its use by other authors.

WEB SITES

<www.rpg.net/quail/labyrinth/gabo>
Created and maintained by A. Ruch, "Macondo" is a complete and quite reliable site. There are special features, such as news about García Márquez, recent articles, information about new books in the works, and the latest on new motion-picture adaptations. "Macondo" includes an impressive section titled "Biography" that includes a time line with the dates of his major works and the events that helped shape his writing; "Bibliography," which includes works available only in Spanish; "Criticism"; "Audio: Books on Tape"; "Images," which is an on-line gallery of García Márquez images, photographs, paintings, and book covers;

"Papers," including links to essays; "Film," a link to a directory of films based on García Márquez's works; his Nobel Prize lecture; links to other resources; and "Bookstore," linked to Amazon.com for easy ordering. This web site is not only comprehensive, but it is also charming, thought-provoking, and obviously created with considerable affection for the subject. No other website about García Márquez comes close to "Macondo" in its professionalism, enthusiasm, and passion.

<www.levity.com/corduroy/marquez.htm>
Also a García Márquez site, with quotations from his novels, news articles, home pages, biographies, and a link to the website "Macondo." Several of the links may be nonoperational, however, and one, a review of *The General in His Labyrinth,* written for "The Tech," was not particularly illuminating. The "New Readings" link led, not very helpfully, to the "Cambridge On Line Catalog."

<http://lanic.utexas.edu/la/colombia/>
Several links relevant to Colombian culture and politics are available through the Latin American Information Center maintained at the University of Texas website, including a link to a general overview of Colombian history maintained by the Library of Congress: http://lcweb2.loc.gov/frd/cs/cotoc.html.

MASTER INDEX

A

Absalom, Absalom! (Faulkner) 64, 179, 183
Adan Buenosayres (Marechal) 175
Al filo del agua. See *The Edge of the Storm* (Yáñez).
El alcalde de Zalamea (Calderon) 19
"The Aleph" (Borges) 175
Allende, Isabel 175, 180
Amaru 164
El amor en los tiempos del cólera. See *Love in the Time of Cholera* (García Márquez).
Anaya, Rudolfo 178
Antigone (Sophocles) 177
Antioch Review 169
Antony and Cleopatra (Shakespeare) 64
Approaches to Teaching García Márquez's One Hundred Years of Solitude (Valdés & Valdés) 75
Aracataca, Colombia 7–9, 11, 39, 43, 68, 78
Area Handbook for Colombia 182
Arias, Ron 167
Asturias, Miguel Ángel 63, 175

B

Bakhtin, Mikhail 178
Banana workers' strike 7–8, 26, 47, 61, 68, 145, 178, 182
Bell-Villada, Gene 64, 71, 151
Beloved (Morrison) 175, 179–180
Bible 182
The Big House (Samudio) 177–178
"Blacamán el bueno, vendedor de milagros." *See* "Blacaman the Good, Vendor of Miracles" (García Márquez).

"Blacaman the Good, Vendor of Miracles" (García Márquez) 72
Bless Me, Ultima (Anaya) 178
Bloom, Harold 72
Bogart, Humphrey 64
Books Abroad 169, 171
The Boom 66, 71, 151–153
The Boom in Spanish American Literature (Donoso) 59, 151–153, 165, 168
Borda, Orlando Fals 181
Borges, Jorge Luis 70, 72, 88, 106, 144, 153, 175, 179, 182
Braude, Fernand 181
Brave New World (Huxley) 183
Broschetto, Sandra M. 181
Buddenbrooks (Mann) 183

C

Cabrera Infante, Guillermo 59, 71, 152–153, 177
Calderon de la Barca, Pedro 19
Cardwell, Richard 71, 106
Carpentier, Alejo 32, 63, 70–71, 74, 104, 106, 175, 177, 179
"La Casa" (García Márquez) 43
Casa de campo (Donoso) 180
La casa de los espíritus. See *The House of the Spirits* (Allende).
La casa grande. See *The Big House* (Samudio).
Castro, Fidel 5, 69, 157
Celan, Paul 179
Cepeda, Álvaro 13, 93
Cervantes, Miguel de 66, 169, 172, 177
The Church and the Latin American Revolution (Houtart & Pin) 182
Cien años de soledad. See *One Hundred Years of Solitude* (García Márquez).

Kennedy, William 170
The Kingdom of This World (Carpentier)
63, 175

L

Lawrence, D. H. 143
Leaf Storm and Other Stories (García
Márquez) 44, 151
Lecture delivered on *One Hundred Years of
Solitude* (Johnston) 126–141
"Liberals, Conservatives, and Bananas:
Colombian Politics in the Fictions of
Gabriel García Márquez" (Janes) 72,
146–147
Lipset, Seymour Martin 182
El llano en llamas (Rulfo) 179
The Lost Steps (Carpentier) 71, 175
Love in the Time of Cholera (García
Márquez) 58
Luna, Eduardo Umaña 181

M

Macbeth (Shakespeare) 64
The Magic Mountain (Mann) 179
"Magic Realism and the Theme of Incest
in *One Hundred Years of Solitude*" (Will-
iamson) 71, 105–125, 144
"Magical Romance/Magical Realism:
Ghosts in U.S. and Latin American Fic-
tion" (Zamora) 144
La mala hora (García Márquez) 101–102
Mann, Thomas 152, 179, 183
Marechal, Leopoldo 175
Márquez, Nicolás 8–11, 42, 68, 92
Márquez, Tranquilina Iguarán 11–12, 42,
69
Martin, Gerald 72, 137, 144
Marxism 171
Maupassant, Guy de 175
McGuirk, Bernard 71, 106
McMurray, George R. 108, 172
*Me Llamo Rigoberta, Mechu y asi nacio me
concienca.* See *I Rigoberta Mechu, An
Indian Woman in Guatemala* (Menchu).
Mead, Robert G., Jr. 170
Mena, Lucila Inés 59, 75
Menchu, Rigoberta 178
Mendoza, Plinio Apuleyo 41, 57

Merrell, Floyd 74, 147–148
The Metamorphosis (Kafka) 64, 178
Midnight's Children (Rushdie) 175, 180
Mignolo, Walter D. 178
A Modest Proposal (Swift) 157
Morrison, Toni 175, 179–180
Mrs. Dalloway (Woolf) 43, 178
La muerte de Artemio Cruz. See *The Death
of Artemio Cruz* (Fuentes).
Müller-Bergh, Klaus 169
Mundo Nuevo 164
Mutis, Álvaro 45–46, 168

N

Neruda, Pablo 169
1984 (Orwell) 183
No Exit (Sartre) 179
*No One Writes to the Colonel and Other
Stories* (García Márquez) 10, 93, 97,
100–101
Nobel Prize for literature 172
Nostromo (Conrad) 64
Nuñez, Rafael 73

O

Oberhelman, Harley D. 143
The Obscene Bird of Night (Donoso) 175
Obsceno pajarode la noche (Donoso). See
The Obscene Bird of Night (Donoso).
Odyssey (Homer) 177
Oedipus Rex (Sophocles) 177
Los ojos de los enterrados. See *The Eyes of
the Interred* (Asturias).
"On 'Magical' and Social Realism in
García Márquez" (Martin) 72, 144–145
One Hundred Years of Solitude (García
Márquez)
  adaptations 172–173
  as an epic 126–129
  character description 14–25
  conclusion of the novel 139–141
  critical analysis 154–161
  critical approaches 142–154
  critical articles 75–126
  critical summary 66
  critical survey 68–75
  financing 45
  historical reflections 169–172